A Bibliography of Russian Composers

David Moldon

WHITE LION PUBLISHERS LIMITED
London, Sydney and Toronto

Based on a thesis accepted for Fellowship of
the Library Association, 1973

ISBN 0 7284 0101 0

Made and printed in Great Britain
for White Lion Publishers Limited,
138 Park Lane, London W1Y 3DD
by Hendington Limited,
Deadbrook Lane, Aldershot, Hampshire.

Gerard McBurney

London 2 March 96

A BIBLIOGRAPHY OF RUSSIAN COMPOSERS

Contents

Where a composer's name is not followed by a number, this indicates a cross-reference.

Acknowledgements

The compilation of this bibliography has involved visits to a considerable number of libraries, but for the help of whose staff it could not have been completed. I would like to thank the staff of the British Museum Library, both at Bloomsbury, where the greater part of the research was done, and at Colindale. I am grateful to the librarians and staffs of the Westminster Central Music Library and Reference Library; the University of London Music Library and Periodicals Department at Senate House; the B.B.C. Reference Library; the Royal Academy of Music Library; the Library of the Royal College of Music; the Library Association Library; and the Bodleian at Oxford; and to the staffs of several periodicals, including *Musical Opinion:* all of these kindly facilitated my research.

I should like to express thanks to my Supervisor, Mr. A.H. King, for giving so much of his time and such prompt and valuable advice at all stages; thanks are also due to my typist, Mrs. V.R. Skinner; and especially to my friend Graham Barnett for his continued interest in my project over a period of more than five years.

Preface

1. *The need for a bibliography of Russian composers*

I have been unable to trace an extensive published bibliography of Russian composers in English. The latter part of the field is covered by three comprehensive bibliographies. These are William Austin's in his book *Music in the Twentieth Century* (Dent, 1966), mostly arranged by composer; Carroll Wade's bibliography of Stravinsky in Paul Henry Lang's *Stravinsky,* which also appeared in the special Stravinsky issue of *Musical Quarterly* in June 1962; and, thirdly, Paul Magriel's bibliography, also of Stravinsky, in Minna Lederman's *Stravinsky in the Theatre.* All are valuable, all contain minor errors, and all are becoming dated, especially the last-mentioned. Other books contain bibliographies, e.g., Catherine Bowen's *Free Artist,* on the Rubinsteins, the material here being mainly chatty reminiscences, but most Russian composers are very poorly represented. Much of the best literature is still only available in Russian, e.g., the invaluable *Days and Years of P.I. Tchaikovsky* (1940). For Russian material, a start may be made with Paul Horecky's *Basic Russian Publications* (University of Chicago Press, 1962). Horecky's companion volume *Russia and the Soviet Union* (University of Chicago Press, 1965) is also useful for Western-language material.

2. *The field covered*

The word "Russian" includes all composers born in countries comprising the present U.S.S.R., except that Cui is included although born in Poland, and Ussachevsky, born in Manchuria. Non-Russian composers, such as Field, who lived in Russia for many years are excluded. Russians better known in other fields who composed, e.g., Shaliapin, Richter, Rostropovich, Sabaneyev and Slonimsky are included, both material by and about them. For Catherine the Great, who collaborated on several operas, only items dealing with these works are included. Amfiteatrov, Dukelsky and Tiomkin are omitted, but Vladimir Stasov, notable propagandist of "The Five", is included. Coverage of Russian popular music has not been attempted, and folk and church music are only represented when they have been used in actual compositions. Russian horn bands, of great importance in the eighteenth century, are included.

3. *Types of material included*

The aim has been to cover exhaustively English-language books and periodical articles with certain exceptions listed below. The vast quantity of Russian literature has been excluded. Some unpublished works, e.g. theses, are included, though almost invariably it has not been possible to examine these. Theses are omitted if less than half is devoted to Russian composers; so are uncompleted theses. Every effort has been made to personally look at the items listed, but owing to the great number of American periodicals involved, this has not always been possible. For example, there seems to be no complete file of *Modern Music* available in the U.K. All items not examined are asterisked, and unfortunately I cannot vouch for the (sometimes incomplete) bibliographical information noted for these items. Also, it has not been possible to discover the dates of some of the minor composers. Only material published before January 1st. 1971 has been included, except that books (but not articles) published from 1971 to 1973 inclusive have been added. Numbers followed by "a", "b" etc. represent late amendments to the text.

The following have been omitted:

a) Parts of books not exclusively or largely concerned with Russian music, e.g. Galina von Meck's *As I Remember Them* which contains material on Tchaikovsky. There are a few exceptions, e.g. the Newmarch and Tovey programme notes.

b) Articles in encyclopaedias and dictionaries, as these tend to be derived from other works.

c) Short articles (under half a page), especially if anonymous; also short obituaries, except Sabaneyev's obituary of Ippolitov-Ivanov.

d) General articles on ballet productions, as in *Dance and Dancers,* are omitted unless there is at least a separately-headed section on the music.

e) Articles in newspapers — here *The Current Digest of the Soviet Press* should prove useful for Russian material. Serials like *The Listener, Time and Tide, Radio Times, The Times Literary Supplement* and *The Musical Standard* are not here classed as newspapers, but articles in the *Christian Science Monitor* are excluded.

f) Most music reviews, unless of great importance, e.g., the review of the original version of "Boris Godunov" (published 1928). Only the most important book reviews are included, and record reviews are omitted.

g) Reviews of concerts, operas and ballets, unless virtually the whole article is devoted to the music itself, apart from the performance.

h) Books of programme notes for concerts, opera and ballet,, except those by Newmarch and Tovey.

i) Libretti.

j) Chat and gossip of no lasting value; if doubt has arisen regarding the inclusion of an item, it has been included.

4. *Sources*

The following sources have been used:

a) *The Reader's Guide to Periodical Literature,* 1890-1970

b) *The International Index to Periodicals,* 1920-70.

d) The Library Association *Subject Index to Periodicals, and British Humanities Index,* 1915-70.

e) *The Music Index,* 1949-70.

f) *Bibliographie des Musikschrifftums,* 1936-8 and 1950-64.

g) *R.I.L.M.* abstracts of music literature, 1967-9.

h) *Dissertation Abstracts* (partial run only).

I have drawn on the card index of composers at the B.B.C.

Reference Library, library catalogues, published bibliographies, and bibliographies in books and periodical articles. I have also searched complete or partial runs of over sixty periodicals.

5. *Arrangement*

a) General material on Russian music, including that on groups of composers, arranged by date of publication, earliest first. Items dealing with two Russian composers are generally entered under the one receiving the larger coverage, with a reference from the other.

b) Individual Russian composers, arranged alphabetically. A work on one Russian and a non-Russian composer is entered under the Russian composer. If a Russian composer, e.g. Sabaneyev, is writing on Shostakovitch, the item is filed under Shostakovitch, and Sabaneyev is listed in the index. If Sabaneyev is writing on Russian music generally, it is entered in the general section (5a above) and Sabaneyev listed in the index. But if he is writing about, say, film music, this is entered under Sabaneyev and again indexed.

Sub-division is as follows:

i) General material on the composer and his music.

ii) Items on groups of compositions or on individual works, arranged by musical form, as in the March 1966 edition of the *Gramophone* classical record catalogue, viz., symphonies; miscellaneous orchestral (including ballet: for Prokofiev, Stravinsky and Tchaikovsky, the ballets form the last part of the miscellaneous orchestral section); concerti and other works for solo instrument and orchestra; chamber, including all ensembles of two or more instruments, arranged in descending order of size; instrumental soli; vocal; choral; opera. However, all Rubinstein's stage works are arranged in one sequence. For Stravinsky, who wrote a dance-cantata, a concerto for two solo pianos etc., every effort has been made to place works in the most appropriate categories. Titles of musical works are not italicized but are placed in inverted commas where appropriate.

Items on a particular work are arranged chronologically by date of publication, earliest first, and, if necessary, sub-divided alphabetically by author. Titles of works adopted are those used in the March 1966 edition of the *Gramophone* classical catalogue, or in Grove's *Dictionary of Music and Musicians* (1954) or other standard work of reference, e.g. White's *Stravinsky: the Composer and His Works* for that composer.

6. *Filing order*

For periodical articles where the date of volume plus a part number but no date of part are given, they are entered under the year and filed before those dated January of that year. Exceptions are some periodicals with twelve parts per annum, but with undated part numbers, e.g. *Soviet Literature,* in which case it is assumed that part one represents January, part three March and so on, and filing will be accordingly.

Articles for April 1930 are placed before those for April 1st. Those dated 1929-30 go before those dated January 1930. A periodical issue dated "Spring" is filed before an April issue, "Summer" filed before July, "Autumn" (or "Fall") before October and "Winter" before January. Likewise "Spring-Summer" goes before May and "Fall-Winter" before November. Winter 1949 files before Winter 1949-50.

Where alphabetisation is used to determine the order of entries, the "word by word" (or "nothing before something") system is used. Abbreviated words are spelled out, e.g. Dr. = Doctor.

7. *The Entry*

Entries follow the information given on the title-page of the book or at the head of the periodical article. Any information not taken from these sources is given in square brackets. Three dots indicates an omission of wording. Every effort has been made to follow the book or periodical, but not always as to punctuation and capitalisation, as this sometimes leads to nonsensical entries. Hence the numerous different ways of spelling a composer's name (Calvocoressi himself used at least three forms for "Mussorgsky") or for the title of a work. Hence some quaint phraseology, bad English etc. The *"in* ABRAHAM." form of entry is used for all books whose contents have been indexed. A list of the books indexed is separately appended.

a) *Books and pamphlets*

A work is entered under the author's surname. Generally only the first Christian name is given (or two initials or one name and one initial) unless a second is required to avoid confusion. Initials are used if the author's fornames are better known by initials. Anonymous works are entered under the first word of the title (for indexing purposes the article is ignored), the title occupying the place normally occupied by the author. The contribution of an editor or compiler is indicated by *"comp."* or *"ed."* In the title part of the entry, titles of musical works, e.g. operas, are only placed in inverted commas if they are thus placed in the book or periodical.

The publisher is given in sufficiently distinctive shortened form. Place of publication is included (before the publisher) only when it is not London. If there are two places of publication, one being British, the British one is given. If not given in the work, publisher and place are identified if known; if not known, the letters "n.p." are used. If the year of publication is not given and is not known exactly, an approximate date is given, indicated by "c." or by "?". If no approximate date is possible, the abbreviation "n.d." is used.

The number of pages is specified in the numeration of the work, the first and last numbered pages being given, followed by "p". Illustrations on pages included in the pagination of the work are indicated by "illus.". The number of plates (i.e. pages occupied by illustration, maps, diagrams, tables, etc., not included in the pagination) is given, followed by "pl.". Music examples are indicated by "mus". A bibliography ("bib") is noted only if it appears at the end of the book or article or at the end of chapters, but not if listed in the form of footnotes. A discography is referred to by the abbreviation "disc."

b) *Theses*

It has not always been possible to ascertain whether the work is a thesis or a dissertation: if not known, it is called a thesis. Owing to the variation in the amount of information collected, most of the theses not having been examined, no set pattern of entry has been possible, but an effort has been made to present the bibliographical information in uniform order.

c) *Periodical articles*

Rules for author and title entry are the same as for books and pamphlets (section a)above). If no title is given or known, a conventional title is used and is placed in square brackets. Many periodical titles are entered in abbreviated form, a full list of these abbreviations being tabulated separately. In almost all cases, the word "The" at the start of a periodical title has been omitted in entries.

The volume number, date of part and page numbers are given, all volume numbers being quoted in Arabic numerals. If there is no volume number, the part number is noted, as with *Composer* and *Tempo.* If there is no date of part, the date of the volume is noted with the part number. For articles in monthly journals, the month and year are specified. The numbers of the first and last numbered pages on which an article appears are given when all the pages are consecutive. If an article is continued on later pages, these are indicated by "+", e.g. "p.2-4+". For the headings of articles in several instalments, Arabic numerals are used even when Roman ones appear in the article. Illustrations, musical examples etc. are indicated as in section 6a) above.

d) *Annotations*

Annotations for books are based on reviews in periodicals such as *Musical Times, Musical Quarterly, Music and Letters,* Music Library Association *Notes, Tempo* and *Musical Opinion,* and on my own examination of the work itself. They indicate the content, extent and level of the book or article, and, where applicable, note the presence of a list of compositions. It may be assumed that a book has an index unless otherwise stated. Errors are pointed out selectively. Annotations for articles generally explain or enlarge on the title.

e) *Transliteration*

Owing to the numerous different practices adopted in the transliteration of Russian names, all composers' names in section headings and annotations are spelled as in *Baker's Biographical Dictionary of Musicians* (fifth edition, 1958, with supplements).

f) *Cross references and running numbers*

Each full entry is given a running number. In a few instances, if a periodical entry is reprinted with a different title or in abridged form, it is entered again and given a new number. "See" references refer to further or related entries under other composers or works; they are arranged chronologically in with the entries and are not numbered. "See also" references refer to other entries, mostly under the same composer and are provided wherever they help to clarify connections between items, particularly to unravel the complexities of the literature of Stravinsky.

List of books indexed

This list refers to the indexing of chapters, essays or sections on Russian composers only.

	Date	*Entry number*
ABRAHAM Eight Soviet composers	1943	165
On Russian Music	1939	147
Slavonic and Romantic music (part only)	1968	353
Studies in Russian music	1935	127
Tchaikovsky. A symposium	1945	2736
ARMITAGE Igor Stravinsky	1936	2068
BLOM Tchaikovsky orchestral works	1927	2734
BORETZ *and* **CONE** Perspectives on Schoenberg and Stravinsky (part only)	1968	2339
BROOK Six great Russian composers	1946	197
CALVOCORESSI A survey of Russian music	1944	176
CALVOCORESSI *and* **ABRAHAM** Masters of Russian music	1936	133
CORLE Igor Stravinsky	1949	2134
DAVIDSON Stories from the Russian operas	1922	71
KREBS Soviet composers and the development of Soviet music	1970	362
LEDERMAN Stravinsky in the theatre	1951	2153
LIPOVSKY Lenin Prize winners (part only)	1967?	347
MOISENCO Realist music. 25 Soviet composers	1949	220
Twenty Soviet composers	1942	158
MONTAGU-NATHAN Contemporary Russian composers	1917	47
An introduction to Russian music	1916	37
NEWMARCH The concert-goer's library of descriptive notes (part only)	1928-48	90
SABANEYEFF Modern Russian composers	1929	96
SHOSTAKOVITCH *and others* Russian symphony. Thoughts about Tchaikovsky	1947	2749
TOVEY Essays in musical analysis (part only)	1935-9	128
ZETLIN The Five	1959	295

General abbreviations

Apr. – April
Aug. – August
bib. – bibliography
bull. – bulletin
c. – circa
comp. – compiled, compiler
Dec. – December
disc. – discography
ed. – edited, editor
Feb. – February
illus. – illustrated (collation)
i.s. – illustrated series
j. – journal
Jan. – January
mag. – magazine
Mar. – March
mus. – music example(s)
n.d. – date not known
n.i.s. – new illustrated series
n.p. – publisher not known
n.s. – new series
Nov. – November
o.s. – old series
Oct. – October
op. – opus
p. – page(s)
pl. – plate(s)
rev. – review
s.s. – second series
Sept. – September
tr. – translated, translator
v. – volume (collation)
vol. – volume (annotation)

Abbreviations of periodical titles

Note: bull. – bulletin; j. – journal; mag. – magazine; rev. – review.
Periodicals with only these words abbreviated in their titles are not listed below.

AM – Atlantic Monthly
ASJ – Anglo-Soviet Journal
C – The Composer
Ch – The Chesterian
CL – Newmarch. The Concert-goer's Library of Descriptive Notes (1928-48)
DA – Dissertation Abstracts
DD – Dance and Dancers
DI – Dance Index
DT – The Dancing Times
E – Etude
FR – Fortnightly Review
G – The Gramophone
H – Hinrichson's Year Book (with year)
HF – High Fidelity (New York, 1951 onwards)
JAMS – Journal of the American Musicological Society
L – The Listener
LLA – Littell's Living Age
LME – London Musical Events
M – Music (Chicago, 1888 onwards)
MA – Musical America
MC – Musical Courier
MJ – Music Journal (Delaware, 1942 onwards)
MJIMS – Monthly Journal of the International Musical Society
ML – Music and Letters
MM – Modern Music
MMR – Monthly Musical Record
MMu – Music and Musicians
MO – Musical Opinion
MQ – Musical Quarterly
MR – Music Review (Cambridge, 1940 onwards)
MS – Musical Standard
MSt – Music Student
MT – Musical Times
MTe – Music Teacher
Mu – Musician (Philadelphia, 1895 onwards)
N – Music Library Association Notes
Na – Nation (New York, 1865 onwards)
NMR – New Music Review
NR – New Republic
NS – New Statesman
O – Opera
ON – Opera News
PAMS – Papers of the American Musicological Society

PMA – Proceedings of the Musical Association (pre 1944)
PNM – Perspectives of New Music
PRMA – Proceedings of the Royal Musical Association (post 1944)
QMIMS – Quarterly Magazine of the International Musical Society
RR – Russian Review (New York, 1941 onwards)
RT – Radio Times
Rev. of revs. – Review of Reviews
S – The Score
SCR – S.C.R. Soviet Music Bulletin
SL – Soviet Literature (formerly International Literature)
Slavonic rev. – Slavonic and East European Review
Sp. – Spectator
SR – Saturday Review (New York, 1924 onwards)
T – Tempo
UU – U.S.S.R. Union of Composers Information Bulletin (Moscow)
USSR illus. monthly – U.S.S.R. Illustrated Monthly
U.S. Dept. of State bull. – U.S. Department of State Bulletin

GENERAL

1. **EDWARDS, H. Sutherland**
Russian coronation music.
Musical rev., 1, 17 Mar. 1883, p.171-2.

2. **BARRETT, W. A.**
Russian music.
MT, 27, Aug. 1886, p.452-7. mus.

3. **SHEDLOCK, J. S.**
Russian music.
MMR, 18, Nov. 1888, p.244-5.

4. **ZIELINSKI, J. de**
[The] present state of music in Russia.
MS, n.s., 45, 2 Dec. 1893, p.446-7.
9 Dec. 1893, p.462-3.
16 Dec. 1893, p.483.

*5. **POUGIN, A.**
Music in Russia.
M, 14, Feb. 1898, p.443.

*6. **SIMPSON, E. E.**
Musical conditions in Russia.
M, 15, 1898, p.426.

7. **KEETON, A. E.**
The Russian school of opera.
Gentleman's mag., 289, Aug. 1900, p.117-27.

8. **ROWBOTHAM, J. F.**
Russian music.
MO, 24, Dec. 1900, p.181-2.
Jan. 1901, p.269-70.

9. **BARRY, C. A.**
Recent Russian music in England.
Edinburgh rev., 194, Oct. 1902, p.363-89. bib.

10. **NEWMARCH, Rosa**
The development of national opera in Russia.
PMA, 28, 1901-2, p.67-88.

11. **EVANS, Edwin**
Modern Russian instrumental music.
MS, i.s., 18, 29 Nov. 1902, p.337-8.
6 Dec. 1902, p.349-50.
13 Dec. 1902, p.366-7.
20 Dec. 1902, p.382-3.
27 Dec. 1902, p.308-9.
19, 3 Jan. 1903, p.6-7.
10 Jan. 1903, p.22-3.
17 Jan. 1903, p.36-7.

12. **NEWMARCH, Rosa**
National opera in Russia (Third paper).
PMA, 29, 1902-3, p.99-113.

*13. **THE DEVELOPMENT of Russian music.**
Rev. of revs., 29, Apr. 1904, p.494-5.

14. **BRUNEAU, Alfred**
Russian music.
MS, i.s., 21, 9 Apr. 1904, p.234-5.
Translated from his book *Musique de Russie et musiciens de France.*

*15. **QUARTER of a century of Russian music.**
Rev. of revs., 34, Aug. 1906, p.231-3.

16. **GILMAN, L.**
Music from Russia.
Harper's weekly, 51, 3 Feb. 1907, p.278. illus.

17. **TIDEBÖHL, Ellen von**
Music in Russia.
MMR, 37, Mar. 1907, p.55-6.

18. **LYMN, Henry**
The music of "Holy Russia".
MS, i.s., 29, 16 May 1908, p.306-7.

*19. **TRACY, J. M.**
Russian composers and pianists.
Mu, 14, Aug. 1909, p.351.

*20. **CALVOCORESSI, M. D.**
Conservatism and progress in Russian music.
NMR, 10?, Mar. 1911, p.?

21. **CALVOCORESSI, M. D.**
Music in St. Petersburg.
MMR, 42, Apr. 1912, p.94-5.

*22. **RUSSIAN music and Tolstoy's views about it.**
Rev. of revs., 45, May 1912, p.611-12.

23. **EVANS, Edward**
Modern Russian pianoforte music.
MJIMS, 14, Jan. 1913, p.105-9.
Feb. 1913, p.126-30.

24. **MUSICAL institutions in Russia.**
MJIMS, 14, Apr. 1913, p.214-15.

25. **MONTAGU-NATHAN, M.**
A short history of Russian music.
MS, n.i.s., 1, 26 Apr. 1913, p.350-2.

26. **MONTAGU-NATHAN, M.**
A history of Russian music.
William Reeves. 1914. vi-viii, 1-346p. illus., 1pl.
Despite some now outdated views of Tchaikovsky, this has long been a standard work, the first in English on its subject. An appendix lists composers not dealt with in the main part of the book.

27. **NEWMARCH, Rosa**
The Russian opera.
Herbert Jenkins. 1914. viii-xv, 1-430p. illus., 16pl.
Straight-forward treatment by the doyenne of writers on Russian music who met many of the composers dealt with. It includes a name index and an index of operas.

28. **BENSUSAN, S.L.**
The Russian movement in music.
Windsor mag., 40, June 1914, p.105-12. illus.
Several of the dates of birth are inaccurate.

29. **MONTAGU-NATHAN, M.**
The influence of women on the Russian School.
MT, 55, July 1914, p.442-4.

30. **NEWMAN, Ernest**
Russian opera and Russian "nationalism".
MT, 55, Aug. 1914, p.505-8.

31. **MONTAGU-NATHAN, M.**
A musician's difficulty of today. The spelling and pronunciation of Russian names.
MSt, 7, Sept. 1914, p.1-3.

32. **MONTAGU-NATHAN, M.**
Russian literature and Russian music.
PMA, 41, 1914-15, p.113-34.

33. **POUGIN, Arthur**
A short history of Russian music. Tr. by Lawrence Haward.
Chatto and Windus. 1915. v-x, 2-231p.
One of the earliest histories published in English, it lacks depth and scholarship. Montagu-Nathan's surveys are much to be preferred.

*34. **RUNCIMAN, John F.**
Young Russians.
Saturday rev., 17, July 1915, p.62-3.

35. **NEWMARCH, Rosa**
The outlook in Russia.
MT, 56, Sept. 1915, p.521-3.

36. **MONTAGU-NATHAN, M.**
The conservative element: Serof, Tchaikovsky, the Rubinsteins, Taneyef and Glazounof.
in MONTAGU-NATHAN. An introduction to Russian music, p.58-62.

37. **MONTAGU-NATHAN, M.**
An introduction to Russian music.
Palmer and Hayward. 1916. 12-70p.
Chapters on Balakirev, Borodin, Cui, Dargomyzhsky, Glinka, Mussorgsky, Rimsky-Korsakov, "The conservative element" (Tchaikovsky, the Rubinsteins etc.) and "The new age" (Scriabin etc.). The lack of an index mars this otherwise excellent account.

38. **MONTAGU-NATHAN, M.**
The new age.
in MONTAGU-NATHAN. An introduction to Russian music, p.64-70.
Deals with Scriabin, Rachmaninoff etc.

39. **MONTAGU-NATHAN, M.**
News from Russia.
MO, 39, July 1916, p.647.

40. **MONTAGU-NATHAN, M.**
Music in Russia.
MT, 57, Aug. 1916, p.364-5.

41. **MONTAGU-NATHAN, M.**
News from Russia.
MO, 39, Aug. 1916, p.701.

42. **SOME Russian composers.**
Musical news, 51, 19 Aug. 1916, p.121-2.
26 Aug. 1916, p.137-8.

43. **MONTAGU-NATHAN, M.**
The story of Russian music.
MSt, 9, Sept. 1916, p.5-15. illus.
Oct. 1916, p.64-6.
Nov. 1916, p.99-101. illus.
Dec. 1916, p.140+.
The first article is general and the others deal respectively with Glinka, Dargomyzhsky and Balakirev.

44. **ALTSCHULER, Modest**
The music of the people in Russian masterpieces.
Musical news, 51, 2 Sept. 1916, p.146-9.
From *Etude.* Includes a comprehensive list of "the best-known Russian works for orchestra", many based in part on folk-songs.

45. **NEWMARCH, Rosa**
Sources of Russian operas and ballet.
Country life, 40, 14 Oct. 1916, p.467-9. illus.

46. **RIENZI, Alexis**
The Russian opera.
Russian rev., 2, Nov. 1916, p.234-9.

47. **MONTAGU-NATHAN, M.**
Contemporary Russian composers.
Palmer and Hayward. 1917. xiii-xv, 3-329p. illus., 12pl.
The first English-language book dealing solely with twentieth century Russian composers and still of some value, although rather wordy. Chapters on Glazunov, Gretchaninov, Medtner, Rachmaninof Rebikov, Scriabin, Stravinsky, Taneyef and N. Tcherepnin.

48. **MONTAGU-NATHAN, M.**
The younger generation.
in MONTAGU-NATHAN. Contemporary Russian composers, p.287-317. illus.

49. **ZIELINSKI, Jaroslaw de**
Russian hunting music.
MQ, 3, Jan. 1917, p.53-9. 1pl.
Includes information on horn bands.

50. **TIDEBÖHL, Ellen von**
A musical jubilee in Moscow.
MMR, 47, Feb. 1917, p.31-3.
The fiftieth anniversary of the Moscow Conservatoire.

51. **ANDERTON, H. Orsmond**
The folk-songs of the Allies. 2. Russia.
MO, 40, Mar. 1917, p.349-51. mus.
Mostly anthologies of Russian folk-songs, e.g., Rimsky-Korsakov's.

52. **MONTAGU-NATHAN, M.**
Russian musical criticism - past and present.
MT, 58, Mar. 1917, p.119

53. **HULL, A. Eaglefield**
Programme annotations for the Russian organ album.
MMR, 47, Apr. 1917, p.77.
Augener's *Album series* no. 105. Notes on ten pieces by Arensky, Mussorgsky, Rachmaninoff, Rebikov and Scriabin (mostly arrangements of piano pieces).

54. **TIDEBÖHL, Ellen von**
The Moscow musical season (October 1916 to January 1917).
MMR, 47, Apr. 1917, p.82-3.

55. **MONTAGU-NATHAN, M.**
Pages of Russian musical criticism.
MO, 40, May 1917, p.482-3.

56. **WESTON, Annie**
The teaching of Russian music.
MSt, 9, July 1917, p.330+.
Also *in Musical herald,* no. 831, June 1917, p.172.

57. **MONTAGU-NATHAN, M.**
The influence of Belayef on modern Russian music.
MSt, 9, Aug. 1917, p.355-6.
M. P. Belaiev (1836-1904) was the publisher of the music of many Russian composers.

58. **MONTAGU-NATHAN, M.**
Notes on the Russian music.
MT, 58, Sept. 1917, p.417-18.

59. **TIDEBÖHL, Ellen von**
Music during the recent Russian Revolution.
MMR, 47, Oct. 1917, p.222-3.

60. **TIDEBÖHL, Ellen von**
Opera in Moscow. 1916-1917.
MMR, 47, Dec. 1917, p.272-3.

61. **CORELLI-GREEN, Mrs.**
Lyricism, realism and fancy as interpreted in Russian music.
MS, n.i.s., 11, 8 June 1918, p.307-9.
22 June 1918, p.322-4.

62. **MONTAGU-NATHAN, M.**
Belaiev — Mæcenas of Russian music.
MQ, 4, July 1918, p.450-65. 2pl.

63. **MARTENS, Frederick H.**
The modern Russian pianoforte sonata (based on an interview with M. Serge Prokofieff).
MQ, 5, July 1919, p.357-63.
There seems to be no evidence of Prokofiev's hand in the article which covers many Russian composers.

64. **NORDEN, N. Lindsay**
A brief study of the Russian liturgy and its music.
MQ, 5, July 1919, p.426-50. mus.
Includes information on early composers and composed settings of the liturgy.

65. **SAMINSKY, Lazare**
The Russian school and its youngest exponents.
Ch, n.s., no.3, Dec. 1919, p.76-8.

66. **HENDERSON, A.**
Russian church music.
PMA, 46, 1919-20, p.1-11.
On composed church music.

67. **TIERSOT, Julien**
Russian composers as described by themselves. Tr. by Frederick H. Martens.
MQ, 7, July 1921, p.376-98.

68. **CATALOGUE of chamber music.**
Russian Music Agency. [1922]. 4-9p.
Arrangement is by musical form sub-divided alphabetically by composer. Titles are mostly in French; prices and opus numbers are given, breakdown being indicated within each opus number.

69. **CATALOGUE of piano music.**
Russian Music Agency [1922]. 4-15p.
Classified arrangement, sub-divided by composer. Much of the information is not to be found elsewhere, e.g., a page is devoted to a list of Glazunov's piano duets.

70. **CATALOGUE of vocal music.**
Russian Music Agency. [1922]. 4-17p.
Again arrangement is by musical form, choruses, songs and opera being included. The lists are very detailed, e.g., the breakdown of the score of "Prince Igor", and there is a page on the works of Alpheraky.

71. **DAVIDSON, Gladys**
Stories from the Russian operas.
T. Werner Laurie. [1922]. v-ix, 2-238p. 9pl.
Covers Borodin's "Prince Igor", Cui's "Mademoiselle Fifi", Dargomyzhsky's "The Stone Guest", Mussorgsky's "Boris Godunov" and "Khovantschina", Rachmaninoff's "Aleko" and "Francesca de Rimini", Rimsky-Korsakov's "The Golden Cockerel", "The Maid of Pskov", "May Night" and "Mozart and Salieri", Rubinstein's "The Demon", Stravinsky's "The Nightingale" and Tchaikovsky's "Eugene Onegin", "Iolanta" and "The Queen of Spades". Chatty treatment, but especially useful for the little-known operas.

72. **SAMINSKY, Lazare**
Music of the peoples of the Russian orient.
MQ, 8, July 1922, p.346-52. mus.

73. **SCHOLES, Percy**
Russian music.
School music rev., 31, 1 Nov. 1922, p.107-8.

74. **SAMINSKY, Lazare**
Letter from Russia.
Ch, n.s., no. 27, Dec. 1922, p.90.

75. **TRINCHIERI, Alfredo**
Facts about the "Russian Opera".
E, 41, Nov. 1923, p.750.

76. **ABRAHAM, Gerald**
Liszt's influence on the Russian nationalists.
MMR, 64, Mar.-Apr. 1924, p.57-8. mus.
Also *in* ABRAHAM. On Russian music, p.80-90, the title being *Liszt's influence on "The Mighty Handful".*

77. **DUTORDOIT, Coralie**
Some Russian music and musicians.
MS, n.i.s., 23, 3 May 1924, p.142-3.

78. **MODERN Russian composers and some of their works.**
MS, n.i.s., 23, 17 May 1924, p.166.
A list of the most well-known works.

79. **BELAIEV, V.**
Letter from Moscow.
Ch, 6, Dec. 1924, p.92-3.

80. **BELAIEV, V.**
Letter from Moscow.
Ch, 6, July 1925, p.269.

81. **BELAIEV, Victor**
Russia: present tendencies.
Sackbut, 6, Sept. 1925, p.46-9.

82. **FINDEISEN, N.**
The early days of chamber music in Russia. Tr. by M.D. Calvocoressi.
MMR, 55, Sept. 1925, p.262-3.
Oct. 1925, p.292-3.
Essay commissioned by W.W. Cobbett for his *Cyclopedic survey of chamber music.*

83. **OLIPHANT, E. H.**
A survey of Russian song.
MQ, 12, Apr. 1926, p.196-230.
Lists 600 songs, most of which he examined.

*84. **BELAIEV, Victor**
Russia's newest composers.
MM, 3, May 1926, p.33-5.

85. **SWAN, Alfred J.**
The present state of Russian music.
MQ, 13, Jan. 1927, p.29-37.

86. **GIL-MARCHEX, Henri**
Back from a trip to Russia.
Ch, 8, Jan.-Feb. 1927, p.115-21.

87. **MILHAUD, Darius**
Music in "Red" Russia.
MT, 68, Feb. 1927, p.131-2.
An interview with the composer, who had recently toured Russia.

88. **BELAIEF, Victor**
The latest Russian quartets. Tr. by S.W. Pring.
MMR, 57, May 1927, p.132-3.
Quartets written since about 1924 by minor Russian composers.

89. **TIDEBÖHL, Ellen von**
New operas in Moscow.
MMR, 57, June 1927, p.168.
Triodion's "Stenka Razin", Yurasovsky's "Trilby" and Zolotarev's "The Decembrists".

90. **NEWMARCH, Rosa**
The concert-goer's library of descriptive notes.
O.U.P. 1928-48. 6v.
Mostly the programme notes written for the Queen's Hall Orchestra, 1908-27. 332 works are covered, including thirty-eight by eleven Russian composers as follows: Tchaikovsky fifteen, Rimsky-Korsakov six, Rachmaninoff four, Borodin and Mussorgsky three each, Glinka two and Balakirev, Glazunov, Prokofiev, Rubinstein and Scriabin one each.

91. **ABRAHAM, Gerald**
The elements of Russian music.
ML, 9, Jan. 1928, p.51-8. mus.
The text is almost identical to that of *The essence of Russian music in* ABRAHAM. Studies in Russian music, p.1-20 (no.125).

92. **BELAIEV, Victor**
An English operatic manager in eighteenth century Russia.
Tr. by S.W. Pring.
Dominant, 1, Jan. 1928, p.18-20.
The manager was Maddox, who managed one of Moscow's theatres.

*93. **SAMINSKY, Lazare**
Russian composer in review.
MM, 5, Jan. 1928, p.36-8.

94. **SABANEYEFF, Leonid**
The American group of Russian composers.
in SABANEYEFF. Modern Russian composers, p.226-8.
Saminsky, Achron etc.

95. **SABANEYEFF, Leonid**
The Leningrad group.
in SABANEYEFF. Modern Russian composers, p.222-5.
Steinberg, Tcherepnin, etc.

96. **SABANEYEFF, Leonid**
Modern Russian composers. Tr. from the Russian by Judah A. Joffe. Martin Lawrence [1929?] 5-253p.
Despite many errors, e.g. wrong birth-dates for Stravinsky, Prokofiev and seven other composers, and the lack of an index, this is still a valuable set of essays. Covers Akimenko, Feinberg Gnessin, Gretchaninov, A. Krein, G. Krein, Medtner, Miaskovsky, Prokofiev, Rachmaninoff, Rebikov, Rosslavetz, Scriabin, Stanchinski, Taneyev, Tchaikovsky, Yavorski, and chapters on six groups of minor composers.

97. **SABANEYEFF, Leonid**
The Moscow group of conservatives.
in SABANEYEFF. Modern Russian composers, p.214-21.
Catoire, Conus, Glière etc.

98. **SABANEYEFF, Leonid**
The musical creative art of the Russian Revolution.
in SABANEYEFF. Modern Russian composers, p.242-9.

99. **SABANEYEFF, Leonid**
... The Russian National School.
in SABANEYEFF. Modern Russian composers, p.251-2.
This is the same as "The Five".

100. **SABANEYEFF, Leonid**
The Russian-Parisian School.
in SABANEYEFF. Modern Russian composers, p.235-41.
Lourié, A. Tcherepnin etc.

101. **SABANEYEFF, Leonid**
The young composers of Russia.
in SABANEYEFF. Modern Russian composers, p.229-34.
Knipper, Shebalin etc.

102. **BOUGHTON, Rutland**
Music of Soviet Russia: an estimate.
Sackbut, 9, Feb. 1929, p.226-35+.
Mar. 1929, p.259-65.

103. **SABANEEV, Leonid**
Russian music in the light of European influences. Tr. by S.W. Pring.
MO, 52, Feb. 1929, p.447-9.

104. **COWELL, Henry**
Conservative music in radical Russia.
NR, 59, 14 Aug. 1929, p.339-41.

105. **SABANEEV, Leonid**
Musical tendencies in contemporary Russia. Tr. by S.W. Pring.
MQ, 16, Oct. 1930. p.469-81.

106. **SOKOLOFF, Nikolai**
Symphonic music in Soviet Russia.
MQ, 17, Apr. 1931, p.219-26.

107. **HOLT, Richard**
Notes on the Russian operas.
G, 9, June 1931, p.7.

*108. **FLEISHER, E. A.**
Music in present day Soviet Russia.
E, 49, Oct. 1931, p.695-6. illus.
Nov. 1931, p.774+.

109. **OULD, Hermon**
The spirit behind Russian music.
RT, 34, 29 Jan. 1932, p.245+.
Reprinted in B.B.C. Symphony Orchestra programme notes, 3 Feb. 1932.

*110. **CORNWALL, F. J.**
Some Russian backgrounds in music.
E, 50, Feb. 1932, p.139.

*111. **GATES, W. F.**
Music of Soviet Russia.
E, 50, Feb. 1932, p.138.

112. **MUSGRAVE, Francis**
Musical life in Soviet Russia.
MT, 73, Aug. 1932, p.712-13

113. **LOURIÉ, Arthur**
The Russian School. Tr. by S.W. Pring.
MQ, 18, Oct. 1932, p.519-29.

*114. **BRAUDO, Eugene**
The Russian panorama.
MM, 10, Jan. 1933, p.79-86.

115. **ABRAHAM, Gerald**
The whole-tone scale in Russian music.
MT, 74, July 1933, p.602-4. mus.
Also *in* ABRAHAM. On Russian music, p.62-71. mus.

116. **FINDEISEN, Nicholas**
The earliest Russian operas. Tr. by M.D. Calvocoressi.
MQ, 19, July 1933, p.331-40. illus., mus.

117. **POSITION of composers in modern Russia.**
MTe, 12, Aug. 1933, p.385+.

118. **SABANEEV, L.**
Music and musicians in the U.S.S.R. Tr. by S.W. Pring.
ML, 15, Jan. 1934, p.55-60.

119. **ABRAHAM, Gerald**
"Mlada", a curious episode in Russian musical history.
MO, 57, June 1934, p.769-70. mus.
July 1934, p.866-7. mus.
Aug. 1934, p.947-8. mus.
The opera-ballet composed jointly by Borodin, Cui, Mussorgsky, Rimsky-Korsakov and Minkus. *See also* no.146.

120. **LOCKSPEISER, Edward**
Music in Soviet Russia.
John O'London's weekly, 31, 21 July 1934, p.575+. illus.

121. **LOCKSPEISER, Edward**
Leningrad Musical Festival.
Ch, 15, July-August. 1934, p.169-70.

122. **ABRAHAM, Gerald**
The oriental element in Russian music.
MMR, 64, Sept. 1934, p.145-7.
Also *in* ABRAHAM. On Russian music, p.72-80, the title being *Oriental elements in Russian music.*

123. **CALVOCORESSI, M.D.**
From my notebook.
MO, 58, Nov, 1934, p.113.
Miscellaneous notes on Russian music.

124. **KERRIDGE, W.H.**
The Union of Soviet Composers.
MT, 75, Dec. 1934, p.1073-5.

125. **ABRAHAM, Gerald**
The essence of Russian music.
in ABRAHAM. Studies in Russian music, p.1-20. illus., mus.
The text is almost identical to that of no. 91.

126. **ABRAHAM, Gerald**
The folk song element.
in ABRAHAM. Studies in Russian music, p.43-67. illus., mus.

127. **ABRAHAM, Gerald**
Studies in Russian music.
William Reeves [1935]. vi, 1-355 p. illus., 8pl., mus.
Fifteen illuminating essays, mostly on "The Five" and especially on Rimsky-Korsakov, some having appeared before (in slightly different forms) in periodicals. A standard work by the doyen of Western writers on the subject.
Contents: The essence of Russian music.- Glinka and his achievement. - The folk-song element. -"The Stone Guest". - Tolstoy and Mussorgsky. - Borodin as a symphonist. - Rimsky-Korsakov's first opera. - Rimsky-Korsakov's Gogol operas. - "Snegurochka" ("Snow Maiden"). - "Sadko". -"The Tsar's Bride". - "Kitezh". -"The Golden Cockerel". - Balakirev: a flawed genius. - Tchaikovsky revalued.

128. **TOVEY, *Sir* Donald**
Essays in musical analysis.
O.U.P. 1935-9. 6v. mus.
Notes on 254 works, most being reprints from programmes for the "Reid" concerts in Edinburgh. Tovey later lamented his innumerable slips in the musical examples, but the books are thought-provoking, sometimes brilliant and superbly written. A chamber music volume, edited by Hubert Foss, was completed after Tovey's death. Only four Russian works are included: Tchaikovsky's Fifth and Sixth Symphonies, Glazunov's First Piano Concerto and Rimsky-Korsakov's "Conte Féerique", op.29.

129. **BRILL, Charles**
Music in the U.S.S.R.
MT, 76, May 1935, p.405-7.

130. **CALVOCORESSI, M. D.**
A bird's eye-view of Russian music.
MT, 76, June 1935, p.505-7.

131. **HOLT, Richard**
Russian music. 1. Some main characteristics.
G, 13, Oct. 1935, p.183-4.

132. **HOLT, Richard**
Russian music 2. The records and a little history.
G, 13, Dec. 1935, p.296-70. illus., discs.

133. **CALVOCORESSI, M. D.** *and* **ABRAHAM, Gerald**
Masters of Russian music.
Duckworth. 1936. 9-511p. 13pl., bib.
A well-written, informative and valuable survey, now something of a classic in its field. It clears up many misunderstandings about "The Five" stemming mainly from Rimsky-Korsakov's memoirs. Covers Balakirev, Borodin, Cui, Dargomyzhsky, Glazunov, Glinka, Liadov, Liapunov, Mussorgsky, Rimsky-Korsakov, Scriabin, Serov, Taneyev and Tchaikovsky.

*134. **SCHNEERSON, Grigori**
The changing course of Russian msuic.
MM, 13, Jan.-Feb. 1936, p.19-24.

135. **CALVOCORESSI, M. D.**
From my notebook.
MO, 59, Feb. 1936, p.398-9.
Deals with ballets which have been created to Russian music.

136. **HOLT, Richard**
Russian music. 3.
G, 13, Feb. 1936, p.361-4. illus., discs.
Discographies arranged by composer.

137. **NADEJINE, Nicholas**
Twenty-five centuries of Russian music.
G, 14, June 1936, p.7-8+.
Aug. 1936, p.131-2.

138. **SABANEEV, L.**
Liszt and Russian music. Tr. by S.W. Pring.
MT, 77, Aug, 1936, p.683-92, illus.

139. **CALVOCORESSI, M. D.**
From my note-book.
MO, 60, Oct, 1936, p.17-18.
Includes information on Glazunov and on Kabalevsky's Symphony no.2.

140. **MELLERS, W. H.**
Russians in Paris.
L, 17, 10 Feb. 1937, p.291.
Mainly on Stravinsky and Prokofiev.

*141. **SLONIMSKY, Nicolas**
[The] development of Soviet music.
Research bull. on the Soviet Union, 2, 30 Apr. 1937, p.31-6.

142. **SABANEEV, Leonid**
Music in the U.S.S.R. Tr. by S.W. Pring.
MT, 78, May 1937, p.413-15.

143. **KOZLENKO, William**
Soviet music and musicians.
MQ, 23, July 1937, p.295-305.

144. **HOLT, Richard,** *tr.*
Songs of famous Russian composers sung by Vladimir Rosing.
Parlophone [1938]. 3-27p.
Entries include brief notes on the composer and songs, and English and phonetic translations of the words.

145. **[CALVOCORESSI, M. D.]**
Musical treasures in the manuscript department of the Public Library, Leningrad. A survey by A.N. Rimsky-Korsakov.
[In Russian].
MT, 79, Dec. 1938, p.902-3.
A review of the book written by Rimsky-Korsakov's son.

146. **ABRAHAM, Gerald**
The collective "Mlada".
in ABRAHAM. On Russian music, p.91-112. mus.
See also no.119.

147. **ABRAHAM, Gerald**
On Russian music.
William Reeves. [1939]. 2-274p. illus., 1pl., mus.
Twenty-one essays, largely devoted to the nineteenth century, most of which appeared in slightly different forms in periodicals. Supplements the author's *Studies in Russian music.*
Contents: "A Life for the Tsar". - "Ruslan and Lyudmila". - Glinka, Dagomizhsky and "The Rusalka". - Dargomizhsky's orchestral pieces. - The whole-tone scale in Russian music. - Oriental elements in Russian music. - Liszt's influence on "The Mighty Handful". - The collective "Mlada". - Rimsky-Korsakov's "Mlada". - "Tsar Saltan". - New light on old friends. - The history of "Prince Igor". - Borodin's songs. - Balakirev's symphonies. - Balakirev's music to "King Lear". -Balakirev's piano sonata. - "The Fair of Sorochintsy" and Cherepnin's completion of it. - "Eugene Onegin" and Tchaikovsky's marriage. - Glazunov: the end of an episode. - Some psychological peculiarities of Russian creative artists. - The evolution of Russian harmony.

148. **ABRAHAM, Gerald**
Some psychological peculiarities of Russian creative artists.
in ABRAHAM. On Russian music, p.234-54.

149. **GRAY, Cecil**
Concerning Russian music.
L, 22, 7 Sept. 1939, p.496.

150. **VODARSKY-SHIRAEFF, Alexandria,** *comp.*
Russian composers and musicians.
New York, H. W. Wilson. 1940. 10-158p. bibs.
Uncritical, sometimes inaccurate and brief biographies of 500-600 musicians.

151. **PLOTNIKOFF, Eugene**
Medallions of Russian masters of yesteryear.
E, 58, Feb. 1940, p.83+.

152. **LIMBERT, K. E.**
Some Russian composers.
Parents' rev. 51, Apr. 1940, p.226-31.
See also no.214.

153. **CALVOCORESSI, M. D.**
The non-Russian in Russian music.
L, 24, 26 Sept. 1940, p.461.

154. **NABOKOV, Nicolas**
Music in the U.S.S.R.
NR, 104, 31 Mar. 1941, p.436-8.
7 Apr. 1941, p.469-71.

155. **CALVOCORESSI, M. D.**
The music of Russia.
L, 26, 24 July 1941, p.141.

156. **EVANS, Edwin**
The oriental element in Russian music.
L, 26, 9 Oct. 1941, p.513.

157. **CALVOCORESSI, M. D.**
Random notes on contemporary Russian music.
MR, 2, Nov. 1941, p.319-23

158. **MOISENCO, Rena**
Twenty Soviet composers.
Workers' Music Association. [1942] 1-64p.
The many errors (Prokofiev's "Scythian Suite" becomes "Scythian Overture") and strong Soviet bias combine to limit its value. More space is devoted to Chishko than to Shostakovitch and there is no index. Covers Asafiev, Brusilovsky, Chiṣhko, Dunayevsky, Gadzhibekov, Glière, Gnessin, Khachaturian, Khrennikov, Kiladze, Kornilov, Miaskovsky, Paliashvili, Prokofiev, Shaporin, Shostakovitch, Spendiarov, Steinberg and Zhelobinsky.

*159 **FOX, S.**
Music: a life ideal in war-torn Russia.
E, 60, Jan. 1942, p.18+. illus.
Feb. 1942, p.92+.

160. **EVANS, Edwin**
Soviet music.
Time and tide, 23, 3 Jan. 1942, p.9.

161. **COWELL, Henry**
Music in Soviet Russia.
RR, 1, Apr. 1942, p.74-9.

162. **ABRAHAM, Gerald**
The music of Soviet Russia.
G, 19, May 1942, p.192-3.

*163. **GNESSINA, E.**
Russian music school in war time.
Mu, 47, Nov. 1942, p.154.

164. **ROTHE, Friede**
Russian music.
Kenyon rev., 4, Winter 1942, p.48-61.

165. **ABRAHAM, Gerald**
Eight Soviet composers.
O.U.P. 1943. 7-102p. mus.
A valuable, thorough and penetrating series of essays, most of which first appeared in *Monthly musical record.* Covers Dzerzhinsky, Kabalevsky, Khatchaturian, Knipper, Prokofiev, Shaporin, Shebalin and Shostakovitch.

166. **BOELZA, Igor**
Handbook of Soviet musicians. Ed. by Alan Bush.
Pilot Press. 1943. v-xiv, 1-101p. illus., 8pl.
Brief sketches of forty Soviet composers (not Stravinsky), arranged alphabetically. The "bibliography" claims to be a complete catalogue of these composers' works. There are some inaccuracies of date.

167. **SLONIMSKY, Nicolas**
Soviet music at quarter-century mark.
MA, 63, 10 Feb. 1943, p.20-1+. illus.

168. **VERNADSKY, Nina**
Lermontov in Russian music.
Slavonic rev., 21, Mar. 1943, p.6-30. mus.
Was reprinted separately in 1943. Includes a list of settings of Lermontov's works. Still gives the previously accepted but inaccurate birth-dates of Borodin (1834) and Glinka (1803).

169. **BOELZA, Igor**
A communication from Moscow. [1].
MQ, 29, Apr. 1943, p.266-8.
Review of works on music published and awaiting publication in the U.S.S.R.

170. **KING, A. Hyatt**
Music in Russia in the eighteenth century.
MO, 66, July 1943, p.329-30.
Includes a section on horn bands.

171. **BUSH, Alan**
Musical life in the U.S.S.R.
L, 30, 1 July 1943, p.25.

172. **BOELZA, Igor**
A communication from Moscow. 2.
MQ, 29, Oct. 1943. p.517-20.
On new Russian music.

173. **ABRAHAM, Gerald**
The key to Soviet music (as introduced in Great Britain).
H, 1944, p.76-81.

174. **BUSH, Alan**
Music in the Soviet Union.
Workers' Music Association. n.d. [1944]. 1-27p. discs.
A short pamphlet derived from two lectures given by Bush.
The discographies are of Soviet concert and operatic music and of popular music.

175. **CALVOCORESSI, M.D.**
A survey of Russian music.
Harmondsworth. Penguin. 1944. v-ix, 11-142p. mus., bib.
A transcription of Calvocoressi's Cramb lectures at Glasgow University (1935), this concentrated and illuminating survey includes valuable coverage of Soviet composers. Recommended.

176. **A HAND list of gramophone records of Soviet and general Russian music, available through the usual channels.**
Anglo-Soviet Public Relations Association. 1944. 1-72p.
A classified list (not exhaustive) intended as a useful guide to the best material.

177. **SEAR, H. G.**
Russian music and Shakespeare.
MT, 85, Mar. 1944, p.78-80+.

178. **SERGEANT, Winthrop**
Russia takes the lead in music.
American mercury, 58, Apr. 1944, p.429-33.

179. **LIST, Kurt**
The music of Soviet Russia.
Politics, 1, May 1944, p.103-8.

180. **BOELZA, Igor**
Music in war-time.
SL, 11, June 1944, p.72-3.

181. **BOELZA, Igor**
Communications. 1. From Moscow.
MQ, 30, July 1944, p.356-8.
Deals with new Soviet music.

182. **BUSH, Alan**
Soviet music in war-time.
ASJ, 5, Autumn 1944, p.29-34.

183. **BOELZA, Igor**
Shakespeare and Russian music.
SL, 11, Dec. 1944, p.66-9. illus.

184. **SLONIMSKY, Nicolas**
Soviet music and musicians.
Slavonic rev., 22, Dec. 1944, p.1-18.
Also issued separately in 1945.

185. **WESTERBY, Herbert**
Introduction to Russian piano music.
William Reeves. [1945]. 6-16p.
A very short survey, first published in *Musical opinion* in 1943.
Includes a list of publishers of Russian piano music.

186. **BOELZA, Igor**
New Soviet chamber music.
T, no.10, Mar. 1945, p.10-11.

187. **BOELZA, Igor**
Ukranian music and the war.
SL, 12, Mar. 1945, p.73-5.

188. **FOLK song collections.**
N, s.s., 2, Mar. 1945, p.105-7.

189. **KEEFER, Lubov**
Opera in the Soviet.
N, s.s., 2, Mar. 1945, p.110-17.

190. **BOELZA, Igor**
British and American music in the U.S.S.R.
SL, 12, May 1945, p.70-3. illus.

*191. **BOELZA, Igor**
New trends in Soviet war-time music.
Mu, 50, June 1945, p.113.

192. **BERTENSSON, Serge**
Ludmila Ivanovna Shestakova - handmaid to Russian music.
MQ, 31, July 1945, p.331-8. 1pl.
Glinka's sister (1818-1906).

193. **BOELZA, Igor**
Communication from Moscow. 4.
MQ, 31, July 1945, p.367-70.
On the publication of editions of the complete works of Borodin, Rimsky-Korsakov and Tchaikovsky.

194. **BOGDANOV-BEREZOVSKY, Valeryan**
Leningrad composers in the days of the blockade.
SL, 12, July 1945, p.67-71.

195. **CARRITT, Graham**
Contemporary Soviet songs.
MMR, 75, July-Aug. 1945, p.123-6.

196. **BEDLINSKY, Kivill**
The development of music in Soviet Bashkiria.
Keynote, 1, Autumn 1945, p.5.

197. **BROOK, Donald**
Six great Russian composers.
Rockliff. 1946. v-x, 1-193p. illus., 23pl., mus.
Concise biographies and comprehensive lists of works for concert-goer and music student, which do not attempt technical analyses. Covers Borodin, Glinka, Mussorgsky, Rimsky-Korsakov, Scriabin and Tchaikovsky.

198. **YAGOLIM, Boris**
Soviet music. Musical education and music making.
Soviet News. 1946. 4-71p. illus.
A descriptive account by a Russian bibliographer.

199. **EVANS, Edwin**
The Soviet musical inheritance.
RR., no.2, Mar. 1946, p.84-99.

*200. **BOELZA, Igor**
Music publishing in Soviet Russia.
Mu, 51, Aug. 1946, p.108.

201. **NESTIEV, P.**
The Soviet song.
ASJ, 7, Winter 1946, p.33-6.
Mostly deals with proletarian and marching songs.

202. **SHOSTAKOVICH, Dmitri**
Soviet music today.
SR, 30, 25 Jan. 1947, p.25.

203. **MONTAGU-NATHAN, M.**
Scottish bards and Russian composers.
MMR, 77, Mar.-Apr. 1947, p.71-3.
Scottish words and folk-tunes set by Russian composers.

204. **RABINOVICH, David**
Soviet pianoforte music.
SL, Apr. 1947, p.62-6.

*205. **GRINEV, M.**
Music in Moscow.
Mu, 52, June 1947, p.41.

*206. **BOELZA, Igor**
Musical criticism in the Soviet Union.
Mu, 52, July 1947, p.53-4.

*207. **ON Soviet music: documents and discussion.**
Hollywood. 1948. 22p.
Issued by the American Russian Institute of South California, it includes statements by Khatchaturian, Prokofiev and Shostakovitch.

208. **SEROFF, Victor I.**
The Mighty Five. The cradle of Russian national music. New York, New York, Allen, Towne and Heath. 1948. 3-280p. 7pl., bib.
The rather slovenly style of the author and a few errors do not seriously mar this useful, if not deeply analytical, study.
The principal compositions of "The Mighty Five" are listed.
Besides sections on Balakirev, Borodin, Cui, Mussorgsky and Rimsky-Korsakov, there is much material on Stasov.

209. **BEHIND the sharps and flats purge.**
Newsweek, 31, 23 Feb. 1948, p.26. illus.
On the 1948 music purge.

209a. **NABOKOV, Nicolas**
The music purge.
Politics, 5, Spring 1948, p.102-6.
An appendix gives the full text of the Soviet music decree condemning "formalism".

210. **ZHDANOV, A. A.**
Soviet music.
SCR, no.1, [Spring 1948?], p.1-12.
Summary of his closing speech at the Conference of Music Workers, January 1948.

211. **BOELZA, Igor**
Current chronicle. U.S.S.R. - 1946.
MQ, 34, Apr. 1948, p.278-82.
Discusses Russian "new music".

212. **CAZDEN, Norman**
What's happening in Soviet music?
Masses and mainstream, 1, Apr. 1948, p.11-24.

*213. **DOWNES, Olin**
The discussion of Soviet music.
Soviet Russia today, [16?]. Apr. 1948, p.15.

214. **LIMBERT, K. E.**
Some Russian composers.
Parents' rev., 59, Apr. 1948, p.377-81.
Mostly the same as the author's article in the same periodical for Apr. 1940 (no.152). According to Limbert, Stravinsky died in 1936.

215. **WERTH, Alexander**
The "reform" of Soviet music.
Na, 166, 10 Apr. 1948, p.393-5.

216. **SHAPORIN, Y.**
Soviet music and its tasks.
SL, June 1948, p.133-4.

217. **YARUSTOVSKY, B.**
The classical tradition and innovation in music.
SL, June 1948, p.126-32.
Largely on Russian music.

218. **SEAR, H. G.**
Music in the U.S.S.R. The background to a controversy.
ASJ, 9, Summer 1948, p.37-41. illus.

219. **LAMBERT, Constant**
Myself and Russian music.
Musical digest, no.8, [Oct. 1948?], p.147-9

220. **MOISENKO, Rena**
Realist music. 25 Soviet composers. Foreword by Adrian Boult.
Meridian Books. 1949. 17-275p. illus. 12pl., mus., bib.
A compilation of cuttings from Soviet musical publications which includes a glossary of musical terms. A supplement which fits into a pocket at the back of the book is mainly devoted to two speeches by Zhdanov delivered in 1948 and the text of the Decree of 10 Feb. 1948. Despite being indifferently thrown together, with a jungle of footnotes, too much jargon and a very pronounced Soviet bias, it still manages to be stimulating. There are some errors of date, e.g., Arensky died in 1906, not 1900. Covers Alexander Alexandrov, Asafiev, Brusilovsky, Chishko, Dunayevsky, Dzerzhinsky, Gadzhibekov, Glière, Gnessin, Khatchaturian, Khrennikov, Kiladze, Kornilov, Miaskovsky, Moldybaev, Paliashvili, Prokofiev, Shaporin, Shostakovitch, Spendiarov, Steinberg, Streikher, Vassilenko, Weissberg and Zhelobinsky.

221. **WERTH, Alexander**
Musical uproar in Moscow.
Turnstile Press. 1949. 10-103p.
Well-documented account of the condemnation of Russian "formalist" composers in 1948. A key work, valuable despite a few slips and the lack of an index.

*222. **SEROFF, Victor**
Musical fireworks behind the Iron Curtain.
E, 67, Jan. 1949, p.5+.

223. **SECOND plenary session of the Board of the Union of Soviet Composers (Dec. 1948).**
SCR, no.2, [c. Feb. 1949], p.1-9.

*224. **THE IRON Curtain falls.**
ON, 13, 14 Feb. 1949, p.7-10. illus.
Deals with the formalism controversy.

225. **WERTH, Alexander**
Soviet music: the new stage.
Na, 168, 5, Mar. 1949, p.277-8.

226. **GAYAMOV, A.**
Soviet women composers.
ASJ, 10, Spring 1949, p.35-6.

227. **ALLEN, Warren**
Music in Russia and the West.
RR, 8, Apr. 1949, p.102-10.

*228. **KHACHATURIAN, Aram**
The rapid decline in quality of the Soviet music [sic].
Musicology, 2, Apr. 1949, p.320-2.

229. **ABRAHAM, Gerald**
Soviet music and Russian esthetics.
SR, 32, 30 Apr. 1949, p.45-6+. illus.

*230. **SHOSTAKOVITCH, D.**
Formalism vs. realism in music.
Music news, 41, May 1949, p.3-4+.

231. **SWAN, Alfred J.**
Harmonizations of the old Russian chants.
JAMS, 2, Summer 1949, p.83-6.

232. **WOOLF, Leonard**
Music in Moscow.
Political quarterly, 20, July-Sept. 1949, p.210-18.

233. **MONTAGU-NATHAN, M.**
A Soviet shindy.
MO, 72, Aug. 1949, p.574-6.
On the formalism controversy.

233a. **NABOKOV, Nicolas**
Russian music after the purge.
Partisan rev., 16, Aug. 1949, p.842-51.

234. **SOVIET music 1948-1949.**
SCR, no.3, [c. Oct. 1949] p.1-4.
A list of eighty-seven compositions of 1948-1949 compiled from the agenda of the second and third plenary sessions of the Board of the Union of Soviet Composers.

*235. **POLYAREVSKY, G.**
Symphonic music in the Soviet Union.
Symphony, 3, Dec. 1949, p.6. illus.

236. **KABALEVSKY, Dmitri**
Soviet music, Tr. by Harold C. Feldt.
ASJ, 10, Winter 1949, p.36-42+. illus.

237. **BUSH, Alan**
Problems of Soviet musical theory.
Modern quarterly, n.s., 5, Winter 1949-50, p.38-47.
On the 1948 "formalism" controversy.

238. **ZHDANOV, A. A.**
On literature, music and philosophy. Tr., prepared and ed. by Eleanor Fox, Stella Jackson and Harold C. Feldt.
Lawrence and Wishart. 1950. 9-112p.
Important statement by the man who carried out Stalin's cultural policies.

*239. **ROSENWALD, H.**
Soviet composers.
Music news, 42, Jan. 1950, p.13.

240. **MONTAGU-NATHAN, M.**
The decomposition of Russian music.
MMR, 80, Mar.-Apr. 1950, p.69-72.
Discusses the standard of Russian music in the late 1940s.

241. **FELDT, H. C.,** *tr.*
Recent developments in Soviet music.
ASJ, 11, Spring 1950, p.44-9.

242. **GORODINSKY, V.**
The national character of Soviet music.
MTe, 29, Apr. 1950, p.177+.

243. **KRYOUKOV, V.**
Current chronicle. U.S.S.R.
MQ, 36, Apr. 1950, p.302-5.
Deals with new works by minor composers.

244. **GROSHEVA, E.**
New works of Soviet music.
SL, June 1950, p.166-71.

*245. **ROSENWALD, H.**
Music of the Russians.
Music news, 42, Sept. 1950, p.10-11.

246. **COOPER, Martin**
The Russian song.
L, 44, 28 Sept. 1950, p.436.

247. **SLONIMSKY, Nicolas**
The changing style of Soviet music.

247. **SLONIMSKY, Nicolas**
The changing style of Soviet music.
JAMS, 3, Fall 1950, p.236-55. mus.

248. **WERTH, Alexander**
Russian music for the people.
L, 44, 9 Nov. 1950, p.494-5.

249. **SOVIET opera and ballet in 1950.**
SCR, no.6, Dec. 1950, p.1-4.

250. **COOPER, Martin**
Russian opera.
Max Parrish. 1951. 9-66p. illus., 1pl., mus.
A brief but informative and well-illustrated history, the only one in English since Rosa Newmarch's book of 1914.

251. **NABOKOV, Nicolas**
Music in the Soviet Union ... a review of the shifting battlefront.
MA, 71, Feb. 1951, p.12+. illus.
Also *in Canon,* 4, June 1951, p.553-4
July 1951, p.598-600.
5, Sept. 1951, p.87-92.
Lists accepted and rejected works in Russia.

251a. **KHRENNIKOV, Tikhon**
New works by Soviet composers.
MTe, 30, June 1951, p.287.

251b. **NABOKOV, Nicolas**
Changing styles in Soviet music.
L, 46, 11 Oct. 1951, p.598-9.

252. **MONTAGU-NATHAN, M.**
Gogol and music.
MMR, 82, May 1952, p.92-8.
Discusses the composers who drew on his works.

253. **GORODINSKY, V.**
English poetry set to music by Russian composers.
News, no. 22, 1 June 1952, p.18-20.
Deals mostly with Shakespeare plays set to music.

254. **NESTYEV, I.**
Notes on Soviet music.
SL, Nov. 1952, p.147-53.

255. **ASAFIEV, B. V.**
Russian music from the beginning of the nineteenth century.
Tr. from the Russian by Alfred J. Swan.
Ann Arbor, Michigan, J.W. Edwards, 1953. iii-vii, 1-329p.
Written in 1928 by an outstanding musicologist and first published in 1939, Swan's translation omits part of the original text. The "list of musical authors" gives no page numbers; there are many inaccuracies (e.g., Mussorgsky died a week after his forty-second birthday, not on it), countless instances of mistranslation and a few typographical errors. *See also* no.388.

256. **MUSIC behind the Iron Curtain – a report.**
MA, 73, Feb. 1953, p.20+. illus.

257. **KOEGLER, Horst**
Aesthetic ideals of Soviet opera.
ON, 17, 23 Mar. 1953, p.14-15, illus.

258. **SIXTH plenary session of the Union of Soviet Composers**
(Jan. 31-Feb. 14 1953).
SCR, no.14, Apr. 1953, p.4-5.

259. **WERTH, Alexander**
Is the Soviet attitude to music changing?
L, 50, 24 Dec. 1953, p.1089-90.

260. **SLONIMSKY, Nicolas**
A new time in Soviet music.
SR, 37, 30 Jan. 1954, p.37+. illus.

*261. **MACKINNON, D.A.**
Music behind the Iron Curtain.
Music clubs mag., 38, Mar. 1954, p.5-6+.

262. **KHACHATURIAN, Aram**
The truth about Soviet music and Soviet composers.
News, no. 64, 1 Mar. 1954, p.17-19. illus.
Also *in* SCR, 1, Aug. 1954, p.1-5.

263. **KELDYSH, Georgi**
Soviet music today.
T, 32, Summer 1954, p.23-8.
Also *in* ASJ, 15, Summer 1954, p.16-20.

264. **BOELZA, Igor**
Current chronicle. U.S.S.R.
MQ, 40, July 1954, p.412-18.
Describes recently written Soviet music.

265. **DZERZHINSKY, I.**
Fight for realistic art !
SCR, 1, Aug. 1954, p.7-11.

266. **SENIOR, Evan**
Russian journey. Part 2 - the Moscow Union of Composers.
MMu, 3, Sept. 1954, p.10-11. illus.

267. **SENIOR, Evan**
Russian journey. Part 4: new operas.
MMu, 3, Nov. 1954, p.16-17. illus.

268. **KHATCHATURIAN, Aram**
The composer in Russia.
MMu, 3, Dec. 1954, p.13+. illus.

269. **OLKHOVSKY, Andrei**
Music under the Soviets. The agony of an art.
Routledge. 1955. vi-xv, 1-427p. bib.
Written by a Russian musicologist resident in the U.S.A., it includes sections on Soviet musical life, policy, aesthetics, musicology and education. Very informative, but difficult to read owing to the extensive use of jargon. The seventy-eight page bibliography is mostly of Russian material and gives American locations. A fascinating indictment of Soviet music policy.

270. **KABAKEVSKY, D.**
Notes on symphonic music. Tr. by Anna Collingwood.
SCH, 2, Sept. 1955, p.1-10.

271. **SHOSTAKOVITCH, Dmitri**
Music for children's concerts.
SCR, 2, Sept. 1955, p.10-12.

*272. **HOVHANNISSIAN, Harpik der**
Armenian music: a cosmopolitan art (Vols. 1 and 2).
Dissertation, Florida State University. 1956. 292p.
Covers church, folk and art music.

273. **LEONARD, Richard A.**
A history of Russian music.
Jarrolds. 1956. 5-395p. 17pl., bib.
Very informative, but marred by inconsistent transliteration and some inaccuracies, e.g., Khatchaturian was born in 1903, not 1904; Rimsky-Korsakov did not have a reliable memory. The most recent date in the bibliography is 1951.

274. **SLUSSER, Robert**
Soviet music since the death of Stalin.
Annals of the American Academy of Political and Social Science, 303, Jan. 1956 p.116-25.

275. **SLOBODSKAYA, Oda**
An approach to the Russian art-song.
T, 39, Spring 1956, p.6-8.

276. **NESTYEV, I.**
Soviet composers on the eve of their second congress.
SL, June 1956, p.214-15.

277. **SLONIMSKY, Nicolas**
Music since Stalin.
NR, 134, 11 June 1956, p.51-2. illus.

278. **WARSON, Joseph**
Contemporary Soviet music.
Canon, 10, Nov. 1956, p.143-5.

279. **SOKOLSKY, M.**
Concerning Soviet symphonic music.
Canon, 10, Apr. 1957, p.292-4. illus.

280. **WERTH, Alexander**
[The] state of Soviet music.
NS, 53, 18 May 1957, p.632.
On the Second Congress of Soviet Composers, Apr.1957.

281. **WERTH, Alexander**
Music in Moscow.
Na, 184, 22 June 1957, p.555-6.
On the Second Congress of Soviet Composers.

282. **ARBATSKY, Yuri**
The Soviet attitude towards music: an analysis based in part on secret archives.
MQ, 43, July 1957, p.295-315.

283. **BUSH, Alan**
Nine days of talk on music.
MMu, 5, July 1957, p.15. illus.
On the Second Congress of the Union of Soviet Composers.

284. **COMPOSERS' Congress.**
SCR, 1, July 1957, p.12-15.
Another article on the Second Congress.

285. **SWAN, Alfred J.**
Russian liturgical music and its relation to twentieth century ideals.
ML, 39, July 1958, p.265-74.

286. **IGNATYEVA, Mariam**
Composers of Soviet Azerbaidjan.
SL, Aug. 1958, p.188-91.

287. **PARKER, Ralph**
More about music.
ASJ, 19, Autumn 1958, p.27-9.
Mainly on the Zhdanov affair.

288. **SHOSTAKOVICH, Dmitry**
Soviet music today.
ASJ, 19, Autumn 1958, p.3-8.
From *Izvestiya, Pravda* and an interview in London.

289. **MYERS, Rollo**
Claude Debussy and Russian music.
ML, 39, Oct. 1958, p.336-42.

290. **THOMSON, Jim**
A note on Russian music.
Canon, 12, Oct. 1958, p.105-6. illus.

291. **NOVIKOV, Anatoli**
The works of composers of the R.S.F.S.R.
SL, Nov. 1958, p.85-9.
This refers to the largest of the republics, the capital being Moscow.

*292. **HARRIS, Roy**
Music education in the U.S.S.R.
International musician, 57, Dec. 1958, p.11+.

293. **HOPKINSON, Cecil**
Notes on Russian music publishers.
[Bath]. [1959]. 10p.
A privately printed guide to lesser-known aspects of Russian music.

*294. **KAY, Ulysees**
Impressions of the Soviet musical scene.
A.C.A. bull., 8, no.3, 1959, p.17-18.

295. **ZETLIN, Mikhail**
The Five. The evolution of the Russian school of music.
Tr. and ed. by George Panin.
New York, International Universities Press. 1959. 7-344p. illus., 7pl.
Chapters on Balakirev, Borodin, Glinka, Mussorgsky, Rimsky-Korsakov and Stasov, but very little on Cui. The approach is a popular one and thereis no index

296. **PARROTT, Cecil**
Music in the Soviet Union.
MT, 100, Jan. 1959, p.14-15.

297. **SELDEN, Margery**
Laurels for Catherine the Great.
ON, 23, 16 Mar. 1959, p.14-15+. illus.
Catherine collaborated on or wrote the libretti for five operas.

298. **LLOYD-JONES, David**
Piano music from Russia.
L, 61, 2 Apr. 1959, p.611.

299. **SEAMAN, Gerald**
The Russian horn band.
MMR, 89, May-June 1959, p.93-9.

*300. **PRYOR, Harold S.** *and* **LOWE, Alberta**
Music education in the Union of Soviet-Socialist Republics.
Music educator's j., 45, June-July 1959, p.28-30.

*301. **SOVIET composers visit U.S.**
U.S. Dept. of State bull., 41, 2 Nov. 1959, p.632-3.

*302. **LEFTWICH, V.**
Report of Soviet composers' press meeting
Music of the West mag., 15, Dec. 1959, p.6.

*303. **SOVIET composers visiting the U.S.A.**
International musician, 58, Dec. 1959, p.3+.illus

304. **JACOBS, Arthur**
Music and myth in Moscow.
NS, 59, 21 May 1960, p.750+.
Discusses the lack of outstanding new composers.

305. **YARUSTOVSKY, Boris**
The young composers. Tr. by Nicolas Slonimsky.
AM, 205, June 1960. p.96-100. illus.

306. **SCHWARTZ, Boris**
Musical thought in Soviet Russia.
L, 64, 7 July 1960, p.16-17+. illus.

307. **INOZEMTSEVA, Galina**
Composers' Union of the Russian Federation. Tr. by Jacob Guralsky.
SL, Aug. 1960, p.176-9.
On its inauguration.

308. **VELIMIROVIC, Milos**
Russian autographs at Harvard.
N, n.s. 17, Sept. 1960, p.539-58. illus. mus.

309. **BROWN, David**
Soviet music: 1960.
MMR, 90, Sept.-Oct. 1960, p.174-9.

310. **POLYAKOVA, Lyudmila V.**
Soviet music. Tr. from the Russian by Xenia Danko. Ed. by Olga Shartse.
Moscow, Foreign Languages Publishing House. [1961] 7-184p. illus.
Arranged by musical form, this is a valuable, if biased, survey, especially for the lesser Soviet composers, and includes material on some works composed before 1917.

311. **POLYANOVSKY, Georgi**
New operas in Moscow.
O, 12, Jan. 1961. p.160.

312. **BROWN, David**
Recent trends in Soviet music.
L, 65, 16 Feb. 1961, p.329.

313. **YARUSTAVSKY [sic], Boris**
Soviet music: 1961.
MA, 81, June 1961, p.28-9.

314. **SEAMAN, Gerald**
The national element in early Russian opera, 1779-1800.
ML, 42, July 1961, p.252-62.

*315. **KREBS, Stanley**
Soviet music instruction: service to the state.
J. of research in music education, 9, Fall 1961, p.83-107.
Summary of higher education in music.

316. **SEAMAN, Gerald**
Professional music in the Soviet Union.
MO, 85, Oct. 1961, p.17.

*317. **SEAMAN, Gerald**
The influence of folk-song on Russian opera in the eighteenth century up to and including the time of Glinka.
D. Phil. thesis, Keble College, Oxford. 1961-2.
A number of errors have been rectified since it was published. Seaman says it should be used in conjunction with his *History of Russian music,* no.349. *See also* no.324.

318. **SEAMAN, Gerald**
Opera-going in Leningrad.
O, 13, Mar. 1962, p.163-7. illus.

319. **SHUMSKAYA, Natalia**
Composers work for children. Tr. by Ralph Parker.
SL, Mar. 1962, p.195-9.

320. **MARTYNOV, Ivan**
What is new in Soviet music? Tr. by George Hanna.
SL, May 1962, p.160-3.

321. **SELDEN, Margery**
Early roots of Russian opera.
JAMS, 15, Summer 1962, p.206-11.
A revision of material from her Yale University Master's thesis, it covers the period up to 1689. The article is discussed and corrected by Velimirovic, no.329.

322. **KABALEVSKY, Dmitri**
Emil Gilels. Tr. by Hilda Perham.
SL, Sept. 1962, p.168-70.

323. **ZHITOMIRSKY, D.**
Schumann and the Russian school.
MJ, 20, Sept. 1962, p.97+.

324. **SEAMAN, Gerald**
Folk-song in Russian opera of the 18th century.
Slavonic rev., 41, Dec. 1962, p.144-57.
See also no. 317.

325. **SHOSTAKOVICH, Dmitri**
New musical works. Tr. by Eve Manning.
SL, Mar. 1963, p.154-6.
This refers to Russian works.

326. **SCHWARZ, Boris**
Soviet music since Stalin.
SR, 46, 30 Mar. 1963, p.55-6+. illus.

327. **DODGSON, Stephen**
Russian journal.
C, 11, Spring 1963, p.4-8+. illus.
Impressions of two weeks as guests of the Union of Soviet Composers.

328. **SEROFF, Victor**
Where is Russian opera?
ON, 27, 6 Apr. 1963, p.8-11. illus.

329. **VELIMIROVIC, Miles**
Early roots of Russian opera revisited.
JAMS, 16, Summer 1963 p.257-60.
Discussion of Selden's article, no.321.

330. **POLYANOVSKY, Georgi**
The soul of music is in its kinship with the people.
SL, Dec. 1963, p.149-51.

331. **SAVINTSEV, Pierre**
Report of the Soviet National Music Committee for 1963.
World of music, 6, Mar-June 1964, p.41-2+.
In English, French and German. Concerns Soviet composers and the dissemination of music within the U.S.S.R.

332. **BELZA, Igor**
Shakespeare and Russian music.
ASJ, 25, Autumn 1964, p.13-18.

333. **SCHWARZ, Boris**
Soviet music since the Second World War.
MQ, 51, Jan. 1965, p.259-81. mus.
Also *in* LANG *and* BRODER. *Contemporary music in Europe* (New York, 1965).

*334. **RIZA, Bayram**
Musical training in the Soviet Union.
Bull. of the Institute for the Study of the U.S.S.R., 12, Mar. 1965, p.22-31.

335. **BUSH, Geoffrey**
Russia 1964.
C, 15, Spring 1965, p.12-13.

*336. **KABALEVSKI, D.B.**
Music education in the U.S.S.R.
International music educator, no. 11, Apr. 1965, p.353-62.
Includes summaries in French and German.

337. **CLAPHAM, John**
Dvorak's visit to Russia.
MQ, 51, July 1965, p.493-506. 2pl.

338. **MAKANOWITZKY, Barbara**
Music to serve the state.
RR, 24, July 1965, p.266-77.
There are some dreadful gaffs in the translation: Bruckner becomes "Brüchner" and Stravinsky's ballet becomes "The Rites of Spring".

339. **SABANEEF, Leonid**
Religious and mystical trends in Russia at the turn of the century.
RR, 24, Oct. 1965, p.354-68.

340. **SEAMAN, Gerald**
The first Russian chamber music.
MR, 26, Nov. 1965, p.326-37, mus.

341. **SCHWARZ, Boris**
The vicissitudes of Soviet music.
Problems of Communism, 14, Nov-Dec. 1965, p.67-82.

342. **BAKST, James**
A history of Russian-Soviet music.
New York, Dodd, Mead and Co. 1966. v-x, 3-405p. illus., 16pl., bib.
Draws heavily on the writings of Asafiev. An informative, thought-provoking and sometimes unreliable survey, which devotes twenty-four pages to Shostakovitch but only eight to Prokofiev. The index is fascinating but inconsistent.

*343. **PETERSON, F.**
Musical aesthetics in Soviet Russia.
MJ, 24, Jan. 1966, p.54+.

344. **ARUTYUNYAN, Margarita**
The music of Armenia.
SL, Mar. 1966, p.194-9.

345. **SEAMAN, G.**
Amateur music-making in Russia.
ML, 47, July 1966, p.249-59.

346. **SEAMAN, Gerald**
The rise of Russian piano music.
MR, 27, Aug. 1966, p.177-93. mus.

347. **LIPOVSKY, Alexander,** *comp.*
Lenin Prize winners. Soviet stars in the world of music.
Tr. by Olga Shartse.
Moscow, Progress Publishers. [1967?] 5-286p. illus.
Twenty-five essays on twelve musicians who won the Lenin Prize between 1957 and 1966, including Shostakovitch and Shneerson on Khatchaturian; Martynov, Shostakovitch and foreign musicians on Prokofiev; Delson and Neuhaus on Richter; Ginsberg on Rostropovitch; Asafiev and Martynov on Shostakovitch; Adigezalova and Zhivov on Solovyev-Sedoi; and Grosheva and Taktakishvili on Sviridov. Also Kabalevsky writes on Gilels and Khatchaturian on Dolukhanova. An index is lacking.

*348. **POSELL, Elsa**
Russian composers.
Boston, Houghton, Mifflin Co. 1967. 181p. illus., bib.
For junior readers. Discusses seventeen composers from Glinka to Shostakovitch.

349. **SEAMAN, Gerald**
History of Russian music. From its origins to Dargomyzhsky.
Vol. 1. Foreword by Gerald Abraham.
Blackwell. 1967. vii-xv, 1-351p. illus., 12pl., mus., bib.
Has the appearance of being a valuable and scholarly work, and there are some useful appendices, e.g., the list of 101 operas, but Velimirovic's scathing review *(Musical quarterly,* 55, July 1969, p.408-17) criticises Seaman's borrowing direct from Russian sources.
See also no. 317.

350. **MARTYNOV, Ivan**
New music.
SL, Feb. 1967, p.171-5.

*351. **JOUVENCEL, M. de** *and* **ROIZMAN, L.**
The organ in Russia during the second half of the eighteenth century.
American organist, 50, May 1967, p.17-20. Translated from *L'Orgue.*

352. **MARTYNOV, Ivan**
Half-century of creative questing.
SL, Oct. 1967, p.109-13.

353. **ABRAHAM, Gerald**
Slavonic and Romantic music. Essays and studies.
Faber. 1968. 9-360p. mus.
A splendid series of essays, most having first appeared in periodicals. Nine of the twenty-nine are on Russian music.
Contents (Russian composers): Anton Rubinstein: Russian composer. - Tchaikovsky: some centennial reflections. - Tchaikovsky's operas. - Mussorgsky's "Boris" and Pushkin's. - The Mediterranean element in "Boris Godunov". - Rimsky-Korsakov as self-critic. - Rimsky-Korsakov's songs. - Random notes on Lyadov. - Glazunov and the string quartet.

*354. **WHITWELL, D.**
Nineteenth century Russian composers - their music for winds.
Instrument, 22, Feb. 1968, p.52-6.

*355. **PLENARY session of the U.S.S.R. Union of Composers in Moscow.**
UU, June 1968, p.4-6.

*356. **CONGRESS of Azerbaijan composers.**
UU, Oct. 1968, p.4.

*357. **ESHPAI, A.**
Trends in Soviet music.
MJ, 27, Mar. 1969, p.35+.

358. **MARTYNOV, Ivan**
Highlights of the music world.
SL, Mar. 1969, p.168-73.
This refers to Soviet music.

359. **GARDEN, Edward**
Classic and romantic in Russian music.
ML, 50, Apr. 1969, p.153-7.

360. **RICKS, Robert**
Russian horn bands.
MQ, 55, July 1969, p.364-71. 2pl., mus.

361. **KARAGICHEVA, Lyudmila**
Music.
SL, Dec. 1969, p.182-8.
A survey of professional music in Azerbaijan.

362. **KREBS, Stanley D.**
Soviet composers and the development of Soviet music.
Allen and Unwin. 1970. 11-364p. mus., bib.
Originating as a Ph.D. dissertation (no part was written after 1963), it is very useful for the sections on minor composers. But the English style is sloppy, and errors and misprints abound: "Rodion Shchedrin" and "Shchedrin, Rodion" are separately listed in the index, which omits non-composers: Prokofiev did not die at sixty-four, but aged 61. There are no music examples for Prokofiev or Khrennikov but thirteen for Karaev.
The following composers are covered in some detail: Amirov, Arakishvili, Asafiev, Balantchivadze, Gadzhibekov, Galynin, Gliere, Ippolitov-Ivanov, Kabalevsky, Karaev, Khatchaturian, Khrennikov, Miaskovsky, Prokofiev, Shaporin, Shchedrin, Shebalin, Shostakovitch, Sviridov, Taktakishvili and Vassilenko.

*363. **NESTYEV, I.**
Russian songs.
Soviet life, no.160, Jan. 1970, p.7-15.

364. **LEVARIE, Siegmund**
Epochs of opera: Slavic countries.
ON, 34, 24 Jan. 1970, p.24-9. illus.
Includes a brief survey of Russian opera.

*364a. **KHRENNIKOV, Tikhon**
Soviet music and its traditions.
MJ, 28, Apr. 1970, p.28-9.

*365. **POPOV, I.**
Great patriotic war in Soviet music.
UU, May 1970, p.3-4.

*366. **KASHA, M.**
Ukrainian music and its cultural heritage.
Guitar rev., no.33, Summer 1970, p.2-10. illus., mus.

367. **TARUSHKIN, Richard**
Realism as preached and practised: the Russian opera dialogue.
MQ, 56, July 1970, p.431-54. illus.

*368. **MELNIKOV, L.**
U.S.S.R.: music and medicine.
MJ, 28, Nov. 1970, p.18.

368a. **SCHWARZ, Boris**
Music and musical life in Soviet Russia 1917-1970.
Barrie and Jenkins. 1972. 4-550p. mus., bib.
The writer is a noted authority on his subject and packs in a vast amount of information. Much more politically slanted than Krebs' survey (no.362), the book is thoroughly documented and well-indexed.

368b. **SWAN, Alfred J.**
Russian music and its sources in chant and folk-songs.
Foreword by Donald Swann.
John Baker. 1973. 5-234p. 17pl., mus., bib.
The author died in 1970 and the final stages were supervised by his widow, Jane. The arrangement is chronological, the first section being on the sources. Sometimes misleading or unhelpful, it is nevertheless a useful survey and interesting for its reminiscences of the composers he knew personally, e.g. Prokofiev and Rachmaninoff. The appendices include a list of Russian folk-song collections.

AKIMENKO, Fyodor (1876-1945)

369. **SABANEYEFF, Leonid**
Fyodor Akimyenko.
in SABANEYEFF. Modern Russian composers, p.195-200.

ALABIEV, Alexander (1787-1851)

*370. **GREENE, Carol A.**
Style in the instrumental chamber music of Alexander Alexandrovich Alabiev.
M.A., Musicology, dissertation, Indiana University.
1969. 72p. mus., bib.

ALEXANDROV, Alexander (1883-1946)

371. **OGOLOVETZ, A.**
Russian composer and combatant.
MT, 83, Sept. 1942, p.267.

372. **MOISENKO, Rena**
Alexander Alexandrov.
in MOISENKO. Realist music, p.41-7. 1pl., mus.

ALEXANDROV, Anatoly (1888-)

373. **BELAIEV, Victor**
Contemporary Russian composers. 3. Anatole Alexandrov.
Sackbut, 6, Nov. 1925, p.95-8.

AMIROV, Fikret (1922-)

374. **RUSSIAN view of England.**
C, 16, July 1965, p.27-8. illus.
Amirov visited England in May 1965.

375. **KREBS, Stanley D.**
Fikret Amirov.
in KREBS. Soviet composers and the development of Soviet music, p.323-30. mus.

ARAKISHVILI, Dmitri (1873-1953)

376. **KREBS, Stanley D.**
Dmitri Arakishvili.
in KREBS. Soviet composers and the development of Soviet music, p.119-31. mus.

ARBATSKY, Yury (1911-63)

*377. **ARBATSKY, Yury**
The Hebrew polyphony in Macedonia.
PAMS, 1951, p.?

378. **ARBATSKY, Yury**
Beating the tupan in the Central Balkans.
Chicago, The Newberry Library. 1953. v-vii, 2-64p. illus., mus. bib.
A dissertation, written 1943-4, the tupan being a two-skinned drum. The translation is by the author.

*379. **ARBATSKY, Yury**
The roga, a Balkan bagpipe, and its medico-magical conjurations.
PAMS, 1953, p.?.

*380. **ARBATSKY, Yury**
An aspect of Balkan musicology; the dipla of Aruman shepherds.
PAMS, 1954, p.?.
The dipla is a double pipe.

381. **THE ARBATSKY Collection.**
Newberry Library bull., 3, July 1954, p.170-6.
In 1954, Arbatsky deposited his valuable collection of Balkan folk music at the Newberry Library.

ARENSKY, Anton (1861-1906)

A. *General.*

382. **TIDEBÖHL, Ellen von**
Anton Arensky.
MMR, 36, May 1906, p.102.

See no. 736.

B. *Works.*

383. **[ABRAHAM, Gerald]**
Arensky's First Symphony.
L, 15, 22 Apr. 1936, p.796.

ASAFIEV, Boris (1884-1949)

A. *General.*

See no. 880.

384. **MOISENCO, Rena**
Boris Asafiev.
in MOISENCO. Twenty Soviet composers, p.6-9.

385. **MOISENKO, Rena**
Boris Assafiev.
in MOISENKO. Realist music, p.48-55. mus.

386. **MONTAGU-NATHAN, M.**
Russian music as she is composed.
MO, 72, Apr. 1949, p.341-2.
Mostly about Asafiev.

387. **MONTAGU-NATHAN, M.**
B.V. Asafiev: 1884-1949.
MMR, 79, May 1949, p.95-9.

388. **SLONIMSKY, Nicolas**
Reviews of books. *Russian music from the beginning of the nineteenth century* by B.V. Asaf'ev (Igor Glebov).
MQ, 40, July 1954, p.425-30.

389. **MONTAGU-NATHAN, M.**
The strange case of Professor Assafiev.
ML, 38, Oct. 1957, p.335-40.

390. **KREBS, Stanley D.**
Boris Asaf'ev.
in KREBS. Soviet composers and the development of Soviet music, p.86-95. mus.

B. *Works.*

391. **HUNT, David**
The Fountain of Bakhchisarai. Music.
DD, 7, Dec. 1956, p.16-17.

BALAKIREV, Mily (1837-1910)

A. *General.*

*392. **POUGIN, A.**
Balakirew and Borodine, Russian musicians.
M, 12, 1897, p.440.

393. **CALVOCORESSI, M. D.**
Mili Balakirev.
MMR, 37, Jan. 1907, p.5-6.

394. **NEWMARCH, Rosa**
The death of Mily Balakirev.
MMR, 40, July 1910, p.149.

395. **CALVOCORESSI, M. D.**
The correspondence between Balakirev and Tchaikovsky.
MT, 53, Nov. 1912, p.712-15.

396. **MONTAGU-NATHAN, M.**
... Balakireff.
MS, n.i.s., 2, 5 July 1913, p.10-11
12 July 1913, p.34.

397. **MONTAGU-NATHAN, M.**

Balakiref.
in MONTAGU-NATHAN. An introduction to Russian music, p.28-31.

398. **LIAPUNOFF, S. M.**

The Balakireff – Rimsky-Korsakoff correspondence, 1862-1898. With a foreword and notes by Professor S.M. Liapunoff. Tr. from the Russian by S.W. Pring.
39, May 1916, p.507-8 226-7. mus.
June 1916, p.569-71.
July 1916, p.629-31. mus.
Aug. 1916, p.695-6. mus.
Sept. 1916, p.762-3. mus.
40, Oct.1916, p.23-5. mus.
Dec. 1916, p.160.
Jan. 1917, p.326-7. mus.
Feb. 1917, p.289-90. mus.
Apr. 1917, p.422-4. mus.
June 1917, p.538-9. mus.
Aug. 1917, p.647-9. mus.
41, Oct. 1917, p.27-8. mus.
Dec. 1917, p.152-3.
Feb. 1918, p.272.
Apr. 1918, p.392-3.
June 1918, p.495-6.
Aug. 1918, p.600-1.
42, Oct. 1918, p.31-2.
Dec. 1918, p.156-7.
Mar. 1919, p.353-4.
May 1919, p.491.
Aug. 1919, p.697.
43, Oct. 1919, p.47.
Dec. 1919, p.209.
Feb. 1920, p.379.
Aug. 1920, p.871.

See no.44.

399. **CALVOCORESSI, M. D.**

The works of Mili Balakiref.
MMR, 51, May 1921, p.101-2+.
June 1921, p.125-7.

400. **NEWMARCH, Rosa**

Some unpublished letters of Balakirev.
Ch, 35, Dec. 1923, p.73-7.

*401. **RIMSKY-KORSAKOFF, N. A.**
Balakireff, a great Russian teacher.
E, 43, Oct. 1925, p.702.

402. **BELAIEV, Victor**
Olenin's reminiscences of Balakirev. Tr. by S.W. Pring.
MQ, 16, Jan. 1930, p.72-82. illus.

403. **ANDREWS, Hilda**
Sidelights on musical history. 9. Mily Alexeivich Balakirev. Founder of the Russian renaissance.
MTe, 8, May 1930, p.283-4. illus., mus.

404. **ABRAHAM, Gerald**
Balakirev, a flawed genius.
in ABRAHAM. Studies in Russian music, p.311-35. illus., mus.

405. **CALVOCORESSI, M. D.**
Mily Balakiref.
in CALVOCORESSI *and* ABRAHAM. Masters of Russian music, p.97-146. 1pl.

406. **CALVOCORESSI, M. D.**
Mily Balakirev, on the centenary of his birth.
MQ, 23, Jan. 1937, p.45-55. 1pl.

407. **SABANEEV, L.**
M.A. Balakirev (Born December 21 1836). Tr. by S.W. Pring.
MT, 78, Jan. 1937, p.21-2.
As so often, Sabaneev is inaccurate: Balakirev died at 73, not 77, and he did not live longer than any other Russian composer (Cui died at 83).

408. **CALVOCORESSI, M. D.**
From my notebook.
MO, 60, Feb. 1937, p.396-7.
On Balakirev's centenary.

409. **SUMNER, T. C.**
M.A. Balakirev: 1837-1910. His influence in music.
Choir, 28, Mar. 1937, p.53-5.

410. **CALVOCORESSI, M. D.**
Balakirev at work.
L, 19, 9 Feb. 1938, p.325.

*411. **LEHMANN, Evangeline**
A great master's principles of composition.
E, 57, June 1939, p.371+. illus.

*412. **HILL, Edward B.**
Russian nationalist composers.
E, 59, Oct. 1941, p.675. illus.
Mainly devoted to Balakirev.

*413. **DEVORE, N.**
Balakireff and the Russian Five.
Mu, 47, Jan. 1942, p.7.

414. **ZETLIN, M. O.**
Balakirev. Tr. by Olga Oushakoff.
RR, 4, Autumn 1944, p.67-82.
Taken from Zetlin's *The Five.*

415. **LOCKSPEISER, Edward**
Balakirev: the man and his work.
L, 34, 11 Oct. 1945, p.417.

See no.208.

*416. **SEROFF, V. I.**
Opera and the Balakirevs.
E, 66, Mar. 1948, p.154+. illus.

417. **MONTAGU-NATHAN, M.** ,*ed.*
Balakirev's letters to Calvocoressi. Ed. and tr. by M. Montagu-Nathan.
ML, 35, Oct. 1954, p.347-60.
Includes Calvocoressi's preface to the letters and extracts from 25 letters dating from 1905 to 1910.

418. **MONTAGU-NATHAN, M.**
Musician and midshipman.
MT, 96, July 1955, p.357-60.
An account of the correspondence between Balakirev and Rimsky-Korsakov, 1862-4.

419. **ZETLIN, Mikhail**
Balakirev.
in ZETLIN. The Five, p.51-69.

420. **ZETLIN, Mikhail**
The Balakirev gang.
in ZETLIN. The Five, p.123-43.
This refers to "The Five".

421. **ZETLIN, Mikhail**
Balakirev in Prague.
in ZETLIN. The Five, p.144-50.

422. **ZETLIN, Mikhail**
Balakirev's "withdrawal into the wilderness".
in ZETLIN. The Five, p.225-36.

See no.1984.

See no.2763.

423. **BROWN, David**
Balakirev, Tchaikovsky and nationalism.
ML, 42, July 1961, p.227-41.

424. **GARDEN, Edward**
Balakirev: a critical study of his life and music.
Faber. 1967. 7-352p. illus., 16pl., mus., bib.
This first study of Balakirev in English is a clearly laid-out, thorough and useful effort, but not the last word on the subject. There are a few errors; the book contains a catalogue of works. Very welcome.

425. **DAVIS, Richard**
Henselt, Balakirev and the piano.
MR, 28, Aug. 1967, p.173-208. mus., bib.
Mostly on Henselt.

426. **GARDEN, Edward**
Balakirev's personality.
PRMA, 96, 1969-70, p.43-55.

B. *Works.*

427. **ABRAHAM, Gerald**
Balakirev's symphonies.
ML, 14, Oct. 1933, p.355-63. mus.
Also *in* ABRAHAM. On Russian music, p.179-92. mus.
Symphonies nos. 1 in C major and 2 in D minor.

428. **ABRAHAM, Gerald**
Balakirev's music to "King Lear".
MMR, 76, Mar.-Apr. 1936, p.49-51. mus.
Also *in* ABRAHAM. On Russian music, p.193-204.
King Lear, overture and incidental music.

429. **HOGARTH, Basil**
The masterpieces of the ballet. 2. Balakirev's Tamara.
G, 13, Aug. 1935, p.99-100.

430. **NEWMARCH, Rosa**
Balakirev. Symphonic poem, "Thamara".
CL, 5, p.1-3.

431. **LEE, E. Markham**
The student-interpreter.
MO, 54, Aug. 1931, p.950-1. mus.
On Balakirev's Sonata for piano in B flat minor, his only sonata.

432. **ABRAHAM, Gerald**
Balakirev's piano sonata.
L, 15, 26 Feb. 1936, p.420.
Also *in* ABRAHAM. On Russian music, p.205-15. mus.

BALANTCHIVADZE, Andrey (1906-)

433. **KREBS, Stanley D.**
Andrei Balanchivadze.
in KREBS. Soviet composers and the development of Soviet music, p.269-76. mus.

BARSUKOV, Sergei (?1912-)

434. **PIANIST and composer.**
Music mag., no.17, Jan. 1965, p.13. illus.

BORODIN, Alexander (1833-87)

A. *General.*

435. **HABETS, Alfred**
Borodin and Liszt. Tr., with a preface, by Rosa Newmarch.
Digby, Long and Co.[1895]. x-liv, 2-199p. 3pl., mus.
Largely based on Stassov's book on Borodin, it contains sections

on Borodin and on Liszt as sketched in Borodin's letters. The first part is a brief history of Russian music, and there is a catalogue of Borodin's works, but no index.

See no. 392.

436. **MONTAGU-NATHAN, M.**
... Borodin.
MS, n.i.s., 2, 26 July 1913, p.87-8.
2 Aug. 1913, p.106-7.
9 Aug. 1913, p.129.
16 Aug. 1913, p.155-6.

437. **MONTAGU-NATHAN, M.**
Borodin.
in MONTAGU-NATHAN. An introduction to Russian music, p.40-3.

438. **MONTAGU-NATHAN, M.**
The story of Russian music. 6. Borodin.
MSt, 9, Feb. 1917, p.195-6. 1pl.

439. **SWAN, Alfred J.**
Borodin as pioneer of national Russian music in Western Europe.
Ch, n.s., no.12, Jan. 1921, p.359-62

*440. **CRUPPI, L.**
Borodin and Liszt.
LLA, 312, 11 Mar. 1922, p.600-5.

441. **EVANS, Edwin**
My first "Modern". A retrospective meditation.
ML, 4, Apr. 1923. p.219-30. mus.

442. **CALVOCORESSI, M. D.**
New facts on Borodin.
MMR, 66, Mar. 1926, p.70-1.

443. **ABRAHAM, Gerald**
Borodin. The composer and his music.
William Reeves. [1927]. 3-205p. 5pl., mus.
A useful, well-written study, but it is not indexed.

444. **FINDEISEN, Nicolas**
Borodin's musical legacy. Tr. by S.W. Pring.
MMR, 57, Feb. 1927, p.34-5.
Mar. 1927, p.74.
Part 2 of the article deals with 5 "unknown" chamber works.

*445. **SCHEFFER, P.**
Borodin's homecoming.
LLA, 333, 15 Sept. 1927, p.503-6.

*446. **NIELSEN, A. K.**
Borodin's swan-song.
LLA, 333, 1 Dec. 1927, p.992-1004.

448. **ONE of the Russian "Five" Alexander Borodin: chemist and musician.**
British musician, 8, Feb. 1932, p.31-6.
Includes a list of his principal works.

449. **ABRAHAM, Gerald**
Borodin for the gramophile.
G, 10, July 1932, p.60-1.

450. **STODDARD, Hope**
Borodin's genius in double-harness.
MO, 57, Mar. 1934, p.502-3. mus.

451. **KURBANOFF, M. M.**
A few reminiscences of Borodin (1884-87). Tr. and arranged by Alfred J. Swan.
Ch, 16, Mar.-Apr. 1935, p.96-9.

452. **CALVOCORESSI, M. D.**
Alexander Borodin.
in CALVOCORESSI *and* ABRAHAM. Masters of Russian music, p.155-77. 1pl.

453. **HUTCHINGS, A. J.**
A study of Borodin. 1. The man.
MT, 77, Oct. 1936, p.881-3.
2. The music.
Nov. 1936, p.980-2. mus.

454. **ABRAHAM, Gerald**
The evolution of Russian harmony. 3. Borodin and Rimsky-Korsakov.
MMR, 68, Feb. 1938, p.37-40. mus.

*455. **HILL, Edward B.**
Russian nationalist composers.
E, 59, Nov. 1941, p.739. illus.
Article on Borodin.

456. **HUTCHINGS, Arthur**
A scientist's music.
L. 26, 24 Dec. 1941, p.865.

457. **CALVOCORESSI, M. D.**
Alexander Borodin: Russian Nationalist.
L, 30, 23 Sept. 1943, p.361.

458. **MONTAGU-NATHAN, M.**
Some unfamiliar Borodin.
L, 33, 24 May 1945, p.585. mus.
Deals with a number of works including Symphony no.1 and the collective "Mlada".

459. **BROOK, Donald**
Borodin.
in BROOK. Six great Russian composers, p.20-38.

See no.208.

*460. **KIDSON, E.**
Alexander Borodin, 1833-1887.
Canon, 8, June 1955, p.423-6.

461. **ZETLIN, Mikhail**
Borodin.
in ZETLIN. The Five, p.70-88.

462. **ZETLIN, Mikhail**
The "Chemical gentleman".
in ZETLIN. The Five, p.283-99.

See no.420.

See no.1984.

See no.2763.

463. **LLOYD-JONES, David**
Borodin's early compositions.
L, 63, 28 Apr. 1960, p.773.

464. **LLOYD-JONES, David**
Borodin in Heidelberg.
MQ, 46, Oct. 1960, p.500-8. 2pl.

465. **LLOYD-JONES, David**
Borodin on Liszt.
ML, 42, Apr. 1961, p.117-26.

466. **SUNDERMAN, F. William**
Alexander Borodin.
American string teacher, 12, no.1, 1962, p.14-16.

467. **DIANIN, Serge**
Borodin. Tr. from the Russian by Robert Lord.
O.U.P. 1963. vii-xi, 2-356p. 13pl., mus.
A revision of the 1955 Russian edition of Dianin's *Life and letters of Borodin,* the author being the composer's grandson by adoption. The scholarly biographical section is superb, but the analysis of the music (with over 300 music examples) is less outstanding. The whole is completely spoiled by a slovenly and very inaccurate translation.

*468. **LLOYD-JONES, D.**
Professor Borodin's indulgence.
HF, 13, June 1963, p.28-31. illus., disc.

*469. **OBER, William B.**
Alexander Borodin, M.D. (1833-1887): physician, chemist and composer.
New York State j. of medicine, 67, Mar. 1967, p.836-45. bib.
Contains a list of Borodin's scientific publications. The same material is covered in no. 470.

470. **OBER, William B.**
Alexander Borodin – the "Sunday" composer.
Hi-fi/stereo rev., 18, Apr. 1967, p.54-8. illus.
See also no.469.

471. **HUTCHINGS, Arthur**
Most professional of amateurs.
Making music, no.64, Summer 1967, p.9-11. illus.

472. **SCHOFIELD, Maurice**
Borodin had two strings to his bow.
Music in education, 33, Nov.-Dec. 1969, p.305.

*473. **SUNDERMAN, F. W.**
Medicine, music and academia.
American string teacher, 20, no.2, 1970, p.42+. illus.

B. *Works.*

Symphonies.

474. **ABRAHAM, Gerald**
Borodin as a symphonist.
ML, 11, Oct. 1930, p.352-9. mus.
Also *in* ABRAHAM. Studies in Russian music. p.102-18. mus.

Symphony no. 1.

475. **CALVOCORESSI, M. D.**
Borodin revised.
MT, 65, Dec. 1924, p.1086-9. mus.
Compares the original version of the First Symphony with the (then) newly published revision by Rimsky-Korsakov and Glazunov.

476. **ABRAHAM, Gerald**
The great unplayed. 4. Borodin's First Symphony.
MS, n.i.s., 25, 30 May 1925, p.183. mus.

Symphony no.2.

477. **NEWMARCH, Rosa**
Borodin. Symphony no. 2 in B minor.
CL, 5, p.12-15.

Symphony no. 3.

478. **CALVOCORESSI, M. D.**
Another unfinished symphony.
L, 22, 23 Nov. 1939, p.1040.

In the Steppes of Central Asia.

479. **NEWMARCH, Rosa**
Borodin. In the Steppes of Central Asia..
CL, 2, p.41.

Petite Suite for piano.

480. **LEE, E. Markham**
The student-interpreter. Borodin's "Petite Suite".
MO, 56, Jan. 1933, p.313-14. mus.

Songs.

481. **ABRAHAM, Gerald**
Borodin's songs.
MT, 75, Nov. 1934, p.983-5. mus.
Also *in* ABRAHAM. On Russian music, p.169-78. mus.

Mlada.

See no. 119

See no. 146

Prince Igor.

482. **NEWMARCH, Rosa**
Prince Igor.
MJIMS, May 1903, p.463-6.

483. **FINCK, Henry**
A Russian professor's opera.
Na, 102, 6 Jan. 1916, p.27-8.

484. **DAVIDSON, Gladys**
Borodin. Prince Igor.
in DAVIDSON. Stories from the Russian operas, p.1-11. illus.

485. **NEWMARCH, Rosa**
Borodin. Ballet suite. Danses Polovtsiennes from "Prince Igor".
CL, 3, p.69-70.

486. **ABRAHAM, Gerald**
Prince Igor; an experiment in lyrical opera.
MQ, 17, Jan. 1931, p.74-83. mus.

487. **ABRAHAM, Gerald**
"Prince Igor".
in ABRAHAM. Studies in Russian music, p.119-41. mus.

488. **ABRAHAM, Gerald**
The history of "Prince Igor".
ML, 16, Mar. 1935, p.85-95.
Also *in* ABRAHAM. On Russian music, p.147-68.

489. **MONTAGU-NATHAN, M.**
The origins of "Igor".
L, 34, 13 Dec. 1945, p.713.

490. **GODDARD, Scott**
Borodin's "Prince Igor".
L, 43, 20 Apr. 1950, p.716.

491. **GRAF, Milan**
Borodin's "unfinished opera".
MMu, 3, Feb. 1955, p.12-13. illus.

492. **WARBURTON, A. O.**
Set works for O Level G.C.E. Borodin: Overture to Prince Igor.
MTe, 48, Feb. 1969, p.17.

*493. **RIZZO, F.**
Dr. Borodin's formula.
ON, 33, 1 Mar. 1969, p.12-13. illus.

The Bogatirs.

494. **LLOYD-JONES, David**
"The Bogatyrs": Russia's first operetta.
MMR, 89, July-Aug. 1959, p.123-30.

BORTNIANSKY, Dimitri (1751-1825)

495. **SEAMAN, Gerald**
D.S. Bortnyansky (1751-1825).
MR, 21, May 1960, p.106-13. mus.

BRUSILOVSKY, Evgenyi (1905-)

496. **MOISENCO, Rena**
Eugene Brussilovsky.
in MOISENCO. Twenty Soviet composers, p.10-12.

497. **MOISENKO, Rena**
Yevgeni Brussilovsky.
in MOISENKO. Realist music, p.58-62. mus.

BUTVILOVSKY, Richard

B. *Works.*

498. **NISNEVICH, Sima**
Three first symphonies. Tr. by Hilda Perham.
SL, Aug. 1962, p.170-80.
By three Byelorussian composers: Butvilovsky, Vladimir Cherednichenko and Dmitri Smolsky.

CHAIKOVSKY – *see* **TCHAIKOVSKY**

CHALIAPIN – *see* **SHALIAPIN**

CHEREDNICHENKO, Vladimir

B. *Works.*

Symphony no. 1.

See no. 498.

CHEREPNIN – *see* **TCHEREPNIN**

CHISHKO, Oles (1895-)

499. **MOISENCO, Rena**
Oles Chishko.
in MOISENCO. Twenty Soviet composers, p.13-16.

500. **MOISENKO, Rena**
Oles Chishko.
in MOISENKO. Realist music, p.63-8. mus.

CUI, César (1835-1918)

A. *General.*

501. **[CUI, Cesar]**
Cesar Cui on the decay of music. Tr. from the Russian by Leo Haendelmann.
MS, i.s., 13, 6 Jan. 1900, p.12-13.
From the preface to an article by Cui which first appeared in the Russian periodical *Artiste* in 1894.

502. **ZIELINSKI, Jaroslaw de**
César Cui.
M, 15, Aug. 1910, p.512-13. illus.

503. **MONTAGU-NATHAN, M.**
... César Cui.
MS, n.i.s., 2, 12 July 1913, p.34-5.
19 July 1913, p.58-9.

504. **TIDEBÖHL, Ellen von**
César Antonovitsh Cui.
MMR, 45, Aug. 1915, p.221-2.

505. **MONTAGU-NATHAN, M.**
Cui.
in MONTAGU-NATHAN. An introduction to Russian music, p.34-7.

506. **MONTAGU-NATHAN, M.**
The story of Russian music. 5. Cui.
MSt, 9, Jan. 1917, p.167-8+. illus.

507. **CESAR Cui**
MO, 41, May 1918, p.449.

508. **CALVOCORESSI, M. D.**
César Cui (1835-1918).
MMR, 65, Jan. 1935, p.2-3.

509. **CALVOCORESSI, M. D.**
César Cui.
in CALVOCORESSI *and* ABRAHAM. Masters of Russian music, p.147-54. 1pl.

See no. 208.

See no. 420.

See no. 1984.

See no. 2763.

B. *Works.*

510. **MONTAGU-NATHAN, M.**
An Anglo-Russian opera. Cui's "A Feast in Plague Time".
MT, 97, Feb. 1956, p.76-7.

511. **DAVIDSON, Gladys**
Cui. "Mademoiselle Fifi".
in DAVIDSON. Stories from the Russian operas, p.12-22. illus.

Mlada.

See no. 119.

See no. 146.

DARGOMYZHSKY, Alexander (1813-69)

A. *General.*

512. **MONTAGU-NATHAN, M.**
... Dargomijsky.
MS, n.i.s., 1, 31 May 1913, p.472-3.

513. **TIDEBÖHL, Ellen von**
Alexander Sergeievitsh Dargomyshski.
MMR, 43, July 1913, p.178-9.

514. **MONTAGU-NATHAN, M.**
The Russian operatic gospel: according to Dargomijsky, Moussorgsky and Rimsky-Korsakoff.
MO, 38, Mar. 1915, p.371-2.
Apr. 1915, p.445-6.
May 1915, p.518-19.
June 1915, p.589-90.
July 1915, p.661-2.
Respectively, two articles about Dargomyzhsky, two on Mussorgsky's fragment "The Matchmaker" (i.e. "The Marriage") and one on Rimsky-Korsakov's "Mozart and Salieri".

515. **MONTAGU-NATHAN, M.**
Dargomijsky.
in MONTAGU-NATHAN. An introduction to Russian music. p.22-6.

See no. 44.

516. **CALVOCORESSI, M. D.**
Dargomyjsky.
in CALVOCORESSI *and* ABRAHAM. Masters of Russian music, p.65-75.

517. **ABRAHAM, Gerald**
The evolution of Russian harmony. 2. Dargomizhsky and Moussorgsky.
MMR, 68, Jan. 1938, p.5-8. mus.

See no. 605.

518. **ALSHVANG, Arnold**
Alexander Dargomyzhsky.
SL, 11, June 1944, p.66-7. illus.

B. *Works.*

Orchestral works.

519 . **ABRAHAM, Gerald**
Dargomizhsky's orchestral pieces.
MMR, 72, May 1937, p.73-5. mus.
Also *in* ABRAHAM. On Russian music, p.52-61. mus.

Russalka.

See no. 605

The Stone Guest.

520. **MONTAGU-NATHAN, M.**
... "The Stone Guest" and "The Five".
MS, n.i.s., 1, 14 June 1913, p.522-3.

521. **DAVIDSON, Gladys**
Dargomijsky. The Stone Guest.
in DAVIDSON. Stories from the Russian operas, p.23-41.

See no. 1343.

522. **ABRAHAM, Gerald**
"The Stone Guest".
in ABRAHAM. Studies in Russian music, p.68-86. illus., mus.

523. **COOPER, Martin**
Don Juan in Russian.
L, 45, 8 Mar. 1951, p.396.

See no. 367.

DUNAYEVSKY, Isaac (1900-55)

524. **MOISENCO, Rena**
Isaak Dunayevsky.
in MOISENCO. Twenty Soviet composers, p.17-20.

525. **MOISENKO, Rena**
Isaak Dunayevski.
in MOISENKO. Realist music, p.69-72.

526. **ISAAC Dunayevsky, 1900-1955.**
SCR, 2, Sept. 1955, p.12-13.

527. **MONTAGU-NATHAN, M.**
Composer for the masses.
MT, 96, Oct. 1955, p.551.

DZERZHINSKY, Ivan (1909-)

528. **MOISENCO, Rena**
Ivan Dzersinsky.
in MOISENCO. Twenty Soviet composers, p.20-4.

529. **ABRAHAM, Gerald**
Ivan Dzerzhinsky.
MMR, 72, Oct. 1942, p.177-83.
Also *in* ABRAHAM. Eight Soviet composers, p.79-88. mus.

530. **MOISENKO, Rena**
Ivan Dzerzhinski.
in MOISENKO. Realist music, p.73-9.

FEINBERG, Samuel (1890-1962)

531. **BELAIEV, Victor**
Contemporary Russian composers. 2. Samuel Feinberg.
Sackbut, 5, June 1925, p.326-9.

532. **SABANEYEFF, Leonid**
Samuil Feinberg.
in SABANYEFF. Modern Russian composers, p.163-71.

FOMIN, Evstigney (1761-1800)

533. **SEAMAN, Gerald**
Evstignei Fomin: 1761-1800.
MMR, 88, Jan.-Feb. 1958, p.21-6. mus.

GABRILOVITCH, Ossip (1878-1936)

*534. **GABRILOWITSCH and Scriabine.**
Independent, 62, 31 Jan. 1907, p.256-7.

535. **CLEMENS, Clara**
My husband Gabrilowitsch.
Harper. 1938. 1-351p. 9pl., mus.
Affectionate reminiscences by the daughter of Mark Twain. The appendices include an appreciation by Bruno Walter. There are a few minor errors.

*536. **GABRILOWITSCH, O.**
A great master of the piano.
Piano teacher, 5, no.4, 1963, p.8-10.
On Leschetizky. Reprinted from *Musical courier,* 27 Dec. 1930.

GADZHIBEKOV, Uzier (1885-1948)

537. **MOISENCO, Rena**
Useir Gadzhibekov.
in MOISENCO. Twenty Russian composers, p.24-9.

538. **MOISENKO, Rena**
Useir Gadzhibekov.
in MOISENKO. Realist music, p.80-7. 1pl., mus.

539. **KREBS, Stanley D.**
Uzeir Gadzhibekov.
in KREBS. Soviet composers and the development of Soviet music, p.132-7.

GALYNIN, German (1922-66)

A. *General.*

540. **KREBS, Stanley D.**
German Galynin.
in KREBS. Soviet composers and the development of Soviet music, p.290-8. mus.

B. *Works.*

541. **MNATSAKANOVA, Elizaveta**
"Death and the Maiden", an oratorio by Herman Galynin.
SL, Mar. 1968, p.178-80.

GLAZUNOV, Alexander (1865-1936)

A. *General.*

542. **DR. Glazunow.**
MT, 48, July 1907, p.454.

*543. **DR. Glazounow and the Society of British Composers.**
Musical world, 7, 16 July 1907, p.?. illus.

544. **MONTAGU-NATHAN, M.**
Glazounof.
in MONTAGU-NATHAN. Contemporary Russian composers, p.81-109. illus.

545. **MONTAGU-NATHAN, M.**
The story of Russian music. 14. Glazunov.
MSt, 10, Dec. 1917, p.140-1.

546. **CALVOCORESSI, M. D.**
Alexander Glazunof.
MMR, 55, Sept. 1925, p.263-4.

547. **SABANEEV, Leonid**
A.K. Glazounov. Tr. by S.W. Pring.
MT, 70, Mar. 1929, p.209-12.

548. **... ALEXANDER Glazounoff.**
MO, 52, July 1929, p.910. illus.

549. **HOLT, Richard**
Alexander Glazounov.
G, 9, July 1931, p.64.

550. **EVANS, Edwin**
... Half a century.
Music lover, 1, 25 June 1932, p.3-4.
On Glazunov's fiftieth anniversary as a composer.

551. **LYLE, Watson**
Glazounow and his music.
Sackbut, 12, July 1932, p.206-10.

552. **CALVOCORESSI, M. D.**
Glazunof.
in CALVOCORESSI *and* ABRAHAM. Masters of Russian music, p.431-5. 1pl.

553. **ABRAHAM, Gerald**
Alexander Constantinovich Glazounov (1865-1936).
MMR, 66, May 1936, p.81-3.

554. **[BRIAN, Havergal]**
Alexander Glazounoff.
MO, 59, May 1936, p.676-7. illus.

555. **SABANEEV, L.**
Glazounov. Tr. by S.W. Pring.
MT, 77, May 1936, p.413-14.

556. **CALVOCORESSI, M. D.**
Alexandre Glazounov.
L, 15, 13 May 1936, p.939.

557. **EVANS, Edwin**
"The last great classical composer?"
RT, 51, 15 May 1936, p.12.

558. **NEWMARCH, Rosa**
Alexander Glazunov.
Slavonic rev., 15, July 1936, p.214-15.

See no. 139.

559. **ABRAHAM, Gerald**
Glazunov: the end of an episode.
in ABRAHAM. On Russian music, p.234-42.

560. **ABRAHAM, Gerald**
A minor master: Alexander Glazunov.
L, 21, 1 June 1939, p.1180.

561. **ANDERSON, W. R.**
Glazunov the reconciler.
L, 26, 18 Sept. 1941, p.417.

562. **CARRITT, Graham**
Alexander Glazunov: master craftsman.
L, 31, 20 Apr. 1944, p.449.

563. **MONTAGU-NATHAN, M.**
A Russian conservative.
L, 34, 30 Aug. 1945, p.249.

564. **AMERONGEN, Alex van**
Glazunov revalued.
T, 33, Autumn 1954, p.31-4. mus.

*565. **MILSTEIN, N.**
Memories of Glazunov's memory.
MJ, 25, Mar. 1967, p.32+.

B. *Works.*

Orchestral music.

566. **STEANE, Leonard**
Glazounov. An assessment of the value of Glazounow's orchestral music, with tributes from various sources.
The author. [1966]. [unpaged]. [1-13p].
A useful little booklet on a neglected composer.

Symphonies.

567. **SEAMAN, Gerald**
The symphonies of Glazunov.
MO, 89, Mar. 1966, p.366-7+.

Symphony no. 6.

568. **[BAUGHAN, Edward A.]**
A new symphony ...
MS, i.s., 11, 7 Jan. 1899, p.6-7.

The King of the Jews, incidental music.

569. **TIDEBÖHL, Ellen von**
Glazounow's music to the drama "The King of the Jews".
MMR, 44, July 1914, p.177-8.

Stenka Razin.

570. **SLONIMSKY, Sergei**
Stenka Razin's victory.
LME, 21, Sept. 1966, p.10-12. illus.

Raymonda.

571. **GOODWIN, Noel**
Raymonda. Music.
DD, 17, Feb. 1966, p.17-19. illus.

Concerto for piano no. 1.

571a. **TOVEY, *Sir* Donald**
Glazounov. Pianoforte concerto in F minor, op. 92.
in TOVEY. Essays in musical analysis, Vol. 3, p.209-10. mus.

572. **NEWMARCH, Rosa**
Glazounov. Pianoforte concerto in F minor (op. 92).
CL, 5, p.41-3.

Concerto for piano no. 2.

573. **BELYAEV, V.**
Glazunov's new pianoforte concerto. Tr. by M. Montagu-Nathan.
MT, 59, Apr. 1918, p.168-70. illus., mus.

Quartets.

574. **ABRAHAM, Gerald**
Glazunov and the string quartet.
T, 73, Summer 1965, p.16-21. mus.
Also *in* ABRAHAM. Slavonic and Romantic music, p.218-24. mus.

Organ works.

575. **THOMAS, A. F. Leighton**
A note on Glazunov's organ music.
MO, 88, Feb. 1965, p.293+. mus.

Piano works.

576. **THIMAN, Eric**
The piano music of Glazounoff.
MO, 51, Dec. 1927, p.273-5. mus.

577. [ABRAHAM, Gerald]
Glazounov: prelude and fugue.
L, 16, 15 July 1936, p.142.
The Prelude and fugue for piano, op. 62.

578. **LEE, E. Markham**
The student-interpreter.
MO, 58, Dec. 1938, p.218-19. mus.
Includes notes on the Prelude in D, op. 25, no.1.

579. **LEE, E. Markham**
The amateur's repertoire. Glazounoff's Variations.
MO, 53, Aug. 1930, p.985-6. mus.
Theme and variations, op. 72.

GLEBOV, Igor – *see* **ASAFIEV, Boris**

GLIÈRE, Reinhold (1875-1956)

*580. **SLONIMSKY, Nicolas**
Reinhold Glière.
American quarterly on the Soviet Union, July 1938, p.52-6.

*581. **NARODNY, Ivan**
Glière's music reconciles old and new Russia.
MA, 59, 10 Feb. 1939, p.321+.

582. **MOISENCO, Rena**
Reingold [sic] Maurice Gliere.
in MOISENCO. Twenty Soviet composers, p.30-4.

583. **MOISENKO, Rena**
Reinhold Glier.
in MOISENKO. Realist music, p.88-96. 1pl., mus.

584. **GLIERE, R.**
The people – the great teacher.
SCR, no. 14, Apr. 1953, p.5-7.

585. **MARTYNOV, I.**
Reinhold Gliere's 80th birthday.
SCR, 2, May 1955, p.15-17.

586. **KREBS, Stanley D.**
Reinhold Glière.
in KREBS. Soviet composers and the development of Soviet music, p.70-81. mus.

B. *Works.*

Symphony no. 3.

587. **TIDEBÖHL, Ellen von**
Letter from Moscow.
MMR, 42, May 1912, p.123-4.
Mainly on Glière's Symphony no. 3.

Concerto for soprano.

See no. 1791.

Album leaf for piano, op. 31, no. 11.

588. **DUMM, Robert**
Sentiment not sentimentality ...
Clavier, 7, Oct. 1968, p.30-2. illus., mus.

GLINKA, Mikhail (1804-57)

A. *General.*

589. **BENNETT, Joseph**
... Glinka.
MT, 28, Jan. 1887, p.12-14.
Feb. 1887, p.78-80.
Mar. 1887, p.143-6.
Apr. 1887, p.207-9.

*590. **POUGIN, A.**
Michel Ivanovitch Glinka, Russian musician.
M, 14, 1808, p.245.

591. **KEETON, A. E.**
Glinka, the father of Russian opera.
Contemporary review, 76, Aug. 1899, p.413-24.
Also *in* LLA, 223, 18 Nov. 1899, p.432-40.
Also précised *in* MS, i.s., 12, 16 Sept. 1899, p.182.

592. **KEETON, A. E.**
Michail Ivànovitch Glinka.
MMR, 34, July 1904, p.125-7.

593. **KEETON, A. E.**
Michail Ivànovitch Glinka. B. June 1st. 1804.
D. February 15th. 1857.
FR, 82, July 1904, p.48.

594. **CENTENARY of Glinka, Russian composer.**
Rev. of revs., 31, Jan. 1905, p.105-7. illus.

595. **MONTAGU-NATHAN, M.**
... Glinka.
MS, n.i.s., 1, 10 May 1913, p.406-8.

596. **MONTAGU-NATHAN, M.**
Glinka.
Constable. 1916. 7-85p. 1pl.
Companion to the Mussorgsky and Rimsky-Korsakov biographies in the *Masters of Russian music* series, this is one of the only books in English on Glinka. There is a list of principal compositions. Glinka wrote over 80 songs, not 70 as the book states.

597. **MONTAGU-NATHAN, M.**
Glinka.
in MONTAGU-NATHAN. An introduction to Russian music, p.16-20.

See no. 44.

598. **MONTAGU-NATHAN, M.**
Glinka revalued.
MT, 58, May 1917, p.212-13.

599. **KALL, Alexis**
Nationalism in Russian music.
Art and archaeology, 13, Feb. 1922, p.78-82.
Mainly devoted to Glinka.

600. **ABRAHAM, Gerald**
Glinka and his achievement.
ML, 9, July 1928, p.255-64. mus.
Also *in* ABRAHAM. Studies in Russian music, p.21-42. mus.

*601. **INCH, Herbert**
A bibliography of Glinka.
New York. 1925. 28p. [typescript].

*602. **GOODWIN, A. S.**
Glinka's musical education.
E, 53, Jan. 1935, p.49.

603. **ABRAHAM, Gerald**
Glinka.
in CALVOCORESSI *and* ABRAHAM. Masters of Russian music, p.13-64. 1pl.

604. **ABRAHAM, Gerald**
The evolution of Russian harmony. 1. Glinka.
MMR, 67, Dec. 1937, p.225-6. mus.
Also *in* ABRAHAM. On Russian music, p.255-74. mus.

605. **ABRAHAM, Gerald**
Glinka, Dargomizhsky and "The Rusalka".
in ABRAHAM. On Russian music, p.43-51. mus.

606. **SOLODUKHO, Ivan**
Glinka.
ASJ, 5, Autumn 1944, p.35-9.

607. **ASSAFYEV, Boris**
Mikhail Glinka (1804-1857).
SL, Oct. 1944, p.64-7.

608. **BROOK, Donald**
Glinka.
in BROOK. Six great Russian composers, p.1-20. illus.

609. **ANDERSON, W. R.**
Michael Ivanovitch Glinka (1804-1857).
MTe, 29, Jan. 1950, p.31+.

610. **SHAPORIN, Y.**
Film of a great Russian composer.
SL, Jan. 1952, p.162-5.

611. **COLLINGWOOD, Frances**
A musical oak from an acorn.
MMu, 5, Feb. 1957, p.11. illus.

612. **ZETLIN, Mikhail**
Glinka.
in ZETLIN. The Five, p.20-50.

613. **GLINKA, Mikhail Ivanovich**
Memoirs. Tr. from the Russian by Richard B. Mudge.
Oklahoma, University of Oklahoma Press. 1963. v-xi, 3-264p. 8pl., mus.
The first English translation of Glinka's *Notes,* written in 1855. There is a useful list of Glinka's relatives, brief synopses of the operas and a helpful index.

*614. **GRUNFELD, F.**
Coachmen's music.
Reporter, 29, 10 Oct. 1963, p.56+.

*615. **JOUVENCEL, M. de** *and* **ROIZMAN, L.**
Glinka and the organ culture in Russia.
American organist, 50, June 1967, p.14-16.

B. *Works.*

*616. **SMITH, A. G.**
Glinka and orchestral music.
E, 53, Feb. 1935, p.120.

617. **NEWMARCH, Rosa**
Glinka. Kamarinskaya (orchestral fantasia).
CL, 2, p.45-7.

Farewell to Petersburg. No. 10, The Lark.

618. **WHITEMORE, Cuthbert**
Studies in pianoforte interpretation. The Russians.
MTe, 4, Jan. 1925, p.20.

*619. **HAMBOURG, Mark**
Master lesson on The Lark, a song by Glinka.
E, 46, Nov. 1928, p.842. illus.

620. **LLOYD-JONES, David**
Glinka and the opera.
L, 66, 12 Oct. 1961, p.581.

A Life for the Tsar.

621. **ABRAHAM, Gerald**
"A Life for the Tsar": a notable centenary.
MO, 59, Feb. 1936, p.401-2. mus.
Mar. 1936, p.497-8. mus.
Also *in* ABRAHAM. On Russian music, p.1-19.

622. **COOPER, Martin**
"Ivan Susanin".
L, 37, 3 Apr. 1947, p.520.

623. **SEAMAN, Gerald**
"A Life for the Tsar".
L, 62, 31 Dec. 1959, p.1175.

Russlan and Ludmila.

624. **MONTAGU-NATHAN, M.**
.. "Russlan and Ludmilla".
MS, n.i.s., 1, 17 May 1913, p.422-4.
31 May 1913, p.471-2.

625. **CALVOCORESSI, M. D.**
Glinka's "Russlan and Ludmila".
MT, 66, Sept. 1925, p.785. mus.

626. **NEWMARCH, Rosa**
Glinka. Overture, "Russlan and Ludmilla".
CL, 4, p.66.

627. **ABRAHAM, Gerald**
The foundation-stone of Russian music.
ML, 18, Jan. 1937, p.50-62. mus.

628. **ABRAHAM, Gerald**
"Russlan and Lyudmilla".
in ABRAHAM. On Russian music, p.20-42. mus.

629. **CALVOCORESSI, M. D.**
Ruslan and Ludmila.
L, 28, 3 Dec. 1942, p.733.

GNESSIN, Mikhail (1883-1957)

630. **SABANEYEFF, Leonid**
Mikhail Gnyesine.
in SABANEYEFF. Modern Russian composers, p.172-80.

631. **MOISENCO, Rena**
Mikhail Fabian Gnessin.
in MOISENCO. Twenty Soviet composers, p.34-5.

632. **MOISENKO, Rena**
Mikhail Gnessin.
in MOISENKO. Realist music. p.97-9.

*633. **GNESSIN, Michael**
Autobiography [abstract].
Tatzlil, no. 6, 1966, p.100.

*634. **GNESSIN, M.**
The Armenian method of reading the Book of Psalms [abstract].
Tatzlil, no. 6, 1966, p.101.

GRETCHANINOV, Alexander (1864-1956)

A. *General.*

635. **MONTAGU-NATHAN, M.**
Grechaninof.
in MONTAGU-NATHAN. Contemporary Russian composers, p.275-83. illus.

636. **GILCAR, Silas**
Alexander Gretchaninoff.
Musical news, 63, 23 Sept. 1922, p.262.

637. **SABANEEV, Leonid**
Gretchaninov. Tr. by S. W. Pring.
Dominant, 1, May 1928, p.18-21.

638. **SABANEYEFF, Leonid**
A. Gryechaninoff.
in SABANEYEFF. Modern Russian composers, p.144-8.

*639. **GRETCHANINOFF, Alexander T.**
Reflections from a busy musical life.
E, 54, Dec. 1936, p.763-4. illus.

640. **NADEJINE, Nicolai**
A. Gretchaninov.
G, 15, Mar. 1938, p.419-21. illus.

*641. **ALL, N. N.**
Sixty years among the masters.
E, 60, July 1942, p.439+. illus.
All interviews Gretchaninov.

*642. **SEAGARD, John**
Vocal style of Russian church music as seen in the works of Alexander Gretchaninoff.
M.M. thesis, Eastman School of Music, University of Rochester, New York. 1949.

*643. **HEYLBUT, R. ,** *ed,*
Russian masters of yesterday; a conference with Alexandre Gretchaninoff.
E, 67, June 1949, p.344+. illus.

644. **GRETCHANINOFF, Alexandre**
My life. Introduced and tr. by Nicolas Slonimsky.
New York, Coleman-Ross. 1952. 1-204p. 2pl., mus.
Well-translated, and containing an invaluable annotated list of (over 200) compositions, it lacks an index.

645. **CRAIG, Mary**
"To remember A. Gretchaninoff".
MC, 150, Oct. 1954, p.8-9. illus.
An interview with the composer.

646. **MONTAGU-NATHAN, M.**
Alexander Grechaninov.
MT, 97, Mar. 1956, p.151.

647. **MONTAGU-NATHAN, M.**
A. T. Grechaninov: 1864-1956.
MMR, 86, Mar.-Apr. 1956, p.52-6.

B. *Works.*

648. **[ABRAHAM, Gerald]**
Grechaninov's songs.
L, 15, 29 Apr. 1936, p.848.

649. **PASTUKHOV, V. L.**
The songs and romances of A.T. Gretchaninoff. Tr. by Mirra Ginsburg
T, no. 25, Autumn 1952, p.11-18

*650. **GORALI, M.**
Wandering Melodies [abstract].
Tatzlil, no. 1, 1960, p.47.

651. **YASSER, Joseph**
Gretchaninoff's "Heterodox" compositions.
MQ, 28, July 1942, p.309-17. 2pl.
A considerable number of his sacred choral works are designated "Heterodox" by Yasser.

IPPOLITOV-IVANOV, Mikhail (1859-1935)

652. **SABANEEV, Leonid**
Obituary. M. M. Ippolitov-Ivanov.
MT, 76, Apr. 1935, p.367.

*653. **KARAPETOFF, V.**
Personal memory of Ippolitoff-Ivanoff.
E, 56, Mar. 1938, p.146.

654. **KREBS, Stanley D.**
Ippolitov-Ivanov.
in KREBS. Soviet composers and the development of Soviet music, p.65-9.

KABALEVSKY, Dmitri (1904-)

A. *General.*

655. **ABRAHAM, G.**
Dmitri Kabalevsky.
MMR, 72, July-Aug. 1942, p.129-34.
Also *in* ABRAHAM. Eight Soviet composers, p.70-8. mus.

656. **BUSH, Alan**
Dmitry Kabalevsky.
L, 32, 10 Aug. 1944, p.165.

657. **MONTAGU-NATHAN, M.**
Kabalevsky and Soviet realism.
L, 41, 17 Mar. 1949, p.464.

658. **KABALEVSKY, Dmitri**
Soviet composer's replies to questions. Tr. by Eleanor Fox.
ASJ, 11, Summer 1950, p.21-3.
Questions by Leonard Cassini to Kabalevsky.

659. **MONTAGU-NATHAN, M.**
"Curtain up?".
MO, 73, July 1950, p.577-8.
On Kabalevsky's address to the (London) Society for Cultural Relations.

660. **KABALEVSKY, D.**
Notes on opera on contemporary themes. Tr. by Harold Feldt.
SCR, no. 9, Oct. 1951, p.1-8.

*661. **CLARK, F.**
Student material: Kabalevsky and Prokofieff.
Repertoire, 1, Nov. 1951, p.76-9.

662. **KABALEVSKY, Dmitry**
Music and the people.
News, no. 40, 1 Mar. 1953, p.8-10.
On English music.

663. **KABALEVSKY, Dmitri**
A Soviet look at musical America.
Hi fi/stereo rev., 5, July 1960, p.35-41. illus.

*664. **KABALEVSKY, D.**
A Russian traveller's view of American music.
Music educator's j., 49, Nov.-Dec. 1962, p.71-2.
Tr. from *Literaturnaya Gazeta.*

*665. **KABALEVSKY, D.**
The composer and music for children.
Music educator's j., 50, 1964, no. 4, p.49-50.

666. **KABALEVSKY, Dmitry**
Emil Gilels playing.
in LIPOVSKY. Lenin Prize winners, p.240-4. illus.

*667. **KABALEVSKY, Dimitri**
Mutual enrichment of children of various countries.
Music educator's j., 53, Feb. 1967, p.45-7.

*668. **KABALEVSKI, D.**
The importance of contemporary music for music education.
International music educator, no. 15, Mar. 1965. p.491-9. illus.
In English, French and German.

*669. **KABALEVSKI, D.**
Technical media for mass dissemination of music and the musical culture of our time.
International music educator, no. 18, Oct. 1968, p.609-18.
English and French text.

*670. **KABALEVSKY, D.**
On mass musical education.
UU, Feb. 1969, p.3-17.

671. **KREBS, Stanley D.**
Dmitri Kabalevsky.

in KREBS. Soviet composers and the development of Soviet music, p.233-56. mus.

B. *Works.*

Symphony no. 2.

See no. 139.

*672. **DUMM, Robert**
The performer's analysis - a lesson on Kabalevsky's "Rondino".
Clavier, 6, no. 3, 1967, p.32-5. illus., mus.

673. **MONTAGU-NATHAN, M.**
A Soviet piano sonata.
L, 40, 26 Aug. 1948, p.321.
Kabalevsky's Sonata for piano no. 3.

674. **BRYANT, Celia**
Color this modern - a Kabalevsky sonatina.
Clavier, 7, Mar. 1968, p.34-5. mus.
Sonatina, op. 13, no. 1.

675. **BRYANT, Celia**
Playing tricks on a scale.
Clavier, 7, Nov. 1968, p.18-25. mus.
The Variations for piano. op. 40.

676. **KABALEVSKY, Dmitri**
The story of a Requiem. Tr. by Louis Zelikoff.
SL, May 1962, p.175-7.
The work is based on Robert Rozhdestvensky's poem *Requiem.*

677. **MARTYNOV, Ivan**
Dmitri Kabalevsky's "Requiem". Tr. by Hilda Perham.
SL, Oct. 1963, p.190-2.

KALINNIKOV, Vassili (1866-1901)

A. *General.*

678. **SEAMAN, Gerald**
V. S. Kalinnikov (1866-1900).
MR, 28, Nov. 1967, p.289-99. mus.
Includes a list of his compositions. In fact he died in 1901.

B. *Works.*

679. **GREW, Sydney**
Kalinnikov's Symphony in G minor.
MO, 33, May 1910, p.549-50. mus.
Symphony no. 1.

KARAEV, Kara (1918-)

680. **KREBS, Stanley D.**
Kara Karaev.
in KREBS. Soviet composers and the development of Soviet music
p.307-22. mus.

KASTALSKY, Alexander (1856-1926)

A. *General.*

681. **TIDEBÖHL, Ellen von**
Alexander Dmitrijevitch Kastalsky and the Moscow Synod Choir.
MMR, 46, June 1916, p.166.

682. **KASTALSKY, A.**
My musical career and my thoughts on church music. Tr. by S.W. Prir
MQ, 11, Apr. 1925, p.231-47.
Written in 1913.

683. **GLEBOV, Igor**
Kastalsky and Russian church music. Tr. by S. W. Pring.
MMR, 57, Aug. 1927, p.228-9.
Glebov was the pen-name of Boris Asafiev.

684. **BELAIEV, Victor**
Kastalsky and his Russian folk polyphony. Tr. by S. W. Pring.
ML, 10, Oct. 1929, p.378-90. mus.

*685. **BECKWITH, Robert**
A. D. Kastal'skii (1856-1926) and the quest for a native Russian choral style.
DA, 31, July 1970, p.412A-13A.
PhD dissertation, Cornell University, Ithaca, New York. 1969, 528p.

B. *Works.*

686. **NEWMARCH, Rosa**
A Requiem for the Allied Heroes.
MT, 58, Nov. 1917, p.496-7.
The "Requiem for the Fallen Heroes of the Allied Armies".

KATUAR – *see* **CATOIRE**

KHATCHATURIAN, Aram (1903-)

A. *General.*

687. **SLONIMSKY, Nicolas**
Aram Khachaturian.
American (quarterly) rev. on the Soviet Union, 3, Feb. 1941, p.23-5.

688. **MOISENCO. Rena**
Aram Khatchaturian.
in MOISENCO. Twenty Soviet composers, p.36-8.

689. **CALVOCORESSI, M. D.**
Music from Armenia.
L, 27, 8 Jan. 1942, p.61.
Mainly on Khatchaturian.

690. **ABRAHAM, G.**
Aram Khachaturyan.
MMR, 72, Mar.-Apr. 1942, p.56-61.
Also *in* ABRAHAM. Eight Soviet composers, p.43-51. mus.

691. **ALSHWANG, Arnold**
Aram Khachaturyan.
SL, 12, Nov. 1945, p.69-71. illus.

692. **CULSHAW, John**
Aram Khachaturyan.
G, 25, Sept. 1947, p.50-1.

693. **RISING Russian.**
Time, 50, 10 Nov. 1947, p.31-2. illus.

694. **MOISENKO, Rena**
Aram Khachaturyan.
in MOISENKO. Realist music, p.100-7. 1pl., mus.

695. **KHATCHATURYAN, A.**
People I met in Iceland.
News, no. 1, 15 July 1951, p.28-31. illus.

696. **KHACHATURYAN, Aram**
Symphony of friendship.
News, no. 37, 15 Jan. 1953, p.10-11.
Harris's Symphony no. 5.

697. **KHACHATURIAN, Aram**
Originality and inspiration in music.
SCR, 1, Jan. 1954, p.1-9.
Also *in* ASJ, 15, Spring 1954, p.38-44.

698. **MITCHELL, Donald**
A Russian composer speaks.
MT, 96, Jan. 1955, p.33.
On Khachaturian's lecture of 13 Nov. 1954.

699. **KHACHATURYAN, Aram**
Aram Khachaturyan says: Let's meet more often.
News, no. 85, 16 Jan. 1955, p.22-3. illus.

700. **KHACHATURYAN, Aram**
George Gershwin, master of melody.
News, no. 103, 16 Oct. 1955, p.13. illus.

701. **KHACHATURYAN, Aram**
Contribution to pre-Congress discussions.
SCR, 3, Mar. 1956, p.5-8.
The exact congress is not specified.

702. **KHACHATURYAN, A.**
Encounters in Britain. Tr. by Anna Collingwood.
ASJ, 17, Spring 1956, p.4-8.

703. **SHNEERSON, Grigory**
Aram Khachaturyan. Tr. from the Russian by Xenia Danko.
Ed. by Olga Shartse.
Moscow, Foreign Languages Publishing House. 1959.
7-102p. 19pl., mus.
Well-illustrated but brief biography containing a list of principal compositions, but no index.

704. **WORNER, Karl, H.**
Current chronicle. U.S.S.R.
MQ, 45, Apr. 1959, p.249-54.
Discusses Khatchaturian's music.

705. **NESTYEV, Israel**
Aram Khatchaturian. Tr. by Hilda Perham.
SL, Nov. 1963, p.174-7.

*706. **MEDVEDEV, A.** *and* **MENDELEYEV, A.**
Philosophy of music.
U.S.S.R. illus. monthly, no. 11, Nov. 1964, p?. illus.
A week with Khatchaturian.

707. **KHACHATURYAN, Aram**
An outstanding singer of our times.
in LIPOVSKY. Lenin Prize winners, p.278-80. illus.
The singer is Zara Dolukhanova.

708. **SHNEERSON, Grigory**
An impassioned musician.
in LIPOVSKY. Lenin Prize winners, p.85-113.
Excerpts from Shneerson's book *Aram Khachaturyan,* no. 703.

709. **SHOSTAKOVICH, Dmitry**
A striking personality.
in LIPOVSKY. Lenin Prize winners, p.82-4. illus.

*710. **MAYER, W.**
The composer in the U.S. and Russia: a frank talk between Copland and Khachaturian.
ASCAP today, 3, no. 1, 1969, p.22-5. illus.
Reprinted from *America illustrated.* An extract appeared *in Composer* (Houston), 2, 1970, no. 2, p.44-7.

*711. **MAYER, W.**
Copland and Khachaturian - historic meeting.
MJ, 27, Mar. 1969, p.25-7+. illus.

712. **KREBS, Stanley D.**
Aram Khachaturian.
in KREBS. Soviet composers and the development of Soviet music, p.217-32. mus.

*713. **KHACHATURIAN, Aram**
The development of music.
MJ, 28, July 1970, p.32+. illus.

B. *Works.*

714. **SPARTACUS. A new Khachaturian ballet.**
SCR, 1, Oct. 1954, p.13-14.

715. **BRYANT, Celia**
Tuning in to student interest.
Clavier, 9, Apr. 1970, p.29-31. mus.
On the Sonatina of 1959.

KHRENNIKOV, Tikhon (1913-)

716. **MOISENCO, Rena**
Tikhon Khrennikov.
in MOISENCO. Twenty Soviet composers, p.38-40.

717. **MOISENKO, Rena**
Tikhon Khrennikov.
in MOISENKO. Realist music, p.108-14. 1pl., mus.

718. **KHRENNIKOV, Tikhon**
With the people, for peace!
News, no. 2, 30 July 1951, p.14-16. illus.
Deals with the British Musicians' Organization for Peace.

*719. **KHRENNIKOV, Tikhon** *and* **SHOSTAKOVICH, D.**
Impressions of American music.
MJ, 18, Mar. 1960, p.10-11+.

*720. **KHRENNIKOV, Tikhon**
Education of the young.
MJ, 26, Jan. 1968, p.25-6+.
Feb. 1968, p.23-4+.

*721. **KHRENNIKOV, T.**
For further flourishing of our musical art.
UU, Jan. 1969, p.3-28.

722. **KREBS, Stanley D.**
Tikhon Khrennikov.
in KREBS. Soviet composers and the development of Soviet music, p.257-60.

*723. **KHRENNIKOV, T.**
Strike fire from men's hearts.
UU, Feb.-Mar. 1970, p.13-20.

KILADZE, Grigory (1903-62)

724. **MOISENCO, Rena**
Grigori Varfolomei Kiladze.
in MOISENCO. Twenty Soviet composers, p.40-2.

725. **MOISENKO, Rena**
Grigori Kiladze.
in MOISENKO. Realist music, p.115-20.

KNIPPER, Lev (1898-1974)

726. **ABRAHAM, Gerald**
Lev Knipper.
MMR, 72, May 1942, p.75-81.
Also *in* ABRAHAM. Eight Soviet composers, p.52-60. mus.

KORNILOV, Feodor (1879-1939)

727. **MOISENCO, Rena**
Feodor Kornilov.
in MOISENCO. Twenty Soviet composers, p.42-3.

728. **MOISENKO, Rena**
Feodor Kornilov.
in MOISENKO. Realist music, p.121-6. mus.

KOVAL, Marian (1907-71)

729. **KOVAL, Marian**
Life and song. Tr. by A. Collingwood.
SCR, 1, Apr. 1954, p.8-13.
Given at the seventh plenary session of the Union of Soviet Composers.

KREIN, Alexander (1883-1951)

730. **SABANEYEFF, Leonid**
Alyeksandr Krein.
in SABANEYEFF. Modern Russian composers, p.181-6.

KREIN, Grigory (1879-1955)

731. **SABANEYEFF, Leonid**
Grigoriy Krein.
in SABANEYEFF. Modern Russian composers, p.187-9.

KRYZHANOVSKY, Ivan (1867-1924)

732. **KRYZHANOVSKY, Ivan Ivanovich**
The biological basis of the evolution of music. Tr. from the author's unpublished manuscript by S. W. Pring.
O.U.P. 1928. iii-iv, 1-57p. illus.
Abstruse dissertation, one of the appendices being devoted to Mendeleev's periodic system. There is also a short biographical note on the composer.

LADIJENSKY, Nicholas (c.1845-1916)

733. **MONTAGU-NATHAN, M.**
Russian music. Two links with the past.
MMR, 46, Aug. 1916, p.214-15.
Deals with Ladijensky, one of Balakirev's circle, and Sacchetti, teacher and librarian.

LIADOV, Anatol (1855-1914)

734. **TIDEBÖHL, Ellen von**
Anatoli K. Liadow (Died August 28, 1914).
MMR, 45, Jan. 1915, p.9-10.

735. **PRING, S. W.**
A great Russian composer.
MSt, 7, May 1915, p.165-6.
A resumé of N. Malkoff's article in *Russian musical gazette* of September 1914.

736. **MONTAGU-NATHAN, M.**
The story of Russian music. 13. Lyadof and Arensky.
MSt, 10, Oct. 1917, p.68+.

737. **SWAN, Alfred**
Liadov - the wizard of the Russian fairy tale and folk song.
Ch, n.s., no. 18, Oct. 1921, p.45-8.

738. **CALVOCORESSI, M. D.**
Anatole Liadov.
in CALVOCORESSI *and* ABRAHAM. Masters of Russian music, p.424-30. 1pl.

739. **ABRAHAM, Gerald**
Random notes on Lyadov.
MR, 6, Aug. 1945, p.149-53. mus.
Also *in* ABRAHAM. Slavonic and Romantic music, p.212-17. mus.

740. **MONTAGU-NATHAN, M.**
A. K. Lyadov: a man of letters.
MO, 69, Apr. 1946, p.197-8.
May 1946, p.230-1.

741. **ABRAHAM, Gerald**
Anatoly Lyadov: 1855-1914.
L, 54, 18 Aug. 1955, p.273.

LIAPUNOV, Sergey (1859-1924)

A. *General.*

742. **NEWMARCH, Rosa**
Serge Liapounov.
Ch, 6, Jan.-Feb. 1925, p.116-18.

743. **CALVOCORESSI, M. D.**
Sergei Liapunof.
in CALVOCORESSI *and* ABRAHAM. Masters of Russian music, p.436-8. 1pl.

B. *Works.*

744. **DAVIS, Richard**
Sergei Lyapunov (1859-1924). The piano works: a short appreciation.
MR, 21, Aug. 1960, p.186-206. mus.
Includes a list of his compositions for piano solo.

745. **CALVOCORESSI, M. D.**
A little-known Russian sextet.
L, 23, 22 Feb. 1940, p.390.
Sextet for piano and strings.

LIATOSHINSKY, Boris (1895-1968)

746. **HORNSTEIN, Gena,** *and others.*
Some impressions from those who entertained our visitors this summer, Boris Lyatoshinsky and Kiril Molchanov.
C, no. 8, Autumn 1961, p.30-1.

LISSENKO, Nikolai (1842-1912)

B. *Works.*

*747. **NIKOLAI Lysenko's opera "Sappho".**
UU, no. 7-8, July-Aug. 1968, p.15.

LOPATNIKOFF, Nikolai (1903-)

*748. **LOPATNIKOFF, Nikolai**
New life in Berlin.
MM, 6, May 1929, p.25-8.

*749. **LOPATNIKOFF, Nikolai**
Christophe Colomb.
MM, 7, July 1930, p.36-8.
The title refers to an opera by Milhaud.

*750. **LOPATNIKOFF, Nicolai**
Independents in Central Europe.
MM, 8, May 1931, p.29-32.

*751. **LOPATNIKOFF, Nikolai**
America in Berlin.
MM, 9, Jan. 1932, p.90-2.

*752. **LOPATNIKOFF, Nikolai**
Finnish Youth Movement.
MM, 11, Jan. 1934, p.85-8.

753. **LOPATNIKOFF, Nicolai**
England's young composers.
MM, 14, May-June 1937, p.204-7.

LOURIÉ, Arthur (1892-1966)

754. **SABANEEV, Leonid**
Three Russian composers in Paris. Tr. by S. W. Pring.
MT, 68, Oct. 1927, p.882-4.
Lourié, Obouhov and Vyshnegradsky.

*755. **LOURIÉ, Arthur**
An enquiry into melody.
MM, 7, Dec. 1929, p.?

756. **LOURIÉ, Arthur**
Sergei Koussevitzky and his epoch: a biographical chronicle.
Tr. from the Russian by S. W. Pring.
New York, Knopf. 1931. vii-xiv, 3-253, i-vp. illus., 16pl.
The only book by Lourié published in English, it includes a considerable amount of information on the Russian school.

*757. **LOURIÉ, Arthur**
The crisis in form.
MM, 8, May 1931, p.3-11.

758. **LOURIÉ, Arthur**
The crisis of form. Tr. by S. W. Pring.
ML, 14, Apr. 1933, p.95-103.

759. **LOURIÉ, Arthur**
Musings on music.
MQ, 27, Apr. 1941, p.235-42.
Calvocoressi comments on the article in *Musical opinion,* 64, July 1941, p.439-40.

760. **LOURIÉ, Arthur**
Notes on the "New Order".
MM, 19, Nov.-Dec. 1941, p.3-9.
Refers to music and other arts since about 1939.

761. **LOURIÉ, Arthur**
The approach to the masses.
MM, 21, May-June 1944, p.203-7.

762. **LOURIÉ, Arthur**
A tribute to Kussevitzky.
MQ, 33, July 1944, p.270-6. 2pl.

763. **CULSHAW, John**
Arthur Lourié.
NMR, 77, Mar.-Apr. 1947, p.68-71.

764. **DAVENSON, Henri**
Arthur Lourié (1892-1966).
PNM, 5, Spring-Summer 1967, p.166-9.

LVOV, Alexey (1798-1870)

See no. 1722.

765. **MONTAGU-NATHAN, M.**
Composer of the Russian national anthem.
MT, 56, Feb. 1915, p.82-4.

LYADOV – *see* LIADOV

LYAPUNOV – *see* LIAPUNOV

MARKEVITCH, Igor (1912-)

A. *General.*

*767. **THOMSON, Virgil**
Igor Markevitch: little Rollo in big time.
MM, 10, Nov. 1932, p.19-23.

768. **CALVOCORESSI, M. D.**
From my note-book.
MO, 57, May 1934, p.689.

769. **MELLERS, W. H.**
Markevitch and Vogel.
L, 19, 12 Jan. 1938, p.213.

770. **MARKEVITCH, Igor**
Made in Italy. Tr. by Darina Silone.
Harvill Press. 1949. v-xi, 1-226p. illus., 9pl.
"A testimony to my love of Italy" (foreword) by the well-known conductor-composer. An index is lacking.

771. **PROFILE– Igor Markévitch.**
LME, 5, Feb. 1950, p.23-4. illus.

772. **KLOPFENSTEIN, René**
Covent Garden artists. Igor Markevitch.
O, 5, Jan. 1954, p.22-3. illus.

*773. **SKULSKY, A.**
The Markevitch nobody knows.
Hi-fi music at home, 3, July-Aug. 1956, p.25+. illus.

*774. **KUPFERBERG, H.**
Markevitch in transit.
HF, 7, May 1957, p.42-4+. illus.
A career sketch.

775. **MAN in demand.**
Newsweek, 50, 8 July 1957, p.86. illus.

776. **CRAIG, Mary**
Igor Markevitch; man of fire and ice.
MC, 156, Oct. 1957, p.11. illus.

777. **IGOR Markevitch - musician of two worlds.**
World of music, no. 3, Jan. 1958, p.1-2. illus.
Interviewed about the Latin American scene.

*778. **SKULSKY, A.**
... Igor Markevitch suggests a basic record library of orchestral music for hi-fi reproduction.
Hi-fi music at home, 5, Sept. 1958, p.24+. illus.

779. **IGOR Markevitch: three orchestras, six languages.**
Philips music herald, Winter 1960-1, p.12-13. illus.

780. **DURAZZO, Michelangelo**
Requiem for the Russians.
MA, 81, Aug. 1961, p.34-6. illus.
Markevitch recording the Verdi "Requiem" in Moscow.

*781. **LYON, N.**
Second fame: good food.
Vogue, 145, 1 Apr. 1965, p.190-2. illus.

782. **MARKEVITCH, Igor**
Markevitch talks to Peter Brown.
MMu, 13, July 1965, p.2-22+. illus.

B. *Works.*

783. **GOLDBECK, Frederick**
Current Chronicle.
MQ, 35, Apr. 1949, p.314-15. mus.
On Markevitch's "Icare".

784. **MARKEVITCH, Igor**
The Musical Offering.
T, no. 23, Spring 1952, p.7-9. 1pl.
Relates Bach's work with the version edited by Markevitch.

785. **"LE PARADIS Perdu."**
L, 14, 11 Dec. 1935, p.1088.
Markevitch's cantata "Paradise Lost".

786. **DIAMOND, David**
Paradise Lost and the Fourteenth of July.
MM, 14, Nov-Dec. 1936, p.31-3.

MEDTNER, Nikolai (1880-1951)

A. *General.*

787. **NEWMAN, Ernest**
Medtner.
MT, 56, Jan. 1915, p.9-11.

788. **MONTAGU-NATHAN, M.**
Medtner.
in MONTAGU-NATHAN. Contemporary Russian composers, p.233-51. illus.

789. **MONTAGU-NATHAN, M.**
The story of Russian music. 16. Medtner.
MSt, 10, Apr. 1918, p.307-8.

790. **HENRY, Leigh**
Contemporaries: Nikolaus Medtner.
MO, 45, Dec. 1921, p.226-7.
Jan. 1922, p.318-20. mus.

791. **SWAN, Alfred J.**
Medtner.
MT, 63, Sept. 1922, p.616-19. mus.

*792. **BROWER, H.**
Medtner finds nothing but discord in ultra-modern music.
Mu, 30, Apr. 1925, p.11-12. illus.
An interview with the composer.

793. **RIESEMANN, Oskar von**
Nikolai Medtner. English by Bianca Karpeles.
Sackbut, 5, May 1925, p.302-4.

794. **SWAN, Alfred J.**
Medtner and the music of our time.
ML, 8, Jan. 1927, p.46-54.

795. **SABANEEV, L.**
Two critiques. 2. Medtner. Tr. by S. W. Pring.
ML, 8, July 1927, p.328-34.
The first is on Richard Strauss.

796. **SABANEEV, Leonid**
Nikolai Medtner. Tr. by S. W. Pring.
MT, 69, Mar. 1928, p.209-10.

797. **MEDTNER, Nicholas**
On inspiration. Opinions: Nicholas Medtner.
Ch, 10, Sept.-Oct. 1928, p.14-15.
A group article with about half a page by each composer.

798. **SWAN, Alfred J.**
Nicholas Medtner.
Ch, 10, Dec. 1928, p.77-81.

799. **SABANEYEFF, Leonid**
Nikolay Metner [sic].
in SABANEYEFF. Modern Russian composers, p.129-43.

800. **LYLE, Watson**
Medtner and his music.
Sackbut, 11, May 1931, p.260-6.
Includes a list of works arranged by opus number to op. 53.

801. **LYLE, Watson**
Modern composers. 6. Nicolas Raslovitch Medtner...
Bookman, 82, Sept. 1932, p.297-8. illus.
An interview with the composer, whose second name was Karlovich, not Raslovitch.

802. **SABANEEV, L.**
N. K. Medtner. Tr. by S. W. Pring.
MT, 77, Apr. 1936, p.313-14.

803. **JAROSY, Albert**
Nicolas Medtner.
L, 16, 16 Sept. 1936, p.551-2. illus.

804. **BROWN, William H.**
Nicholas Medtner.
G, 21, Sept. 1943, p.50.

805. **HOLT, Richard**
Medtner and his music. A tribute to a great Russian composer. Ed. by Fred Smith.
Rimington, Van Wyck. [1948?]. 5-24p. illus., 1pl.
Eulogistic essays by Medtner's friend and champion. The detailed list of compositions stops at op. 59 (1945).

806. **NICHOLAS Medtner records.**
MO, 71, July 1948, p.414.
On the first issue of the Medtner Society's edition of his works with Medtner playing the piano in each case. *See also* no. 819
See also no. 819.

807. **PROFILE - Nicholas Medtner.**
LME, 5, Jan. 1950, p.23. illus.

808. **SCHEREK, Jeffreys**
Nicholas Medtner.
Canon, 3, May 1950, p.596-9.

809. **MEDTNER, Nicholas**
The muse and the fashion, being a defence of the foundations of the art of music. Tr. (with some annotations) by Alfred J. Swan.
Haverford, Pa., Haverford College Bookstore. 1951. i-iii, 1-146p.
Was provoked "by the phenomena of modern music" and deals with "the essentials and foundations of music". First published in 1935, the translation was completed in 1945 and then corrected and annotated by the composer.

810. **HOLT, Richard**
Nicholas Medtner (1880-1951).
G, 29, Dec. 1951, p.149-50.

811. **ALEXANDER, Arthur**
Nicholas Medtner: an appreciation.
T, no. 22, Winter 1951-2, p.3-4.

812. **AUSTIN, Michael**
Nicholas Medtner (1880-1951).
Canon, 5, Mar. 1952, p.387-90. illus.

813. **BOYD, C. M.**
Medtner reconsidered.
MMR, 82, Dec. 1952, p.260-4. mus.

814. **GILLELS [sic], E.**
Nikolai Medtner.
SCR, 1, Apr. 1954, p.1-3.

815. **CONUS, Georges**
A Medtner recital in 1911.
in HOLT, *ed.* Nicolas Medtner (1879-1951) ..., p.102-3.

816. **HOLT, Richard,** *ed.*
Nicolas Medtner (1879-1951). A tribute to his art and personality.
Dobson. 1955. 5-238p. 10pl., mus., disc.
Over 30 articles by friends and contemporaries. There is a list of compositions and the discography mainly comprises recordings by the composer himself. Medtner was born Jan. 5 1880 (N.S.).

817. **SABANEIEV, Leonid**
Medtner and his age.
in HOLT, *ed.* Nicolas Medtner (1879-1951) ..., p.77-85.

818. **TRUSCOTT, Harold**
Nicolas Medtner.
Ch, 31, Summer 1956, p.1-9.

See no. 1254.

B. *Works.*

819. **HOLT, Richard,** *ed.*
[Handbook to accompany gramophone records].
Hayes, The Gramophone Company. 1948-9. [3 v.] mus.
Notes by Holt on piano concertos nos. one to three, plus a few piano solos and songs. The records were issued for the Medtner Society by the Gramophone Company and recorded under the auspices of the Maharajah of Mysore's Musical Foundation. Some of the records are reviewed in *Musical opinion,* no. 806.

820. **GERSTLÉ, Henry S.**
The piano music of Nicolai Medtner.
MQ, 10, Oct. 1924, p.500-10. mus.

821. **MILLER, Sidney**
Medtner's piano music. An appreciative study.
1. MT, 82, Oct. 1941, p.361-3. mus.
2. Nov. 1941, p.393-5. mus.
Covers op. 17 to op. 56.

*822. **COVATTA, Sister M. Annette**
Document: the piano solo music in smaller forms of Nicolas Medtner (1880-1951).
Thesis, Boston University. 1965.

823. **LEE, E. Markham**
The student-interpreter. Medtner's "Fairy tale", op. 9, no. 1 and "Dithyramb", no. 3, op. 10 [sic].
MO, 58, Mar. 1935, p.508-9. mus.

824. **LEE, E. Markham**
The student-interpreter.
MO, 54, Dec. 1930, p.223-4. mus.
On Medtner's "Conte", no. 3 in F minor of the Fairy Tales for piano, op. 26, plus two non-Russian works.

*825. **LOFTIS, Bobby Hughes**
The piano sonatas of Nicolai Medtner.
Ph.D dissertation, West Virginia University. 1970. 232p.

826. **TRUSCOTT, Harold**
Medtner's Sonata in G minor, op. 22.
MR, 22, May 1961, p.112-23. mus.
This was Medtner's third piano sonata.

827. **MONTAGU-NATHAN, M.**
The violin music of Nicholas Medtner.
Strad, 25, Mar. 1915, p.356-9.
Sonata for violin and piano no. 1 in B minor, op. 21 and the Three Nocturnes for violin and piano, op. 16.

828. **BLOM, Eric**
Medtner and his songs.
L, 28, 1 Oct. 1942, p.445.

829. **DRINKER, Henry S.**
English texts for the songs of Nicholas Medtner.
[Hinrichson]. 1946. iii-xxiv p.
Texts of 103 songs, arranged in order of opus number.
There is also a two page biographical note by Alfred Swan.

830. **MONTAGU-NATHAN, M.**
Medtner and his songs.
L, 42, 21 July 1949, p.124.

831. **BOYD, Malcolm**
The songs of Nicolas Medtner.
ML, 46, Jan. 1965, p.16-22. mus.

MIASKOVSKY, Nikolai (1881-1950)

A. *General.*

832. **BELAIEV, Victor**
Contemporary Russian composers. 1. Nicholas Miaskovsky.
Sackbut, 5, May 1925, p.296-9.

833. **SABANEYEFF, Leonid**
Nikolay Myaskovski.
in SABANEYEFF. Modern Russian composers, p.149-62.

834. **CALVOCORESSI, M. D.**
Soviet music at the cross-roads.
L, 19, 5 Jan. 1938, p.50.
Mostly devoted to Miaskovsky.

835. **BUSH, Alan**
Nikolai Myaskovsky.
ASJ, 2, July 1941, p.253-5. illus.

836. **MOISENCO, Rena**
Nicolai Miaskovsky.
in MOISENCO. Twenty Soviet composers, p.43-8.

*837. **BOELZA, Igor**
Wartime productivity of N. Miaskovsky.
Mu, 48, June 1943, p.76.

838. **SHEBALIN, Vissarion**
Dean of Soviet composers.
MM, 21, Nov.-Dec. 1943, p.16-17. illus.

839. **IKONNIKOV, Alexei A.**
Myaskovsky: his life and work.
New York, Philosophical Library. 1946. 1-162p. 1pl., mus.
This useful account includes only a short biographical section. The list of compositions ends at 1943, and there is no index.

840. **MOISENKO, Rena**
Nikolai Myaskovsky.
in MOISENKO. Realist music, p.156-63. 1pl., mus.

841. **KREBS, Stanley D.**
Nikolai Miaskovsky.
in KREBS. Soviet composers and the development of Soviet music, p.96-118. mus.

B. *Works.*

842. **BELAIEV, Victor**
Russian symphony and the symphonies of Miaskovsky.
Ch, 6, Oct. 1924, p.5-11.

843. **BROWN, David**
Soviet symphonist.
L, 66, 20 July 1961, p.112.

844. **CALVOCORESSI, M. D.**
On Miaskovsky, Prokofiev, Shostakovich.
L, 11, 24 Jan. 1934, p.156.
Deals with Miaskovsky's Seventh and Eighth Symphonies, "The Gambler" and "The Nose".

845. **BOELZA, Igor**
Nikolai Myaskovsky's new orchestral works.
MT, 84, Apr. 1943, p.108-9. mus.
Symphonies nos. 22 and 23 and the Overture for brass, op. 60.

MOLCHANOV, Kiril

See no. 746.

MOLDYBAEV, Abdylas (1906-).

846. **MOISENKO, Rena**
Abdylas Moldybaev.
in MOISENKO. Realist music, p.127-49. mus.

MOUSSORGSKY – *see* MUSSORGSKY

MUKHAMEDJANOV, Sadykh

B. *Works.*

847. **TIFTIKIDI, Nikolai**
The first Kazakh oratorio.
SL, Dec. 1961, p.164-6
Mukhamedjanov's "Voice of the Ages".

MURADELI, Vano (1908-70)

A. *General.*

848. **KANN, Elizaveta**
Vano Muradyelli. Tr. by H. Yaffe.
ASJ, 6, Summer 1945, p.25-8. illus.

B. *Works.*

*849. **HERO worship in Soviet music: symphony about Kirov being written by Vanno Muradeli.**
LLA, 355, Dec. 1938, p.376-7.

MUSSORGSKY, Modest (1839-81)

A. *General.*

850. **A RUSSIAN genius.**
MS, i.s., 6, 18 July 1896, p.26.

*851. **POUGIN, A.**
M. P. Moussorgsky, Russian musician.
M, 13, 1897, p.438.

852. **VISETTI, Albert**
Moussorgski and his methods.
MMR, 39, Aug. 1909, p.173.

853. **TIDEBÖHL, Ellen von**
Modest Petrovitch Moussorgsky.
M, 16, June 1911, p.374-5. illus.

854. **RUSSIA'S foremost composer.**
Literary digest, 44, 20 Apr. 1912, p.812-13.

855. **COLLES, H. C.**
Moussorgsky.
MT, 53, Aug. 1912, p.503-8. mus.

856. **MONTAGU-NATHAN, M.**
... Moussorgsky.
MS, n.i.s., 2, 23 Aug. 1913, p.174-5.
30 Aug. 1913, p.203-4.
6 Sept. 1913, p.222-3.

857. **MONTAGU-NATHAN, M.**
... The last phase.
MS, n.i.s., 2, 8 Nov. 1913, p.442-3.
15 Nov. 1913, p.463.

858. **MONTAGU-NATHAN, M.**
Moussorgsky.
PMA, 40, 1913-14, p.15-35.

859. **CALVOCORESSI, M. D.**
The new Moussorgsky.
MT, 55, Mar. 1914, p.157-9.

860. **HUNEKER, James**
A musical primitive: Modeste Moussorgsky.
Forum, 53, Feb. 1915, p.269-76.

861. **MONTAGU-NATHAN, M.**
Moussorgsky.
Constable. 1916. 5-100p. 1pl.
Another short but useful biography in the *Masters of Russian music* series. There is a list of the principal published works, and synopses of the operas are also given.

862. **MONTAGU-NATHAN, M.**
Moussorgsky.
in MONTAGU-NATHAN. An introduction to Russian music, p.46-9.

863. **RIENZI, Alexis**
M. P. Moussorgsky as a man.
Russian rev., 2, July-Aug. 1916, p.53-7.

864. **MONTAGU-NATHAN, M.**
The story of Russian music. 7. Moussorgsky.
MSt, 9, Mar. 1917, p.229-30. illus.

865. **HULL, A. Eaglefield**
Debussy and Musorgsky.
MMR, 48, July 1918, p.149-50.

866. **CALVOCORESSI, M. D.**
Mussorgsky. The Russian musical nationalist. Tr. by A. Eaglefield Hull.
Kegan, Paul, Trench, Trubner and Co. [1919]. 2-215p. illus., 1pl., mus., bib.
First published by Alcan of Paris (1908) as *Moussorgsky. Les maitres de la musique,* it includes a comprehensive catalogue of works. The author later admitted *(Proceedings of the Musical Association,* 60, 1933-4, p.87) that it was inaccurate, and Montagu-Nathan claimed (in *Musical opinion,* 43, Nov. 1919, p.117) that the translation contained "upwards of 900 errors".

867. **CALVOCORESSI, M. D.** *and* **HULL, A. Eaglefield**
The national music of Russia – Mussorgsky and Scriabin.
Waverley Book Co.[n.d.] 2v. in 1.
Nos. 866 and 1633 bound together.

868. **HULL, A. Eaglefield**
Debussy's forerunner.
MMR, 52, May 1922, p.100-1.

869. **CALVOCORESSI, M. D.**
The unknown Mussorgsky.
ML, 3, July 1922, p.237-44. mus.
On the original versions of the music.

870. **GODET, Robert**
The death of Mussorgsky.
Ch, n.s., no. 27, Dec. 1922, p.59-76.

871. **SWAN, Alfred J.**
Some unknown Mussorgsky letters.
Ch, n.s., no. 27, Dec. 1922, p.81-9.
They date from 1874-9.

872. **SWAN, Alfred J.**
The three styles of Moussorgsky (1839-1881).
Ch, n.s., no. 27, Dec. 1922, p.77-80.

873. **CALVOCORESSI, M. D.**
Mussorgsky's letters to his friends.
MQ, 9, July 1923, p.432-42. mus.

874. **CALVOCORESSI, M. D.**
Stassof and Mussorgsky.
MMR, 54, Dec. 1924, p.359-60.

875. **CALVOCORESSI, M. D.**
Mussorgsky's realism.
MMR, 55, Apr. 1925, p.99-101.

876. **SWAN, Alfred J.**
Moussorgsky and modern music.
MQ, 11, Apr. 1925, p.271-80. mus.

877. **CALVOCORESSI, M. D.**
Mussorgsky's autobiography.
MMR, 55, June 1925, p.167-8.
The three autobiographical sketches were discovered about 1914 and published in Russia in 1917.

878. **CALVOCORESSI, M. D.**
Moussorgsky as seen by one of his friends.
MT, 67, Mar. 1926, p.214-16.
Discusses a long article by N. Kompaneisky on the composer's early years.

879. **BELAIEFF, Victor**
Some recent Musorgsky researches. Tr. by S. W. Pring.
MMR, 57, July 1927, p.195-6.

880. **CALVOCORESSI, M. D.**
A Russian critic on Mussorgsky's orchestration.
Dominant, 1, May 1928, p.24-6.
The critic is Glebov (i.e. Asafiev).

881. **CALVOCORESSI, M. D.**
Early criticism of Moussorgsky in Western Europe.
MO, 52, Apr. 1929, p.642-3+.
May 1929, p.736-8.

882. **BELAIEV, Victor**
Mussorgsky's two lives. Tr. by S. W. Pring.
Dominant, 2, May-June 1929, p.17-19.
As composer and civil servant. Lists appointments he held.

883. **FERROUD, P. O.**
Moussorgsky and Chabrier.
Ch, 10, July-Aug. 1929, p.256-61.

*884. **MEDIA, J.**
The tragedy of Moussorgsky.
E, 48, Feb. 1930, p.87-8. illus.

885. **TURNER, W. J.**
Moussorgsky the realist.
Ninteenth century, 107, Mar. 1930, p.407-18.

886. **ABRAHAM, Gerald**
Tolstoy and Moussorgsky.
ML, 12, Jan. 1931, p.54-9.
Also *in* ABRAHAM. Studies in Russian music, p.87-101.

887. **SABANEEV, Leonid**
Moussorgsky (Died March 29, 1881). [Tr. by S. W. Pring].
MT, 72, Apr. 1931, p.311-14.

888. **CALVOCORESSI, M. D.**
Moussorgsky's musical style.
MQ, 18, Oct. 1932, p.530-46. mus.

889. **CALVOCORESSI, M. D.**
Moussorgsky's letters.
MMR, 63, July-Aug. 1933, p.129-30.

890. **CALVOCORESSI, M. D.**
Mussorgsky's youth and early development.
PMA, 60, 1933-4, p.87-104.

891. **CALVOCORESSI, M. D.**
Mussorgsky's youth in the light of the latest information.
MQ, 20, Jan. 1934, p.1-14. mus.

892. **RIESEMANN, Oskar von**
Moussorgsky. Tr. from the German by Paul England.
New York, Tudor Publishing Co. 1935. vii-ix, 3-412, iii-xviiip. bib.
Includes many excerpts from Mussorgsky's letters and a detailed catalogue of works, but there are a few errors. Does not rival Leyda and Bertensson's or Calvocoressi's studies of the composer.

*893. **POORE, C.**
Moussorgsky the realist.
Mu, 40, Aug. 1935, p.8+.

894. **CALVOCORESSI, M. D.**
Moussorgsky's ideas in 1863.
MMR, 65, Nov. 1935, p.202.

895. **ABRAHAM, Gerald**
Modest Mussorgsky.
in CALVOCORESSI *and* ABRAHAM. Masters of Russian music, p.178-248. 1pl.

896. **LOCKSPEISER, Edward**
Musorgsky and Debussy.
MQ, 23, Oct. 1937, p.421-7.

See no. 518.

897. **CALVOCORESSI, M. D.**
From my notebook.
MO, 61, June 1938, p.778.
On the true date of Mussorgsky's birth.

898. **ABRAHAM, Gerald**
Modeste Mussorgsky, 1839-1881.
L, 21, 16 Mar. 1939, p.601.

899. **KLEIN, John W.**
Modeste Mussorgsky: 1839-81. A centennial tribute.
MO, 62, Apr. 1939, p.595-7.

900. **CALVOCORESSI, M. D.**
From my note-book.
MO, 62, May 1939, p.688-9.

901. **CALVOCORESSI, M. D.**
Mussorgsky and drink.
MO, 63, Dec. 1939, p.106-7.

*902. **KEEFER, Lubov**
Musorgsky: a sketch.
Peabody bull., 36, Dec. 1939, p.22-4.

*903. **BERTENSSON, S.**
Modest Moussorgsky's last hours.
E, 59, July 1941, p.441+. illus.

904. **ALSHWANG, Arnold**
Modest Moussorgsky.
SL, 4, Nov. 1945, p.69-72. illus.

905. **BROOK, Donald**
Mussorgsky.
in BROOK. Six great Russian composers, p.39-72. illus.

906. **CALVOCORESSI, M. D.**
Mussorgsky.
Dent. 1946. v-viii, 1-216p. 8pl., mus., bib.
One of the *Master musicians* series, Calvocoressi's third book on Moussorgsky was left unfinished at his death (1944) and completed by Gerald Abraham. This valuable study contains a comprehensive list of works and a notable chapter on his style and technique.

907. **LEYDA, Jay** *and* **BERTENSSON, Sergei**
The Musorgsky reader. A life of Modeste Petrovich Musorgsky in letters and documents.
New York, Norton. 1947. ix-xxiii, 1-474p. illus., 10pl., mus., disc.
Over 200 letters and documents from 1856-1880, copiously annotated. Contains all Mussorgsky's known correspondence, except casual messages, including the letters to Golenishchef-Kutuzof, originally published separately in 1939. Appendices include a chronology of Mussorgsky's life, list of compositions (Lamm edition) and a list of his letters with present locations. The index is rather scrappy, but otherwise the book is definitive and indispensable.

908. **GRAY, Cecil**
Moussorgsky: psychologist.
Musical digest, 1, Autumn 1947, p.33-5.

See no. 208.

*909. **WILL, Roy**
A stylistic analysis of the works of Moussorgsky.
PhD, Theory, dissertation, Eastman School of Music, University of Rochester, New York. 1949.

910. **FOSS, Hubert**
Mussorgsky.
Novello. [1950] . 4-16p.
Brief survey with abridged list of compositions.

911. **SCHEREK, Jeffreys**
Modest Petrovitch Moussorgsky.
Canon, 6, Apr. 1953, p.365-7.

912. **CALVOCORESSI, M. D.**
Modest Mussorgsky. His life and works.
Rockliff. 1956. vii-xix, 1-322p. 7pl., mus.
The second of "Calvo" 's three books on Mussorgsky, written between 1911 and 1939, and seen through the press by Gerald Abraham. The life and music are dealt with in one continuous narrative, and there is a classified catalogue of works. Slonimsky *(Notes,* 15, Mar. 1958, p.209) calls it "the most satisfying biography of this composer available in any Western language".

913. **GRUNFELD, Fred**
An ensign takes command.
ON, 20, 5 Mar. 1956, p.8-9+. illus.

914. **HOOVER, Kathleen**
Mussorgsky: the handwriting on the wall; the Metropolitan acquires a Mussorgsky letter.
ON, 22, 2 Dec. 1957, p.14-15. illus.

915. **ZETLIN, Mikhail**
The decline (Mussorgsky after "Boris").
in ZETLIN. The Five, p.237-54.

916. **ZETLIN, Mikhail**
The end of Mussorgsky.
in ZETLIN. The Five, p.255-82.

917. **ZETLIN, Mikhail**
Mussorgsky's credo.
in ZETLIN. The Five, p.151-75.

918. **ZETLIN, Mikhail**
The young Mussorgsky.
in ZETLIN. The Five, p.89-109.

See no. 420.

See no. 1984.

See no. 2763.

919. **GINSBURG, Lev**
Modeste Musorgsky. (On the occasion of the 125th anniversary of his birth). Tr. by Jim Riordan.
SL, Sept. 1964, p.154-9.

B. *Works.*

Night on the Bare Mountain.

920. **NEWMARCH, Rosa**
Moussorgsky. Fantasia for orchestra, "Une nuit sur le mont chauve".
CL, 2, p.52-4.

Piano works.

921. **HULL, A. Eaglefield**
The piano pieces of Musorgsky.
MMR, 49, Sept. 1919, p.196-8.
Oct. 1919, p.212-21.
Nov. 1919, p.244-5.

*922. **FRITZ, Thomas**
The development of Russian piano music as seen in the literature of Mussorgsky, Rachmaninov, Scriabin and Prokofiev.
Dissertation, University of Southern California. 1958.

Pictures from an Exhibition.

923. **HULL, A. Eaglefield**
Moussorgsky's "Tableaux d'une exposition".
MMR, 45, Feb. 1915, p.38-9. mus.

924. **MONTAGU-NATHAN, M.**
Hartmann and the "Pictures from an Exhibition".
MMR, 46, July 1916, p.191-3.

925. **MONTAGU-NATHAN, M.**
New light on Moussorgsky's "Pictures".
MMR, 47, May 1917, p.105-6.

926. **NEWMARCH, Rosa**
Moussorgsky (Orchestrated by Sir Henry J. Wood). Suite "Pictures from an exhibition".
CL, 3, p.38-41.

927. **CALVOCORESSI, M. D.**
From my note-book.
MO, 61, Oct. 1937, p.15-16.
Tries to disprove Diaghilev's claim that he met Mussorgsky and heard him play "Pictures from an Exhibition".

928. **CALVOCORESSI, M. D.**
From my note-book.
MO, 62, Dec. 1938, p.202.
Compares the original with Ravel's orchestral arrangement.

929. **FRANKENSTEIN, Alfred**
Victor Hartmann and Modeste Musorgsky.
MQ, 25, July 1939, p.268-91. 8pl., bib.
Lists Hartmann's pictures traced by Frankenstein. Reprinted in abridged form in *Musical America,* no. 930.

930. **FRANKENSTEIN, Alfred**
Victor Hartmann and Moussorgsky ... Pictures at an exhibition.
MA, 69, Feb. 1949, p.20-1+. illus.
Abridged reprint from *Musical quarterly,* no. 929.

Songs.

931. **HULL, A. Eaglefield**
Musorgsky: a great song writer.
MO, 43, Oct. 1919, p.42-3. mus.
Nov. 1919, p.125. mus.

932. **EVANS, Edwin**
Moussorgsky: the man and his songs.
Sackbut, 2, Mar. 1922, p.7-13.

933. **NEWMAN, Ernest**
Moussorgsky as a song writer.
1. MT, 64, Feb. 1923, p.93-5.
2. Mar. 1923, p.165-8. mus.

934. **HOLT, Richard,** *tr.*
The songs of Modeste Moussorgsky sung by Vladimir Rosing.
Parlophone. [1935] 3-23p.
Fourteen songs are covered, with English and phonetic translations of the words.

935. **LLOYD-JONES, David**
The songs of Moussorgsky.
L, 64, 14 July 1960, p.74.

*936. **KUZMICH, Natalie**
The role of text in the songs of Musorgsky.
MA., Musicology, dissertation, University of Toronto. 1968. 162p. mus., bib. [typescript]

Hopak.

937. **LEE, E. Markham**
The amateur's repertoire.
MO, 53, Mar. 1930, p.523-4. mus.
On "Hopak", Rachmaninov's "In the silent night" and Pergolesi's "The Coquette".

Songs and Dances of Death.

*938. **MIDDAUGH, B.**
Modest Mussorgsky's "Songs and Dances of Death".
N.A.T.S. bull., 26, no. 2, 1969, p.2+. illus., bib.

Sunless.

939. **HULL, A. Eaglefield**
Mussorgsky's "Sunless".
MMR, 47, Feb. 1917, p.22-8.
Mar. 1917, p.51-2. mus.

Operas.

940. **NEWMARCH, Rosa**
Moussorgsky's operas.
MT, 54, July 1913, p.433-9. 1pl.

941. **BAUGHAN, E. A.**
Moussorgsky's operas.
FR, 94, 1 Sept. 1913, p.539-45.
Also *in* LLA, 279, 22 Nov. 1913, p.474-8.

Boris Godunov.

*942. **SCHINDLER, Kurt**
"Boris Godounoff" and the life of Moussorgsky.
New York, North American Review Publishing Co. 1913. 12p.
See also no. 943.

943. **SCHINDLER, Kurt**
"Boris Godounoff".
North American rev., 197, Feb. 1913, p.256-67.
Was also issued separately, no. 942.

*944. **OPERA** revealing the soul of the Russian people: Boris Godunoff.
Current opinion, 54, May 1913, p.385-6.

945. **MONTAGU-NATHAN, M.**
... "Boris Godounoff".
MS, n.i.s., 2, 13 Sept. 1913, p.251-2.
4 Oct. 1913, p.321-2.
11 Oct. 1913, p.342-3.

946. **NEWMAN, Ernest**
... A note on "Boris Godounov".
Nation, 15, 13 June 1914, p.415-16.
Calls Mussorgsky "an amateur with moments of genius".

947. **BOUGHTON, Rutland**
Moussorgsky's great melodrama.
MO, 37, July 1914, p.798-800. mus.

948. **DAVIDSON, Gladys**
Moussorgsky. Boris Godounov.
in DAVIDSON. Stories from the Russian operas, p.42-60.
Places the death of Boris last.

949. **GODET, Robert**
The true and false Boris.
Ch, n.s., no. 23, May 1922, p.193-9.

950. **COOKE, James Francis**
"Boris Godounow".
E, 41, Mar. 1923, p.199.
Includes brief resumé of the plot by Edward Hipsher.

951. **CALVOCORESSI, M. D.**
"Boris Godunov": genuine and otherwise.
MT, 65, Feb. 1924, p.117-19. mus.
The original versions and the Rimsky-Korsakov revisions.

952. **BENISEVICH, M.**
"Boris Godunov". Tr. by Mrs. Gertrude Senschan.
MS, n.i.s., 25, 10 Jan. 1925, p.12.

*953. **THE ORIGIN of Moussorgsky's Boris.**
E, 45, Jan. 1927, p.28.

954. **EVANS, Edwin**
Boris redivivus.
Ch, 8, Mar. 1927, p.145-9.
On Rimsky-Korsakov's editing of "Boris".

955. **CALVOCORESSI, M. D.**
New chapters in the history of "Boris Godunov".
MT, 68, June 1927, 512-13.

956. **BELAIEV, Victor**
Musorgsky's Boris Godunov and its new version. Tr. from the Russian by S. W. Pring.
O.U.P. 1928. iii-vii, 1-58p. mus.
Informative coverage of the various versions.

957. **CALVOCORESSI, M. D.**
The opening motive in "Boris Godunov".
MT, 69, Jan. 1928, p.19-20. mus.
Discusses the opening prelude and the leitmotives.

958. **CALVOCORESSI, M. D.**
"Boris Godunov" as Moussorgsky wrote it. 1. The facts of the case.
MT, 69, Apr. 1928, p.318-20.
2. The initial version.
MT, 69, May 1928, p.408-12. mus.
3. The complete "Boris Godunov".
MT, 69, June 1928, p.506-8. mus.

959. **CALVOCORESSI, M. D.**
The genuine "Boris Godunof" discovered.
Dominant, 1, Apr. 1928, p.26-9.

960. **BELAIEV, Victor**
A contribution to the "Boris" controversy. Tr. by S. W. Pring.
Dominant, 1, June 1928, p.17-19. 2pl.

961. **BORIS Godunoff.**
MO, 51, July 1928, p.994.

962. **JACOBSON, Maurice**
The five versions of Boris Godunov.
Sackbut, 8, July 1928, p.369-72.

963. **SCHMID, Willy**
"Boris Godounov" again.
Ch, 9, July-Aug. 1928, p.245-51.

964. **GRAY, Cecil**
The real "Boris".
Nation, 43, 22 Sept. 1928, p.791-2.

965. **CALVOCORESSI, M. D.**
The genuine scoring of "Boris Godunof".
MMR, 58, Nov. 1928, p.328-31. mus.

966. **GODDARD, Scott**
Editions of "Boris Godunov".
ML, 10, July 1929, p.278-86. mus.

967. **HAGGIN, B. H.**
Boris Godunov as Moussorgsky wrote it.
Theatre arts, 14, Feb. 1930, p.142-4.

968. **CALVOCORESSI, M. D.**
The genuine Boris Godounov.
L, 11, 11 Apr. 1934, p.625-6. illus.

969. **CALVOCORESSI, M. D.**
The experience of "Boris Godounov".
MMR, 64, July-Aug. 1934, p.123-4.

970. **CALVOCORESSI, M. D.**
From my notebook.
MO, 58, Sept. 1935, p.1001.

971. **CALVOCORESSI, M. D.**
From my note-book.
MO, 59, Oct. 1935, p.114.

972. **CALVOCORESSI, M. D.**
From my note-book.
MO, 59, Dec. 1935, p.206-7.

973. **CALVOCORESSI, M. D.**
From my notebook.
MO, 59, June 1936, p.757-9.

974. **ABRAHAM, Gerald**
The Carthaginian element in "Boris Godunov".
MT, 83, Jan. 1942, p.9-12. mus.
Also *in* ABRAHAM. Slavonic and Romantic music, p.188-94. mus.
The article is here called *The Mediterranean element in "Boris Godunov".*

*975. **SQUIRES, Paul**
Act IV of Musorgsky's "Boris".
J. of musicology, 3, Spring 1942, p.229.

976. **ABRAHAM, Gerald**
Mussorgsky's "Boris" and Pushkin's.
ML, 26, Jan. 1945, p.31-8.
Also *in* ABRAHAM. Slavonic and Romantic music, p.178-87.

977. **SEMEONOFF, Boris**
Boris Godunov.
Record collector, 2, Nov. 1947, p.6-16. disc.
A synopsis and discography together in one sequence, arranged by scene.

978. **ABRAHAM, Gerald**
Mussorgsky. Boris Godunov (Rimsky-Korsakov version).
Boosey and Hawkes. 1948. 5-31p. illus., 8pl., bib.
Includes plot synopsis of Rimsky-Korsakov's 1906-8 version, notes on the composition of the opera and a short biography of Mussorgsky.

979. **MONTAGU, George**
Moussorgsky's "Boris Godounow".
LME, 3, May 1948, p.15-17. illus.

980. **KUDRAVETZ, Boris**
A page of history in music.
ON, 17, 23 Mar. 1953, p.12-13. illus.

981. **MERKLING, Frank**
Boris the Ninth.
ON, 17, 23 Mar. 1953, p.6-8+. illus., mus.
On the various versions.

982. **THE POWERS behind Boris.**
ON, 17, 23 Mar. 1953, p.10-11. illus.
On Karol Rathaus, who modified the 1874 version and conducted the Met. production.

983. **HINES, Jerome**
Psychological interpretation of Boris Godounoff.
MA, 74, 1 Feb. 1954, p.5+. illus.

984. **ASHBROOK, William S.**
Boris Godounov: portraits at an exhibition.
ON, 18, 22 Feb. 1954, p.4-7+. illus.
Deals with the characters in the opera.

985. **FRIEDLANDER, Maryla**
Boris before and after.
ON, 18, 22 Feb. 1954, p.12-13. illus.

986. **FREEMAN, John W.**
Pattern of power.
ON, 20, 5 Mar. 1956, p.4-7+. illus., mus.

987. **MITROPOULOS, Dimitri**
... Mitropoulos on Boris Godunov.
ON, 20, 5 Mar. 1956, p.14+. illus.

988. **LAWRENCE, A. F.**
Boris Godunov, 1928.
Bull. of the British Institute of Recorded Sound, 4, Spring 1957, p.9-13. disc.
On the recording made at Covent Garden in 1928.

989. **DUNLOP, Lionel**
Opera on the gramophone. 6. "Boris Godunov".
O, 9, Oct. 1958, p.636-45+. illus.

990. **ZETLIN, Mikhail**
At the pinnacle of fame (Boris Godunov).
in ZETLIN. "The Five", p.194-224.

991. **FREEMAN, J. W.**
Boris and Dmitri.
ON, 25, 7 Jan. 1961, p.14-15. illus.
Discusses the various versions, especially Shostakovitch's.

992. **McDONALD, Katherine**
Figures of rebellion.
ON, 25, 7 Jan. 1961, p.21. mus.

993. **MUSSORGSKY'S Boris Godunov.**
ON, 25, 7 Jan. 1961, p.18-19. illus., bib.

994. **GORKY, Maxim**
Chaliapine and Boris Godunov.
London mag., 6, July 1966, p.51-60. 2pl.
Extract from Shaliapin's *Autobiography as told to Maxim Gorky,* no. 1771.

995. **BLUSTAIN, Jonah**
"Boris Godunov" – for the descendants of the Orthodox.
RR, 27, Apr. 1968, p.177-94.
Deals with the historical background.

996. **PRIORY, Hugh**
Boris Godunov.
About the house, 3, Mar. 1970, p.4-9. illus.

The Fair at Sorochintsy.

997. **TIDEBÖHL, Ellen von**
Moussorgsky's opera "The Fair at Sorotshinsk".
MMR, 44, Aug. 1914, p.209-10.

998. **NEWMARCH, Rosa**
Moussorgsky. Gopak (From "The Fair at Sorochinsk").
CL, 3, p.134.

*999. **VERNON, G.**
Fair at Sorochintzy.
Commonweal, 13, 17 Dec. 1930, p.188.

1000. **ABRAHAM, Gerald**
Moussorgsky's "Fair of Sorochintsy".
MMR, 66, Nov. 1936, p.195-6.

1001. **CALVOCORESSI, M. D.**
"The Fair at Sorochinski".
L, 16, 18 Nov. 1936, p.972.

1002. **ABRAHAM, Gerald**
"The Fair at Sorochintsy" and Cherepnin's completion of it.
in ABRAHAM. On Russian music, p.216-24.

1003. **KLEIN, John W.**
Mussorgsky's comic opera.
Ch, 34, Autumn 1959, p.49-54.

Khovantschina.

1004. **MONTAGU-NATHAN, M.**
... Khovantchina.
MS, n.i.s., 2, 18 Oct. 1913, p.369-70.
25 Oct. 1913, p.395-6.
1 Nov. 1913, p.417-18.

1005. **DAVIDSON, Gladys**
Moussorgsky. Khovanstchina.
in DAVIDSON. Stories from the Russian operas, p.61-76. illus.

1006. **GILMAN, Lawrence**
... Unknown opera, Khowantchina.
North American rev., 217, Jan. 1923, p.117-20.

1007. **CALVOCORESSI, M. D.**
The genuine "Khovanshchina".
MO, 60, Jan. 1937, p.305-6.
Feb. 1937, p.404-5. mus.
Mar. 1937, p.500-1. mus.

1008. **EATON, Quaintance**
Khovanchina – prize patchwork of opera.
MA, 70, Feb. 1950, p.106-7+. illus.

*1009. **PEYSER, H. F.**
For deeper enjoyment of Khovanchina.
ON, 14, 20 Feb. 1950, p.5-9. illus.

*1010. **SCHAUENSEE, M. de**
Debut on horseback.
ON, 14, 20 Feb. 1950, p.10-11+.

1011. **KLEIN, John W.**
Mussorgsky's neglected masterpiece.
Ch, 31, Autumn 1956, p.47-54.

1012. **LLOYD-JONES, David**
Mussorgsky's "Khovanshchina".
O, 10, Dec. 1959, p.778-86. illus.

1013. **RICHNELL, D. T.**
"Khovanshchina" as a film.
ASJ, 21, Autumn 1960, p.29-34.
Here the opera was edited and orchestrated by Shostakovitch.

1014. **JACOBS, Arthur**
"Khovanshchina" – opera and film.
O, 13, Aug. 1962, p.520-2

1015. **DREW, David**
Khovanshchina.
NS, 64, 21 Sept. 1962, p.372.
Includes discussion of Shostakovitch's edition.

1016. **KLEIN, John W.**
Mussorgsky's "Khovanshchina".
MO, 86, June 1963, p.529+.

1017. **WEISSMAN, John**
A Russian epic on the opera stage.
LME, 18, June 1963, p.10-11.

The Marriage.

See no. 514.

1018. **CALVOCORESSI, M. D.**
Mussorgsky's "The Marriage".
MO, 57, Oct. 1933, p.20-1. mus.
Nov. 1933, p.118-20. mus.

Mlada.

See no. 119.

See no. 146.

Sorochintsy Fair, opera – *see The Fair at Sorochintsy.*

NABOKOV, Nicolas (1903-)

A. *General.*

1019. **NABOKOV, Nicolas**
Music under dictatorship.
AM, 169, Jan. 1942, p.92-9.
On music in the U.S.S.R. and Germany.

1020. **NABOKOV, Nicolas**
Specter of Nijinsky.
AM, 184, Aug. 1949, p.43-5.
Also *in* SR, 34, 24 Feb. 1951, p.22.

1021. **NABOKOV, Nicolas**
Sergei Diaghilev.
AM, 185, Jan. 1950, p.24-9.
Feb. 1950, p.66-73.
Mar. 1950, p.64-70.
Later published *in Old friends and new music,* no. 1022.

1022. **NABOKOV, Nicolas**
Old friends and new music.
Hamish Hamilton. 1951. 7-243p.
Shrewd, witty and engaging reminiscences, parts of which first appeared *in Atlantic monthly.* The two chapters on Stravinsky also appeared in Corle's symposium, no. 2134. Especially valuable are the chapters on Stravinsky, Prokofiev and Shostakovitch.
See also nos. 1021, 1023, 2137 and 2144.

1023. **NABOKOV, Nicolas**
Music under the generals.
AM, 187, Jan. 1951, p.49-54.
Music in Berlin 1945-6. Later appeared *in Old friends and new music,* no. 1022.

1024. **NABOKOV, Nicolas**
Festivals and the twelve-tone row.
SR, 34, 13 Jan. 1951, p.56+. illus.

1025. **SORIA, Dorle**
Artist life.
HF, 18, Apr. 1968. p.MA6-8.

B. *Works.*

1026. **NABOKOV, Nicolas**
Don Quixote. Nabokov's musical synopsis, June 1964.
DD, 16, Aug. 1965, p.16-17.
Gives timings of some items.

*1027. **JACOBI, Frederick**
Nabokoff's oratorio "Job".
MM, 12, Nov. 1934, p.43-4.

1028. **HALBIK, Charlotte**
An opera on Rasputin.
Ricordiana, 5, Apr. 1960, p.11-12. illus.
Nabokov's "The Death of Grigori Rasputin".

OBOUHOV, Nicolas (1892-1954)

See no. 754.

OLENIN, Alexander (1865-1944)

A. *General.*

See no. 402.

B. *Works.*

1029. **TIDEBÖHL, Ellen von**
The opera season in Moscow, 1915-16.
MMR, 46, Nov. 1916, p.289-90.
Useful for its information on Olenin's opera "Kudeyar".

ORNSTEIN, Leo (1892-)

*1030. **MARTENS, Frederick H.**
Leo Ornstein: the man, his ideas, his work.
New York, Breitkopf and Hartel. 1918. 89p. illus.

1031. **BUCHANAN, Charles L.**
Ornstein and modern music.
MQ, 4, Apr. 1918, p.174-83. illus.

*1032. **EASTMAN, J. A.**
A bibliography of Leo Ornstein.
1935.
A manuscript in New York Public Library.

PALIASHVILI, Zakharia (1872-1933)

1033. **MOISENCO, Rena**
Zakharia P. Paliashvili.
in MOISENCO. Twenty Soviet composers, p.48-51.

1034. **MOISENKO, Rena**
Zakhary Paliashvili.
in MOISENKO. Realist music, p.164-72. mus.

PROKOFIEV, Sergey (1891-1953)

A. *General.*

1035. **MONTAGU-NATHAN, M.**
Sergei Prokofiev.
MT, 57, Oct. 1916, p.465-6.

*1036. **MERRICK, Frank**
Sergei Prokofiev.
Musical news, 64?, 31 March 1923, p.306.

1037. **HENRY, Leigh**
Contemporaries: Serge Prokofief.
MO, 47, May 1924, p.806-7.
July 1924, p.999-1001.

1038. **SACKVILLE-WEST, Edward**
Serghei Prokofiev.
Sp, 134, 7 March 1925, p.360.

1039. **SABANEEV, Leonid**
Two more Russian critiques. Tr. by S. W. Pring.
ML, 8, Oct. 1927, p.425-36.
The first (up to p.431) is entitled *Sergei Prokofiev* and the second *The composer-critic.*

1040. **SABANEYEFF, Leonid**
Sergey Prokofyeff.
in SABANEYEFF. Modern Russian composers, p.87-102.

*1041. **SABANEYEFF, Leonid**
Russia's strong man.
MM, 6, Jan. 1929, p.3-9. illus.

1042. **FRASER, Andrew**
Serge Prokofieff.
Ch, 10, Apr.-May 1929, p.181-6.

1043. **LAMBERT, Constant**
Prokofieff.
Nation, 47, 27 Sept. 1930, p.792.

1044. **LYLE, Watson**
Modern composers. 4. Serge Prokofieff. An interview...
Bookman, 82, June 1932, p.177-8. illus.

1045. **CALVOCORESSI, M. D.**
Prokofiev and classicism.
L, 9, 10 May 1933, p.756.

1046. **MYERS, Rollo**
Prokofiev and twentieth century music.
L, 16, 14 Oct. 1936, p.742.

*1047. **PROKOFIEV, Sergei Sergeievich**
Musical America.
LLA, 357, 1939, p.89.

1048. **SLONIMSKY, Nicolas**
Serge Prokofiev: his status in Soviet music.
American quarterly on the Soviet Union, 2, Apr. 1939, p.37-44.
Includes a list of works up to op. 78 compiled by Prokofiev for Slonimsky.

1049. **PROKOFIEFF, Serge**
Musical America.
SL, Apr.-May 1939, p.198-200. illus.

1050. **STOCKDALE, Alan**
Prokofiev, playboy of modern music.
G, 17, Aug. 1939, p.101-2.

1051. **BAYLISS, Stanley**
Serge Prokofiev.
Choir, 32, Apr. 1941, p.54-5.

1052. **MOISENCO, Rena**
Sergei Prokofiev.
in MOISENCO. Twenty Soviet composers, p.51-5.

1053. **NABOKOV, Nicolas**
Sergei Prokofiev.
AM, 170, July 1942, p.62-70.

1054. **ABRAHAM, Gerald**
Prokofiev as a Soviet composer.
MR, 3, Nov. 1942, p.241-7. mus.
Also *in* ABRAHAM. Eight Soviet composers, p.32-42. mus.

1055. **PROKOFIEFF, Sergei**
The war years.
MQ, 30, Oct. 1944, p.421-7.
Describes his own activities during this period.

1056. **[WERTH, Alexander]**
Prokofiev talks to Werth.
L, 33, 1 Feb. 1945, p.121-2.

1057. **COMPOSER, Soviet style.**
Time, 46, 19 Nov. 1945, p.57-8+. illus.

1058. **PROKOFIEFF'S voice is cosmopolitan; his theme is the spirit of Russia**
Newsweek, 26, 19 Nov. 1945, p.82+. illus.

1059. **EISENSTEIN, Sergei**
P-R-K-F-V.
in NESTYEV. Sergei Prokofiev [1946], p.ix-xix.

1060. **NESTYEV, Israel V.**
Sergei Prokofiev: his musical life. Tr. from the Russian by Rose Prokofieva.
New York, Knopf. 1946. ix-xxvii, 3-193, i-xivp. 1pl., mus.
Written in 1941 and drawing freely on the *Autobiography,* this book formed the basis of Nestyev's major biography, published

in England in 1961, the emphasis being on the music rather than on Prokofiev's personal life. Eisenstein's introductory essay P-R-K-F-V does not appear in the later volume. There is a catalogue of works. *See also* no. 1093.

1061. **BOELZA, Igor**
Sergei Prokofyev.
SL, Apr.-May 1946, p.85-8. illus.

1062. **FULLER, Donald**
Prokofiev, the prodigal son.
MM, 23, Summer 1946, p.234.
A review of Nestyev's book.

1063. **PROKOFIEFF, Sergei**
Recollection. Tr. from the Russian by Harris Moss.
AM, 178, Nov. 1946, p.122-4. illus.
On his childhood.

1064. **CULSHAW, John**
Sergei Prokofiev.
G, 25, July 1947, p.18-19.

1065. **PROKOFIEV, Sergei**
My first years in the Conservatory.
AM, 180, July 1947, p.75-80.
On the St. Petersburg Conservatory.

1066. **PROKOFIEV, S.**
My plans.
SL, June 1948, p.134-5.

1067. **PROKOFIEV, S.**
Prokofiev explains.
MT, 89, Aug. 1948, p.233-4.
A translation of a German version of a Russian newspaper article by Prokofiev. He replies to the Russian government's criticism of his music and talks about melody, atonality and recitative.

*1068. **PROKOFIEV, S.**
Somethin' you can hum!
Mu, 53, Sept. 1948, p.83.

1069. **MOISENKO, Rena**
Sergei Prokofiev.
in MOISENKO. Realist music, p.173-87. mus.

1070. **CLOUGH, Francis *and* CUMING, Geoffrey**
Prokofieff on records.
T, n.s., no.11, Spring 1949, p.32-4.
Arranged alphabetically by title, it covers the period 1927-49 and includes recordings made by the composer.

1071. **MOREUX, Serge**
Prokofieff: an intimate portrait.
T, n.s., no.11, Spring 1949, p.5-9.

1072. **PROKOFIEFF'S works.**
T, n.s., no.11, Spring 1949, p.23-5.
Arranged by opus no. Incomplete for the later works and omits the childhood works. Inaccurate, e.g., the incidental music to "Boris" is op. 70 bis, not 74. Even so, as complete and as accurate a list as was possible at the time.

1073. **OTTAWAY, Hugh**
Serge Prokofiev and Benjamin Britten.
MO, 73, July 1950, p.576-7.

See no. 661.

1074. **PROKOFIEFF, S.**
Music and life.
News, no. 10, 30 Nov. 1951, p.14-16. illus.
Includes comments on his current activities.

1075. **SABIN, Robert**
Serge Prokofieff – a classicist but "decadent".
MA, 71, 15 Dec. 1951, p.5+. illus.

1076. **SHAWE-TAYLOR, Desmond**
A Russian composer.
NS, 45, 14 Mar. 1953, p.294.
Prokofiev died on March 5th, not March 4th as the article says.

1077. **MITCHELL, Donald**
Serge Prokofieff (1891-1953).
T, no. 27, Spring 1953, p.5.

*1078. **SERGE Prokofiev.**
Musical information record, no. 8, Spring 1953, p.5-6+. mus.
Includes a catalogue of works.

1079. **S. S. PROKOFIEV. 23rd. April, 1891 – 4th March, 1953.**
SCR, no. 14, Apr. 1953, p.1-3.

1080. **WERTH, Alexander**
The real Prokofiev. Now it can be told.
Na, 176, 4 Apr. 1953, p.285-7.

1081. **COOPER, Martin**
Sergei Prokofiev (1891-1953).
LME, 8, May 1953, p.22-3. illus.

1082. **LOCKSPEISER, Edward**
Prokofieff: Russia's Peter Pan of music.
MMu, 1, May 1953, p.12. illus.

1083. **MONTAGU-NATHAN, M.**
Sergei Prokofiev (1891-1953).
MT, 94, May 1953, p.209-11. illus., bib.

*1084. **ULANOV, B.**
The death of Prokofiev.
Metronome, 69, May 1953, p.34.

*1085. **PROKOFIEFF, S.**
My musical creed.
International music news, 45, May-June 1953, p.9.

*1086. **ALTSCHULER, Modest**
[Prokofiev].
International musician, 51, June 1953, p.35.

1087. **GOODWIN, Noel**
Sergei Prokofiev.
MO, 76, June 1953, p.537+.

1088. **STEVENS, Bernard**
Sergei Sergeyevich Prokofiev, 1891-1953.
ASJ, 14, Summer 1953, p.25-6.

*1089. **SERGEI Prokofiev; April 23, 1891 - March 8, 1953.**
American record guide, 19, July 1953, p.339-41. illus.
He actually died on March 5th.

1090. **LOCKSPEISER, Edward**
The unknown Prokofiev.
L, 50, 22 Oct. 1953, p.705.

See no. 2182.

1091. **LOCKSPEISER, Edward**
Prokofiev: the man and his music.
MO, 80, Nov. 1956, p.97.

1092. **SEAMAN, Gerald**
The many-sidedness of Prokofiev.
L, 61, 9 Apr. 1959, p.647.

1093. **NESTYEV, Israel V.**
Prokofiev. Tr. from the Russian by Florence Jonas.
Foreword by Nicolas Slonimsky.
O.U.P. 1961. v-xiv, 1-528p. illus., 13pl., mus.
Written by a close friend of the composer, this biased, sometimes distorted and patchy account is an elaboration of Nestyev's 1946 biography. The index lists musical events in London under "London, Jack" and there is no bibliography. Still the best English-language biography of Prokofiev, it should be supplemented by Seroff's unbalanced book, especially on the composer's personal life. M. H. Brown's article in *Journal of the American Musicological Society* (16, Spring 1963, p.100-8) corrects and adds to the list of compositions. *See also* no. 1060.

1094. **PROKOFIEV, S.**
Autobiography, articles, reminiscences. Comp. and ed., and with notes, by S. Shlifstein. Tr. from the Russian by Rose Prokofieva.
Moscow, Foreign Languages Publishing House. [1961] 7-334p. illus., 25pl.
The autobiography breaks off at 1936; Prokofiev's articles include one dealing with his creative plans for 1953; the reminiscences are by friends and colleagues. There is a detailed catalogue of compositions but no index. Still the most important book in English on Prokofiev. The composer's *Extracts from autobiography (Soviet literature,* 1963, p.158-65) are taken from *The Conservatoire,* part of the second section of the autobiography, which was never finished and is not included in the above book.

1095. **COOPER, Martin**
Playboy or Prodigal?
L, 65, 16 Feb. 1961, p.301.

1096. **SCHWARZ, Boris**
Reviews of books: *Prokofiev* by Israel V. Nestyev.
MQ, 46, Apr. 1961, p.263-70.

1097. **HARRIS, Roy**
Roy Harris salutes Sergei Prokofieff.
MA, 81, May 1961, p.12-14. illus.

1098. **BROWN, Malcolm H.**
... Israel V. Nestyev. *Prokofiev.*
JAMS, 16, Spring 1963, p.100-8.
Lists corrections and additions to Nestyev's catalogue of works.
See also no. 1093.

1099. **SZIGETI, Joseph**
The Prokofiev I knew.
MMu, 11, June 1963, p.10. illus.

1100. **PROKOFIEV, Sergei**
Extracts from autobiography. Tr. by Hilda Perham.
SL, Aug. 1963, p.158-65. illus.
Taken from *The Conservatoire,* part of the second section of autobiography which was never completed, these extracts are not included in Prokofiev; *Autobiography; articles, reminiscences.*

1101. **PROKOFIEFF, Serge**
Music in America. Tr. from the Russian by Florence Jonas.
Listen, 1, Dec. 1963, p.1-2. illus.

1102. **BROWN, Malcolm H.**
Prokofieff in America.
Listen, 1, Dec. 1963, p.2.

1103. **HANSON, Lawrence *and* HANSON, Elizabeth**
Prokofiev. The prodigal son. An introduction to his life and work in three movements.
Cassell. 1964. vii-ix, 3-243p. 9pl., bib.
An inaccurate hack biography. The authors' study of sources on the composer is inadequate. They seem badly informed about his ("first") wife but acknowledge her special help in the preface. The musical analyses are poor and the catalogue of works omits the complete ballets, the Sinfonietta, "Flourish Mighty Land", etc. Not recommended.

1104. **WEINSTOCK, Herbert**
Long, twisting road.
ON, 28, 29 Feb. 1964. p.8-13. illus.

1105. **RAYMENT, Malcolm**
Prokofiev.
Novello. [1965]. 3-24p.
A booklet containing a brief list of compositions and too many slips for its short length.

1106. **SHLIFSTEIN, Semyon**

Sergei Prokofiev.

Moscow, State Music Publishers. 1965. 5-233p. illus., 1pl., mus.

First published in Russia in 1961, it consists of over 500 photographs, many in colour, with Russian and English text and captions. Some of Prokofiev's autograph manuscripts are here published for the first time. There is a detailed chronology of his life and subsequent history of his works up to 1963, but no index. The operas and ballets are especially well covered. One of the three indispensable books on the composer, the others being the autobiography and Nestyev's study.

1107. **ULANOVA, Galina**

Ulanova remembers.

DT, 55, Mar. 1965, p.287-8. illus.

On her early meetings and rehearsals with Prokofiev. Reprinted from the autobiography.

1108. **HARRIS, Roy,** *and others.*

Foreign musicians on Sergei Prokofiev.

in LIPOVSKY. Lenin Prize winners, p.34-41.

Harris' contribution takes over half the article. Others include Hanns Eisler (sic), Auric, Bliss and Stokowski.

1109. **MARTYNOV, Ivan**

In the forefront of his age.

in LIPOVSKY. Lenin Prize winners, p.11-33.

Excerpts from Martynov's book *Sergei Prokofiev,* not available in English.

1110. **SHOSTAKOVICH, Dmitry**

Great music.

in LIPOVSKY. Lenin Prize winners, p.8-10. illus.

1111. **SEROFF, Victor**

Sergei Prokofiev. A Soviet tragedy.

Frewin. 1969. 9-383p. 16pl., bib.

An unbalanced study, first published in New York by Funk and Wagnalls (1968), which pays only scant attention to the music, but includes new information on Prokofiev's "wives". The prose is over-dramatized, the style journalistic, presentation haphazard and transliteration slapdash. Errors and misprints abound: Miaskovsky's dates are given as 1880-1952, not 1881-1950; one caption says Prokofiev died in May when it should read March; Scriabin's D sharp minor étude is from op. 8, not op. 57. There is a chronology of the composer's works. In some ways indispensable, but should be read with caution.

1112. **KREBS, Stanley D.**
Sergei Prokofieff.
in KREBS. Soviet composers and the development of Soviet music, p.138-64.

1112a. **SAMUEL, Claude**
Prokofiev. Translated by Miriam John.
Calder and Boyars. 1971. 8-190p. illus., mus.
Originally published by Editions du Seuil in 1960, it draws heavily on the reminiscences of Mira Mendèlson. There is a list of works in opus number order, including sketches; also a chronology which includes "First Charlie Chaplin film". The book's value lies in its illustrations. There are numerous inaccuracies: Prokofiev did not remarry (compare Seroff, no. 1111); the first version of "War and Peace" was in thirteen scenes, not ten. There is no consistency in the spelling of Russian names and titles of compositions ("Chout" becomes "Schut" and "The Queen of Spades" "The Queen of Diamonds") and the index is scrappy and very incomplete.

B. *Works.*

Orchestral works.

1113. **SWARSENSKI, Hans**
Prokofieff's orchestral works.
T, n.s., 11, Spring 1949, p.10-22. illus., mus.

*1114. **BIANCOLLI, Louis**
Serge Prokofieff and his orchestral music.
New York, Philharmonic Society. 1953. 64p.

Symphonies.

1115. **RAYMENT, Malcolm**
Prokofiev as symphonist.
L, 73, 18 Feb. 1965, p.277.

*1116. **BROWN, Malcolm**
The symphonies of Sergei Prokof'ev.
Ph.D. dissertation, Florida State University. 1967. 537p. [typescript].

Symphonies nos. 1-5.

1117. **SALTER, Lionel**
Prokofiev's symphonies.
L, 36, 15 Aug. 1946, p.225.

1118. **DEL MAR, Norman**
Confusion and error.
S, no. 21, Oct. 1957, p.24-5. mus.
On mistakes in editions of orchestral works.

Symphony no. 1.

1119. **ELKIN, Robert**
Prokofiev's Classical Symphony: an analysis.
Music in education, 28, Nov.-Dec. 1964, p.273-5. illus., mus.

1120. **WARBURTON, A. O.**
Set works for O level G.C.E. Prokofiev's Classical Symphony.
MTe, 44, Apr. 1965, p.162+.

*1121. **ROSS, J.**
"Classical Symphony" – Serge Prokofiev.
American string teacher, 19, no. 3, 1969, p.7+.

Symphony no. 3.

1122. **YAMPOLSKY, I.**
Prokofiev's Third Symphony.
LME, 17, Sept. 1962, p.22-3.

1123. **[MASON, Colin]**
Colin Mason reviews two rediscovered Russian symphonies.
LME, 17, Nov. 1962, p.12.
Prokofiev 3rd. and Shostakovitch 4th.

Symphony no. 4.

1124. **McALLISTER, Rita**
The Fourth Symphony of Prokofiev.
L, 78, 6 July 1967, p.28. illus.

Symphony no. 5.

1125. **AUSTIN, William**
Prokofiev's Fifth Symphony.
MR, 17, Aug. 1956, p.205-20. mus.

Symphony no. 6.

1126. **SHAWE-TAYLOR, Desmond**
Pastoral Prokofiev.
NS, 39, 4 Mar. 1950, p.243-4.

1127. **PERSICHETTI, Vincent**
Current chronicle. Philadelphia.
MQ, 36, Apr. 1950, p.282-5. mus.

Symphony no. 7.

1128. **OTTAWAY, Hugh**
Prokofiev's Seventh Symphony.
MT, 96, Feb. 1955, p.74-5.

1129. **LOCKSPEISER, Edward**
Prokofiev's Seventh Symphony.
T, 37, Autumn 1955, p.24-7. illus.

1130. **PORTER, Andrew**
Prokofiev's Seventh Symphony.
LME, 11, June 1956, p.25-6. illus.

Peter and the Wolf.

*1131. **DEAKIN, Irving**
Peter and the Wolf. Pictures by Richard C. Jones.
O.U.P., 1940.
A biography for children.

1132. **PROKOFIEV, Sergei**
The story of Peter and the Wolf. Illustrated by Alan Howard.
Faber. [1951]. 31p. illus.
A children's book for the very young.

Ballets.

1133. **FERROUD, P. O.**
The ballets of Serge Prokofieff.
Ch, 15, Mar.-Apr. 1934, p.89-93.

1134. **GOODWIN, Noel**
Music for the Kirov.
DD, 12, Aug. 1961, p.29.

Cinderella.

1135. **PROKOFIEV, Serge**
My Cinderella.
MM, 21, Jan.-Feb. 1944, p.67-9.

1136. **HOPE-WALLACE, Philip**
Prokofiev's music for "Cinderella".
Ballet world, 1, Feb. 1949, p.34-7.

1137. **MORLEY, Iris**
"Cinderella" and "Romeo and Juliet".
T, n.s., no. 11, Spring 1949, p.30-2.

1138. **GOODWIN, Noel**
Cinderella. Music.
DD, 17, Feb. 1966, p.34-5+.
Includes a table of the 50 numbers in the Boosey and Hawkes 1949 score.

Pas d'Acier.

See no. 2582.

Romeo and Juliet.

See no. 1137.

1139. **HUNT, David**
Romeo and Juliet. Music.
DD, 7, Nov. 1956, p.11.

1140. **GOODWIN, Noel**
Romeo and Juliet. Music.
DD, 16, Mar. 1965, p.22-4.

1141. **LAVROVSKY, Leonid**
Lavrovsky's tribute.
DT, 55, Mar. 1965, p.288-91. illus.

Concerto for piano no. 1.

1142. **MONTAGU-NATHAN, M.**
Prokofiev's first pianoforte concerto.
MT, 58, Jan. 1917, p.12-13. mus.

Concerto for piano no. 3.

1143. **BLOM, Eric**
Sergey Prokofiev: decorator.
L, 28, 23 July 1942, p.125.
Mainly on the Third Piano Concerto.

Concerto for violin no. 2.

1144. **AURIC, Georges**
A new Prokofiev concerto.
L, 16, 16 Dec. 1936, p.1164.

Concerto for 'cello.

1145. **APRAHAMIAN, Felix**
Prokofieff's 'Cello Concerto, op. 58.
LME, 12, Apr. 1957, p.27-8.

Piano works.

1146. **MERRICK, Frank**
Prokofieff's works for piano solo.
T, n.s., no. 11, Spring 1949, p.26-9. mus.

See no. 922.

*1147. **ASHLEY, Patricia R.**
Prokofiev's piano music: line, chord, key.
DA, 26, Oct. 1965, p.2248.
Ph.D., Theory, thesis, Eastman School of Music, University of Rochester, New York. 1963. 317p.

Sonatas for piano.

1148. **MERRICK, Frank**
Prokofiev's piano sonatas.
PRMA, 75, 1948-9, p.13-21. mus.

*1149. **KINSEY, David L.**
The piano sonatas of Serge Prokofieff: a critical analysis of the elements of their style.
Dissertation, Columbia Teachers' College. 1959.

1150. **LAYTON, Robert**
Prokofiev and the sonatas.
L, 77, 19 Jan. 1967, p.106. illus.

Sonatas for piano nos. 1-5.

1151. **MERRICK, Frank**
Prokofiev's piano sonatas 1 to 5.
MT, 86, Jan. 1945, p.9-11. mus.

Sonata for piano no. 6.

1152. **MERRICK, Frank**
Serge Prokofiev's Sixth Piano Sonata.
MT, 85, Jan. 1944, p.9-11. mus.

Sonatas for piano nos. 7 and 8.

1153. **MERRICK, Frank**
Prokofiev's Seventh and Eighth Piano Sonatas.
MT, 89, Aug. 1948, p.234-6. mus.

Sonata for piano no. 8.

1154. **BROWN, Malcolm H.**
Prokofiev's Eighth Piano Sonata.
T, 70, Autumn 1964, p.9-15. mus.

Sonata for piano no. 9.

1155. **MERRICK, Frank**
Prokofiev's Ninth Piano Sonata.
MT, 97, Dec. 1956, p.649. mus.

Vision Fugitives for piano.

1156. **SLENCZYNSKA, Ruth**
Added color from special pedal techniques.
Clavier, 8, Feb. 1969, p.19-20.

Alexander Nevsky.

1157. **STEVENS, Bernard**
Film music. Prokofiev's "Nevsky" cantata.
Music survey, 2, Winter 1950, p.187-8.

Cantata on the Twentieth Anniversary of the October Revolution.

1158. **NESTYEV, Israel**
Music inspired by the genius of Lenin (A Prokofiev cantata).
SL, Apr. 1969, p.167-71.

Seven, They are Seven.

1159. **DREW, David**
Prokofiev's demon.
NS, 72, 2 Sept. 1966, p.328.
Mainly on "Seven,They Are Seven".

Operas.

1160. **MASON, Colin**
Prokofiev's operas.
L, 50, 10 Dec. 1953, p.1021.

1161. **SWARSENSKI, Hans**
Prokofieff: unknown works with a new aspect.
T, 30, Winter 1953-4, p.14-16.

1162. **LLOYD-JONES, David**
Prokofiev and the opera.
O, 13, Aug. 1962, p.513-17. illus.

1163. **BROWN, David**
Prokofiev and the opera.
L, 68, 23 Aug. 1962, p.297.

1164. **PUGLIESE, Giuseppe**
Unknown world of Prokofiev's operas.
HF, 16, June 1966, p.44-50+. illus., disc.

The Angel of Fire.

1165. **SABANEEV, Leonid**
"The Angel of Fire", Prokofiev's new opera. Tr. by S. W. Pring.
MT, 69, Oct. 1928, p.891-3.

1166. **SWARSENSKI, Hans**
Sergeii Prokofieff: "The Flaming Angel".
T, 39, Spring 1956, p.16-27. mus.

1167. **COOPER, Martin**
Prokofiev's "Flaming Angel".
L, 59, 10 Apr. 1958, p.637.

1168. **THE OPERA that everyone refused.**
Music mag., no. 23, July 1965, p.7. illus.

1169. **[SWAN, Alfred J.]**
Prokofiev's "The Angel of Fire".
LME, 20, July 1965, p.6-7.

1170. **LLOYD-JONES, David**
Prokofiev and "The Angel of Fire".
L, 74, 29 July 1965, p.177.

1171. **JEFFERSON, Alan**
The Angel of Fire.
MMu, 13, Aug. 1965, p.32-5. illus., mus.

1172. **PAYNE, Anthony**
First performances. Prokofiev's "The Fiery Angel".
T, 74, Autumn 1965, p.21-3.

1173. **McALLISTER, Rita**
Natural and supernatural in "The Fiery Angel".
MT, 111, Aug. 1970, p.785-9. mus.

The Fiery Angel, opera – *see The Angel of Fire.*

The Gambler.

See no. 844.

See no. 1180.

1174. **SHLIFSTEIN, Semyon**
"The Gambler". Tr. by Avril Pyman.
SL, July 1964, p.177-80.

The Love of Three Oranges.

1175. **EVANS, Edwin**
The Love for Three Oranges.
L, 14, 3 July 1935, p.20.

1176. **NEWMARCH, Rosa**
Prokofieff. March and scherzo from the opera, "The Love of the Three Oranges".
CL, 5, p.61-2.

*1177. **NEW opera by Serge Prokofieff.**
Music news, 41, Feb. 1949, p.7.

1178. **BLOM, Eric**
Fantastic opera.
L, 56, 23 Aug. 1956, p.285.

1179. **MITCHELL, Donald**
Prokofieff's "Three Oranges": a note on its musical-dramatic organisation.
T, 41, Autumn 1956, p.20-4. 1pl., mus.

1180. **PORTER, Andrew**
Prokofiev's early operas.
MT, 103, Aug. 1962, p.528-30. illus.
On "The Love of Three Oranges" and "The Gambler".

1181. **RAYMENT, Malcolm**
Chicago Oranges.
MMu, 11 Apr. 1963, p.12-13. illus.
On the Chicago production.

Maddalena.

1182. **McALLISTER, Rita**
Prokofiev's early opera "Maddalena".
PRMA, 96, 1969-70, p.137-47.

The Story of a Real Man.

1183. **KELDYSH, Yuri**
Sergei Prokofiev's last opera. Tr. by Abram Alperin.
SL, June 1960, p.176-81.

War and Peace.

1184. **SCHLIFSTEIN, S.**
News from Russia. On "War and Peace".
MM, 20, Mar.-Apr. 1943, p.185-7.

1185. **[PROKOFIEV, Serge]**
Prokofiev's opera "War and Peace".
MT, 86, Feb. 1945, p.51.

1186. **HOOVER, Kathleen**
Prokofiev's War and Peace.
Theatre arts, 34, Oct. 1950, p.44-5+. illus.

1187. **GLIÈRE, Rheinhold**
Prokofiev's "War and Peace": second thoughts on the opera.
SCR, 3, Mar. 1956, p.1-4.

1188. **JACOBS, Arthur**
Prokofiev's "War and Peace".
L, 67, 22 Feb. 1962, p.357.
A timed synopsis.

1189. **BROWN, David**
Prokofiev's "War and Peace".
L, 77, 13 Apr. 1967, p.504. illus.

RACHMANINOFF, Sergey (1873-1943)

A. *General.*

1190. **CARTER, Vivian**
Rachmaninoff.
MS, i.s., 16, 19 Oct. 1901, p.243-4.

*1191. **HILL, E. B.**
Sergei Rachmaninoff... a retrospect.
NMR, 9, Nov. 1910, p.573-5.

*1192. **NARODNY, Ivan**
The art of Sergei Rachmaninoff.
MA, 16, no. 7, 1912, p.?

1193. **MONTAGU-NATHAN, M.**
Rakhmaninoff.
in MONTAGU-NATHAN. Contemporary Russian composers, p.155-76. illus.

1194. **MONTAGU-NATHAN, M.**
The story of Russian music. 15. Rakhmaninov.
MSt, 10, Mar. 1918, p.280+.

*1195. **DISTINGUISHED Russian composer.**
Outlook, 120, 25 Dec. 1918, p.652.

1196. **ROSENFELD, Paul**
Musical evolutionist.
NR, 18, 15 Mar. 1919, p.208-10.

*1197. **[RACHMANINOFF, Sergei]**
National and radical impressions in the music of today and yesterday.
E, 37, Oct. 1919, p.?

*1198. **KORZUCHIN, I.**
[Rachmaninoff].
M, [21], Feb. 1920, p.15-21.

*1199. **MARTENS, Frederick H.**
Rachmaninoff.
New York, Breitkopf and Hartel. 1922. 23p. illus.
One of the *Little biographies* series.

1200. **LYLE, Watson**
Rachmaninoff. A personal sketch.
Musical news, 62, 17 June 1922, p.740.

1201. **RACHMANINOFF, Sergei**
New lights on the art of the piano.
E, 41, Apr. 1923, p.223-4. illus.
An interview with the composer.

1202. **RACHMANINOFF, Sergei**
How Russian students work.
E, 41, May 1923, p.298.

1203. **RACHMANINOFF, Sergei**
[Fortieth anniversary prophecies and greetings].
E, 41, Oct. 1923, p.662.

*1204. **BROWER, H.**
"Beware of the indifferent piano teacher", warns Rachmaninoff.
Mu, 30, Feb. 1925, p.11-12.

1205. **PORTE, John F.**
Gramophone celebrities. 12. Sergei Rachmaninoff.
G, 3, Aug. 1925, p.128-9. 1pl.

*1206. **HENDERSON, W. J.**
Master of piano and orchestra.
Mentor, 14, Mar. 1926, p.38-9. illus.

1207. **BELAIEV, Victor**
Sergei Rakhmaninov. Tr. by S. W. Pring.
MQ, 13, July 1927, p.359-76. 1pl.

1208. **LYLE, Watson**
Rachmaninoff and music today.
Apollo, 8, Aug. 1928, p.81-3. illus.

1209. **SABANEYEFF, Leonid**
Sergey Rakhmaninoff.
in SABANEYEFF. Modern Russian composers, p.103-20.

1210. **HOLT, Richard**
The genius of Rachmaninov.
G, 6, Jan. 1929, p.352-4. illus.

1211. **[ABRAHAM, G.]**
Serge Rachmaninov.
MS, n.i.s., 34, 30 Nov. 1929, p.177. illus.

1212. **RACHMANINOV, Sergej**
Some critical moments in my career.
MT, 71, June 1930, p.557-8.
An interview in which he describes meetings with Tchaikovsky and Tolstoy.

1213. **SERGEI Rachmaninoff.**
MO, 54, Dec. 1930, p.213. illus.

*1214. **RACHMANINOFF, Sergei**
Interpretation depends on talent and personality. Ed. by Florence Leonard.
E, 50, Apr. 1932, p.239-40. illus.

1215. **RIESEMANN, Oskar von**
Rachmaninoff. Recollections told to Oskar von Riesemann.
Tr. by Dolly Rutherford.
Allen and Unwin. 1934. 5-272p. 13pl., mus.
Including a catalogue of compositions, but no index, it contains many inaccuracies, and the transliteration of Russian names is chaotic. Riesemann is said to have invented many of Rachmaninoff's supposed statements. The composer in an interview in 1938 said "The writer states that I dictated it all myself. If so, something must have gone wrong with my mind at the time".

1216. **RACHMANINOV, Sergei**
The composer as interpreter. (In an interview with Norman Cameron).
MMR, 64, Nov. 1934, p.201.

1217. **NADEJINE, Nicholas**
Rachmaninoff.
G, 12, Mar. 1935, p.383. illus.

1218. **MAINE, Basil**
Conversation with Rachmaninoff.
MO, 60, Oct. 1936, p.14-15.

1219. **HENDERSON, A. M.**
Rachmaninoff at home.
MO, 61, Apr. 1938, p.593-4. illus.

1220. **LYLE, Watson**
Rachmaninoff. A biography. Foreword by Leff Pouishnoff.
Reeves. [1939]. 1-247p. 2pl., disc.
Volume one of a projected two volume biography, containing little musical analysis. Appendices include a comprehensive list of works and a critical survey of Rachmaninoff's piano records. The composer later said that though he authorized the book, he could not read beyond the first three chapters.

1221. **TAUBMAN, H.**
Musical triple-threat.
Colliers, 194, 16 Dec. 1939, p.54-5+. illus.
Mostly on Rachmaninoff's daily habits.

1222. **HOWES, Frank**
Musical imagination: the case of Rachmaninov.
L, 23, 22 Feb. 1940, p.391.

1223. **GODDARD, Scott**
Rachmaninov the composer.
L, 26, 11 Sept. 1941, p.385.

*1224. **EWEN, David,** *ed.*
Music should speak from the heart.
E, 59, Dec. 1941, p.804+. illus.

1225. **HULL, Robin**
The problem of Rachmaninoff.
MO, 65, Apr. 1942, p.229.

1226. **GRAY-FISK, Clinton**
Rachmaninoff's seventieth birthday.
MO, 66, Apr. 1943, p.221-2.
In fact he died four days before his seventieth birthday.

1227. **[LAST pictures taken of Rachmaninoff before death].**
Life, 14, 12 Apr. 1943, p.4-5+.
Pictures taken in December 1942.

1228. **HENDERSON, A. M.**
Personal memories of Rachmaninoff.
MO, 66, May 1943, p.257-8. illus.

1229. **HOWES, Frank**
Rachmaninov.
MMR, 73, May 1943, p.81-5.

1230. **MOISEIWITSCH, Benno**
Sergei Rachmaninoff, 1873-1943.
G, 20, May 1943, p.169-70.

1231. **EVANS, Edwin**
Obituary: Sergei Rachmaninov (1873-1943).
MR, 4, Aug. 1943, p.190-2.

1232. **GAISBERG, F. W.**
Notes from my diary. The last of the three giants of the Volga has departed.
G, 21, Aug. 1943, p.37-8.
The three giants were Shaliapin, Gorky and Rachmaninoff.

1233. **SWAN, A. J.** *and* **SWAN, Katherine**
Rachmaninoff. Personal reminiscences.
MQ, 30, Jan. 1944, p.1-19. 2pl.
Apr. 1944, p.174-91. 2pl.

1234. **CULSHAW, John**
Rachmaninov two years after.
G, 22, Mar. 1945, p.116.

1235. **RACHMANINOFF Memorial Fortnight.**
[Soviet] music chronicle, no. 10, Oct. 1945, p.1-8.

1236. **GRONOWICZ, Antoni**
Sergei Rachmaninoff. [Tr. from the Polish by Samuel Sorgenstein and Edna Ruth Johnson]. Illustrated by Woodi Ishmael.
New York, Dutton. 1946. 9-153p. illus., bib.
The popular approach is designed for younger readers. There is a list of Rachmaninoff's works and the bibliography includes Russian material.

1237. **BOELZA, Igor**
Sergei Rachmaninov.
SL, Jan. 1946, p.63-7. illus.

1238. **RACHMANINOFF, Sergei**
Key colour [as told to Oskar von Reisemann].
Musical digest, 1, Winter 1947 [i.e. 1946-7], p.25-6. illus.

*1239. **BERTENSSON, S.**
Rachmaninoff as I knew him.
E, 66, Mar. 1948. p.138+. illus.

1240. **CULSHAW, John**
Sergei Rachmaninov.
Dobson. 1949. 12-174p. 7pl., mus., bib., disc.
Despite irritating slips and many misprints, a sincere and laudatory assessment which contains a list of compositions.

1241. **GREAT Russian.**
Newsweek, 35, 27 Feb. 1950, p.37.

1242. **SEROFF, Victor I.**
Rachmaninoff. Foreword by Virgil Thomson.
Cassell. 1951. vii-xi, 1-247p. 11pl., bib.
Not without interest, but contains too many errors, and is anyway now superseded by Bertensson and Leyda. The bibliography omits Culshaw's biography. There is a catalogue of works. *See also* no. 1249.

1243. **WATERS, Edward T.**
Annual report on acquisitions. Music.
Library of Congress quarterly j., 9, Nov. 1951, p.39-42. illus.
On the Rachmaninoff Archives in the Library of Congress.

1244. **CITKOWITZ, Israel**
Orpheus with his lute.
T, no. 22, Winter 1951-2, p.8-11.
On Rachmaninoff's use of the piano.

1245. **FLANAGAN, William**
Sergei Rachmaninoff: a twentieth century composer.
T, no.22, Winter 1951-2, p.4-8.

1246. **REITHER, Joseph**
Chronicle of exile.
T, no.22, Winter 1951-2, p.29-36.
A survey of the books on the composer and records made by him and of his works.

1247. **YASSER, Joseph**
Progressive tendencies in Rachmaninoff's music.
T, no. 22, Winter 1951-2, p.11-25. 2pl., mus.
A revised and amplified version of an article published in *Musicology,* 2, no.1, 1948, p.1.

1248. **HENDERSON, A. M.**
Rachmaninoff as I knew him.
E, 72, Apr. 1954, p.9+. illus.

1249. **SEROFF, Victor**
Notes on a translation...
SR, 37, 31 July 1954, p.53.
A scathing attack on a French translation of Seroff's own biography. *See also* no. 1242.

*1250. **ERICSON, Raymond**
Rachmaninoff: a discography.
HF, 5, May 1955, p.76+. illus., disc.

1251. **WERTH, Alexander**
The Rachmaninov enigma.
NS, 50, 17 Sept. 1955, p.318-19.

1252. **HENDERSON, A. M.**
Rachmaninov at home.
MMu, 5, Nov. 1956, p.15+. illus.

1253. **SACKVILLE-WEST, Edward**
Rachmaninov.
Bull. of the British Institute of Recorded Sound, 4, Spring 1957, p.13-16.
Deals with his records.

1254. **FRANK, Jonathan**
Rachmaninov and Medtner - a comparison.
MO, 81, Mar. 1958, p.387.

*1255. **FAVIA-ARTSAY, A.**
Rachmaninoff.
Hobbies, 64, Oct. 1959, p.28-9+. illus.

*1256. **QUILTY, G.**
Rachmaninoff... the last romantic composer.
Hi-fi music at home, 3, Oct. 1959, p.26+.

1257. **MOISEIWITSCH, Benno**
Rachmaninoff remembered.
Music mag./MC, 164, May 1962, p.14-15+. illus.

*1258. **MOISEIWITSCH, Benno**
Reminiscences of Rachmaninoff.
MJ, 21, Jan. 1963, p.67-8+.

1259. **BERTENSSON, Sergei *and* LEYDA, Jay**
Sergei Rachmaninoff. A lifetime in music.
Allen and Unwin. 1965. vi-viii, 2-446p. 17pl., mus., disc.
Written with the assistance of Sophia Satina, Rachmaninoff's cousin and sister-in-law, and first published by New York University Press in 1956, it claims to be "the first full-length and definitive biography". There is more emphasis on the man than on the music. Meticulously documented and well indexed, with a detailed list of works and comprehensive discography, it supersedes all previous biographies. Very reliable and highly recommended.

1260. **CULSHAW, John**
Rachmaninov: the legacy.
L, 75, 3 Mar. 1966, p.328. illus.

See also no. 1772.

1261. **FAGAN, Keith**
Rachmaninoff's major works.
MO, 91, May 1968, p.431+.

1262. **WALSH, Stephen**
Flawed but a genius.
MMu, 16, Aug. 1968, p.32-3+. illus.

1262a. **THRELFALL, Robert**
Sergei Rachmaninoff: his life and music.
Boosey and Hawkes. 1973. 5-74p. 4pl., mus.
Treats life and music in one continuous narrative. There is a list of principal works arranged by musical form and giving dates of composition. An index is lacking.

B. *Works.*

Symphony no.2.

1263. **RUBIN, David**
Transformations of the "Dies Irae" in Rachmaninov's Second Symphony.
MR, 23, May 1962, p.132-6. mus.

Symphony no.3.

1264. **HULL, Robin**
Rachmaninov's Third Symphony.
MMR, 67, Nov. 1937, p.201-3.

The Isle of the Dead.

1265. **NEWMARCH, Rosa**
Rachmaninov. Symphonic poem, "The Island of the Dead" (op.29).
CL, 2, p.54-5.

Concertos for piano.

1266. **CHISLETT, W. A.**
Rachmaninov's piano concertos.
G, 12, Aug. 1934, p.84. illus.

1267. **ANDERSON, W. R.**
Rachmaninov and his pianoforte concertos. A brief sketch of the composer and his style.
Hinrichsen. [1947]. 1-24p. mus.
Includes a short biography and coverage of works other than the concertos.

Concerto for piano no.2.

1268. **SEAR, H. G.**
A Rachmaninoff concerto.
MS, n.i.s., 13, 15 Feb. 1919, p.57.

1269. **NEWMARCH, Rosa**
Rachmaninov. Concerto no.2, in C minor for pianoforte and orchestra (op.18).
CL, 5, p.62-3.

Concerto for piano no.3.

1270. **NEWMARCH, Rosa**
Rachmaninov. Concerto no.3, in D minor (op. 30), for pianoforte and orchestra.
CL, 5, p.64-5.

1271. **LYLE, W. G.**
Rachmaninov's last phase.
G, 25, Aug. 1947, p.35-6.
Mostly on Rachmaninoff's own recording of the work.

1272. **YASSER, Joseph**
The opening theme of Rachmaninoff's Third Piano Concerto and its liturgical prototype.
MQ, 55, July 1969, p.313-28. mus.

Rhapsody on a theme of Paganini.

1273. **NEWMARCH, Rosa**
Rachmaninov. Rhapsody on a theme of Paganini, for pianoforte and orchestra.
CL, 5, p.65-7.

Chamber music.

1274. **DOBROKHOTOV, Boris**
Rachmaninoff's unpublished chamber instrumental works.
[Soviet] music chronicle, no. 10, Oct. 1945, p.8-13. mus.
Two unfinished string quartets and a piano trio in D minor.

Piano works.

See no. 922.

Preludes for piano.

1275. **THIMAN, Eric H.**
A note on Rachmaninoff's Preludes.
MO, 49, Sept. 1926, p.1199-1200.

1276. **LEE, H. Markham**
The student-interpreter. Rachmaninoff Preludes in G Major (op. 32, no.5), F minor (op. 32, no.6), G sharp minor (op. 32, no. 12).
MO, 57, Oct. 1933, p.28-9. mus.

*1277. **LAMAGRA, Anthony**
A source book for the study of Rachmaninoff's Preludes.
Thesis, Columbia University Teachers' College. 1966.

1278. **LEE, E. Markham**
The student-interpreter. Rachmaninoff Preludes: op.23, no.3 in D minor; and op. 23, no.10 in G flat major.
MO, 61, May 1938, p. 694-5. mus.

1279. **LEE, E. Markham**
The student-interpreter. Rachmaninoff Preludes: op.23, no.6 in E flat; op. 32, no.7 in F; no.10 in B minor; no.11 in B major.
MO, 61, July 1938, p.869-70. mus.

*1280. **RACHMANINOV, S.**
My Prelude in C sharp minor.
Delineator, 75, Feb. 1910, p.127. illus.

*1281. **MAIER, G**
Rachmaninoff's Prelude in C sharp minor.
E, 63, Aug. 1945, p.432.

Variations for piano.

*1282. **BOLDT, Kenwyn**
The solo piano variations of Rachmaninoff.
D.M. dissertation, Indiana University. 1957. 72p. mus.

Sonata for 'cello and piano.

1283. **SALMOND, Felix**
The sonata of Rachmaninoff for piano and violoncello (op.19).
Strad, 26, Aug. 1915, p.100-2. mus.
Sept. 1915, p.155-7. mus.

Songs.

*1284. **MILLIGAN, H. V.**
[Rachmaninoff's songs of the church]
NMR, 20, Mar. 1921, p.133-6.

1285. **BREWERTON, Erik**
Rachmaninov's songs.
ML, 15, Jan. 1934, p.32-6. mus.

1286. **KURENKO, Maria**
The songs: an appreciation.
T, no.22, Winter 1951-2, p.25-6.

1287. **KURENKO, Maria**
The musical form. The songs of Rachmaninoff.
MC, 147, 1 Jan. 1953, p.4.

Songs, op. 4:- No.3, In the silent night.

See no. 937.

The Bells.

*1288. **WALDO, F. L.**
Rachmaninoff's "The Bells".
Outlook, 124, 25 Feb. 1920, p.318-19. illus.

1289. **HULL, Robert**
Rachmaninov's "The Bells"
MMR, 66, Oct. 1936, p.171-2. mus.

1290. **CALVOCORESSI, M. D.**
"The Bells".
L, 17, 3 Feb. 1937, p.244.

*1291. **ASHTON, L. S.**
The Bells.
E, 70, Mar. 1952, p.54.

Vesper Mass.

*1292. **BAKER, Virginia**
The harmonic style of Sergei Rachmaninoff in the Vesper Mass, op. 37.
M.M. thesis, Eastman School of Music, University of Rochester, New York. 1942.

Operas.

Aleko.

1293. **DAVIDSON, Gladys**
Rachmaninov. Aleko.
in DAVIDSON. Stories from the Russian operas, p.77-83.

The Covetous Knight, opera – *see The Miserly Knight.*

Francesca da Rimini.

1294. **DAVIDSON, Gladys**
Rachmaninov. Francesca da Rimini.
in DAVIDSON. Stories from the Russian operas, p.84-96.

See no. 1295.

The Miserly Knight.

1295. **TIDEBÖHL, Ellen von**
Sergez Rachmaninoff.
MMR, 36, July 1906, p.148-9.
Deals with "Francesca da Rimini" and "The Miserly Knight".

REBIKOV, Vladimir (1866-1920)

A. *General.*

1296. **PARKER, D. C.**
Vladimir Ivanovich Rebikov.
MSt, 9, Sept. 1916, p.31-2.

1297. **MONTAGU-NATHAN, M.**
Rebikof.
in MONTAGU-NATHAN. Contemporary Russian composers, p.179-97. illus.

1298. **MONTAGU-NATHAN, M.**
Rebikov and his mantle.
MT, 58, Aug. 1917, p.356-7. mus.

1299. **VLADIMIR Rebikov.**
MS, n.i.s., 10, 8 Sept. 1917, p.158-9. illus.

1300. **SABANEYEFF, Leonid**
Vladimir Ryebikoff.
in SABANEYEFF. Modern Russian composers, p.121-8.

1301. **ROWLEY, Alec**
Rebikoff.
MR, 4, May 1948, p.112-15. mus.

B. *Works.*

*1302. **DALE, William H.**
A study of the music-psychological dramas of Vladimir Ivanovitch Rebikov.
PhD, Musicology, dissertation, University of Southern California. 1955. vii, 611p. illus.

1303. **VLADIMIR Rebikoff. His opera "Via Grozu".**
MS, i.s., 11, 18 Mar. 1899, p.166.
The English title is "The Storm".

RICHTER, Sviatoslav (1914-)

1304. **RABINOVICH, David**
Svyatoslav Richter.
SL, Aug. 1946, p.63-5. illus.

1305. **SEROFF, Victor**
The unsung Mr. Richter.
SR, 39, 27 Oct. 1956, p.54-5. illus.

1306. **LEGENDARY virtuoso.**
Time, 71, 16 June 1958, p.39. illus.

*1307. **MOOR, Paul**
Sviatoslav Richter: sequestered genius.
HF, 8, Oct. 1958, p.49-51+. illus.

*1308. **ERICSON, R.**
From Bach to Prokofiev – the art of Sviatoslav Richter.
HF, 10, June 1960, p.56-7. illus.

1309. **YAMPOLOSKY, I. M.**
Sviatoslav Richter.
G, 38, June 1960, p.10.

1310. **MASLOWSKI, Igor**
Meeting Richter in Helsinki.
G, 38, Aug. 1960, p.103-4. illus.

1311. **DELSON, V.** *and* **PARKER, Ralph**
The two views of Sviatoslav Richter.
SR, 43, 15 Oct. 1960, p.64-6+. disc.
The article by Delson was translated by S. Ostrofsky.

1312. **HOLCMAN, Jan**
Great artists of our time. 3. Sviatoslav Richter.
SR, 43, 26 Nov. 1960, p.43+. illus.

*1313. **RICHTER, Sviatoslav**
A pianist views America.
MJ, 19, Mar. 1961, p.10+. illus.

1314. **SHNEERSON, Grigori**
The world's greatest pianist for the first time in London.
MMu, 9, Mar. 1961, p.6-7. illus.

1315. **NEUHAUS, H.**
Svyatoslav Richter: a profile.
ASJ, 22, Spring 1961, p.3-5.
By Richter's former teacher.

1316. **KOGAN, Grigori**
Svyatoslav Richter. Tr. by Maya Birman.
SL, Aug. 1961, p.159-60.

1317. **CRAXTON, Harold**
Sviatoslav Richter.
MT, 102, Sept. 1961, p.588-9. illus.

1318. **DELSON, Victor**
His life and art.
in LIPOVSKY. Lenin Prize winners, p.216-37.
Excerpts from his book *Svyatoslav Richter.*

1319. **NEUHAUS, Heinrich**
Portrait of an artist.
in LIPOVSKY. Lenin Prize winners, p.210-15. illus.

RIMSKY-KORSAKOV, Nikolay (1844-1908)

A. *General.*

1320. **NEWMARCH, Rosa**
Rimsky-Korsakov.
MS, i.s., 7, 6 Mar. 1897, p.152-3.
13 Mar. 1897, p.166-8.

*1321. **POUGIN, A.**
Rimsky-Korsakow, Russian musician.
M, 14, 1898, p.17. illus.

1322. **NEWMARCH, Rosa**
The development of national opera in Russia. Rimsky-Korsakov.
PMA, 31, 1904-5, p.111-29.

1323. **NEWMARCH, Rosa**
Rimsky-Korsakov.
MJIMS, 7, Oct. 1905, p.9-12.

*1324. **RIMSKY-KORSAKOV and Russian national music.**
Current literature, 39, Oct. 1905, p.432-3.

1325. **KEETON, A. E.**
Nikolai Andrèyevitch Rimski-Kòrssakov.
Contemporary rev., 89, Apr. 1906, p.539-48.

1326. **NEWMARCH, Rosa**
Rimsky-Korsakov. Personal reminiscences.
MMR, 38, Aug. 1908, p.172-3.

*1327. **RIESEMANN, O. von**
[Rimsky-Korsakov].
NMR, 7, Sept. 1908, p.558-61. illus.

*1328. **TIDEBÖHL, Ellen von**
Incidents from the life of Rimsky-Korsakov.
Mu, 14, Sept. 1909, p.397.

1329. **MONTAGU-NATHAN, M.**
... Rimsky-Korsakoff.
MS, n.i.s., 2, 22 Nov. 1913, p.486-7.
29 Nov. 1913, p.515-6.
6 Dec. 1913, p.537-9.
13 Dec. 1913, p.561-2.
20 Dec. 1913, p.585-6.
27 Dec. 1913, p.609-10.

1330. **MONTAGU-NATHAN, M.**
Rimsky-Korsakov.
Constable. 1916. 7-124p. 1pl.
Like his biographies of Glinka and Mussorgsky, this is part of the series *Masters of Russian music,* an important survey by one of the most notable writers on Russian music. There is a catalogue of works.

1331. **MONTAGU-NATHAN, M.**
Rimsky-Korsakof.
in MONTAGU-NATHAN. An introduction to Russian music, p.52-5.

*1332. **RIMSKY-KORSAKOV, N.**
My musical life.
NMR, 15, Mar. 1916, p.114-17 and following issues.

1333. **MONTAGU-NATHAN, M.**
The inner history of modern Russian music.
MO, 39, Apr. 1916, p.450-1.
May 1916, p.512.
On Rimsky-Korsakov's memoirs.

See no. 398.

1334. **MONTAGU-NATHAN, M.**
The story of Russian music. 8. Rimsky-Korsakof.
MSt, 9, Apr. 1917, p.260+. illus.

1335. **PRING, S. W.,** *tr. and comp.*
Rimsky-Korsakoff's obiter dicta.
MSt, 9, Apr. 1917, p.cxxiv.
The article is by V. V. Yastrebtseff.

1336. **ROSENFELD, Paul**
Rimsky-Korsakov.
Dial, 64, 28 Mar. 1918, p.279-81.

1337. **RIMSKY-KORSAKOV, Nicholas**
Principles of orchestration, with musical examples drawn from his own works. Ed. by Maximilian Steinberg. English translation by Edward Agate.
Berlin, Editions Russe de Musique. 1923. [2v. in 1] viii-xii, 1-152p; 3-333p. mus.
Written over a period of 35 years, and published in Paris and Berlin in 1914. A standard work, in which the composer devotes volume 2 to music examples from his own works. The 1950 edition by Schmid is severely cut.

1338. **THE MUSIC masters of modern Russia. Nikolay Andreyvich Rimsky-Korsakoff.**
E, 42, July 1924, p.459-60. illus.

See no. 1980.

*1339. **LEVENSON, B.**
How Rimsky-Korsakoff taught.
E, 46, Mar. 1928, p.197-8. illus.

1340. **SABANEEV, Leonid**
Rimsky-Korsakov. Tr. by S. W. Pring.
MT, 69, May 1928, p.403-5.

1341. **ISTEL, Edgar**
Rimsky-Korsakov, the oriental wizard. Tr. by Theodore Baker.
MQ, 15, July 1929, p.388-414. mus.

*1342. **RIMSKY-KORSAKOV, Nikolai**
Practical manual of harmony. Tr. from the 12th Russian edition by Joseph Achron.
New York, Carl Fischer. 1930. 142p. illus.
First published in Russian in 1888.

1343. **CALVOCORESSI, M. D.**
Rimsky-Korsakov and "The Stone Guest".
MMR, 62, June 1932, p.106-7. mus.

1344. **ABRAHAM, Gerald**
The unknown Rimsky-Korsakov.
MS, n.i.s., 38, Sept. 1932, p.153-4.

*1345. **ARTHUR, S. G.**
Professor Rimsky-Korsakov.
E, 51, Feb. 1933, p.80.

1346. **CALVOCORESSI, M. D.**
Rimsky-Korsakov: commemoration in Russia.
MT, 74, Sept. 1933, p.801-3.

*1347. **STRASSER, W.**
Personal observations on Rimsky-Korsakoff.
E, 51, Oct. 1933, p.661+. illus.

1348. **MAINE, Basil**
Rimsky re-interpreted.
MO, 57, Feb. 1934, p.409.

1349. **SANDULENKO, A.**
The Korsakoff Wednesdays. Tr. and arranged by Alfred J. Swan.
Ch, 15, July-Aug. 1934, p.165-8.
Reminiscences of the composer, whom Sandulenko visited fortnightly.

1350. **ABRAHAM, Gerald**
Nicholas Rimsky-Korsakof.
in CALVOCORESSI *and* ABRAHAM. Masters of Russian music, p.335-423. 1pl.

1351. **[HERBAGE, Julian]**
Rimsky-Korsakov.
L 15, 1 Jan. 1936, p.46. illus.

See no. 454.

1352. **RIMSKY-KORSAKOV, Nikolay Andreyevich**
My musical life. Tr. by Judah A. Joffe. Ed. with an introduction by Carl van Vechten.
New York, Knopf. 1942. v-xliv, 3-480, 1-xxip. illus., 18pl.
First published in St. Petersburg, 1909, it has run into a welter of editions, some greatly cut. The third U.S. edition of 1942 translated from the fifth revised Russian edition is more satisfactory than that of 1923. It is well indexed, and despite the author's "notoriously faulty memory" (Gerald Abraham), it remains one of the most important source books on Russian music.

1353. **CALVOCORESSI, M. D.**
A musician's autobiography.
L, 27, 18 June 1942, p.797. illus.
On *My musical life.*

1354. **CALVOCORESSI, M. D.**
Rimsky-Korsakov, known and unknown.
L, 28, 15 Oct, 1942, p.509.

1355. **STEINPRESS, Boris**
A great Russian composer.
SL, 11, Mar. 1944, p.66-70. illus.

1356. **GODDARD, Scott**
Nicholas Andreievich Rimsky-Korsakov: 1844-1908.
L, 31, 9 Mar. 1944, p.281.

1357. **KLEIN, John W.**
Nicholas Rimsky-Korsakov: 1844-1908. A centennial appreciation.
MO, 67, Mar. 1944, p.185-6.
Apr. 1944, p.217-18.

1358. **EVANS, Edwin**
Rimsky-Korsakov (1844-1944).
ASJ, 5, Spring 1944, p.46.

1359. **ABRAHAM, Gerald**
Rimsky-Korsakov. A short biography.
Duckworth. 1945. 5-142p. bib.
A first-rate biography, containing an exhaustive catalogue of compositions, but no index. Still a standard life of the composer.

1360. **ABRAHAM, Gerald**
Rimsky-Korsakov's letters to a publisher.
MMR, 75, June 1945, p.105-8.
Sept. 1945, p.152-5.
Oct. 1945, p.182-5.
The publisher is Bessel.

1361. **ZETLIN, M. O.**
The youth of Rimsky-Korsakov. Tr. by Catherine Butakov.
RR, 5, Aug. 1945, p.89-101.
A chapter from Zetlin's book *The Five and others,* published in Russian.

1362. **BROOK, Donald**
Rimsky-Korsakov.
in BROOK. Six great Russian composers, p.137-71. illus.

See no. 208.

1363. **LOCKSPEISER, Edward**
The influence of Rimsky-Korsakov.
L, 51, 7 Jan. 1954, p.37.

See no. 418.

1364. **SLONIMSKY, Nicolas**
Muscovy's musical merlin. Rimsky-Korsakov (March 18, 1844 – June 21, 1908).
Hi fi and music rev., 1, June 1958, p.37-40+. illus., mus., disc.

1365. **ZETLIN, Mikhail**
The delightful child (the young Rimsky-Korsakov).
in ZETLIN. The Five, p.110-22.

1366. **ZETLIN, Mikhail**
The "Herr professor of music".
in ZETLIN. The Five, p.300-34.

See no. 420.

See no. 1984.

See no. 2763.

1367. **RABENECK, Nicolai**
The magic of Rimsky-Korsakov.
ON, 23, 16 Mar. 1959, p.31-3. illus.

1368. **VELIMIROVIĆ, Milos**
An unpublished letter from Rimsky-Korsakov.
JAMS, 15, Fall 1962, p.352-3.
To B. L. Levenson, a pupil of the composer.

1369. **ABRAHAM, Gerald**
Rimsky-Korsakov as self-critic
in ABRAHAM. Slavonic and Romantic music, p.195-201. mus.

B. *Works.*

Legend.

1369a. **TOVEY, *Sir* Donald**
Rimsky-Korsakov. Conte Féerique, op. 29.
in TOVEY. Essays in musical analysis, Vol. 4, p.140-3. mus.
This "Legend" was originally entitled "Baba-Yaga".

Scheherazade.

*1370. **BIART, V.**
Great orchestral masterpieces: Scheherazade.
E, 43, Sept. 1925, p.621-2. illus.

1371. **NEWMARCH, Rosa**
Rimsky-Korsakov. Symphonic suite, "Scheherazade", op. 35.
CL, 3, p.52-6.

1372. **ABRAHAM, Gerald**
The programme of "Scheherazade".
MMR, 63, Sept. 1933, p.154-5.

1373. **ABRAHAM, Gerald**
New light on old friends. A. The programme of "Scheherazade".
in ABRAHAM. On Russian music, p.138-43.

1374. **ROBERTSON, Marion**
L'Oiseau de feu (The Fire Bird) and Scheherazade. With decorations by Joyce Millen.
Newman Wolsey. 1947. 7-94p. [2nd. ed.] illus.
Mostly devoted to the stories of the ballets but also containing background information on the music and composers.

Songs.

1375. **ABRAHAM, Gerald**
Rimsky-Korsakov's songs.
MMR, Mar.-Apr. 1944, p.51-7.
Also *in* ABRAHAM. Slavonic and Romantic music, p.202-11. mus.

Operas.

See no. 514.

1376. **CALVOCORESSI, M. D.**
Rimsky-Korsakov's operas reconsidered.
MT, 72, Oct. 1931, p.886-8. mus.

Christmas Eve.

See no. 1400.

The Golden Cockerel.

1377. **TIDEBÖHL, Ellen von**
Rimsky-Korsakov's last opera – "Zolotoi Petoushok" ("The Golden Cockerel").
MMR, 38, Dec. 1908, p.275-6.

1378. **CLEASBY, Harold**
Le Coq d'or and Roman pantomime.
Na, 108, 17 May 1919, p.799-800.

1379. **DAVIDSON, Gladys**
Rimsky-Korsakov. The Golden Cockerel.
in DAVIDSON. Stories from the Russian operas, p.149-74. illus.

1380. **ABRAHAM, Gerald**
"The Golden Cockerel".
in ABRAHAM. Studies in Russian music, p.290-310. mus.

1381. **NEWMARCH, Rosa**
Rimsky-Korsakov. Suite, "Le Coq D'Or".
CL, 5, p.70-4.

1382. **WOOD, Ralph W.**
"The Golden Cockerel".
L, 40, 30 Sept. 1948, p.500.

1383. **COOPER, Martin**
"Le Coq d'Or".
O, 5, Jan. 1954, p.10-16. illus.

1384. **MONTAGU, George**
Rimsky-Korsakov's "Le Coq d'Or"
LME, 9, Jan. 1954, p.21-2. illus.

1385. **MONTAGU-NATHAN, M.**
The origin of The Golden Cockerel.
MR, 15, Feb. 1954, p.33-8. mus.

1386. **MONTAGU-NATHAN, M.**
King Dodon's love-song.
MMR, 84, Oct. 1954, p.210-12. mus.

1387. **DORATI, Antal**
"The Golden Cockerel": political satire and fairy tale.
O, 13, Nov. 1962, p.713-15. illus.

1388. **MERKLING, Frank**
A cry at dawn.
ON, 32, 23 Sept. 1967, p.6-7. illus., mus.

1389. **FEINBERG, Saul**
Rimsky-Korsakov's Suite from Le Coq d'Or.
MR, 30, Feb. 1969, p.47-64. mus., bib.

1390. **WEAVER, William**
"The Golden Cockerel" by Rimsky-Korsakov.
About the house, 3, Christmas 1969, p.28-33. illus.

Ivan the Terrible, opera – *see The Maid of Pskov.*

The Legend of the Invisible City of Kitezh.

1391. **EDWARDS, Lovett F.**
The Russian "Parsifal".
Sackbut, 2, July 1921, p.21-5. mus.

1392. **ABRAHAM, Gerald**
"Kitezh".
in ABRAHAM. Studies in Russian music, p.261-89. mus.

1393. **COOPER, Martin**
Rimsky-Korsakov's "Kitezh".
L, 45, 18 Jan. 1951, p.116.

1394. **"THE LEGEND of the Invisible City of Kitezh".**
L, 66, 10 Aug. 1961, p.221.
A timed synopsis of the opera.

The Maid of Pskov.

1395. **DAVIDSON, Gladys**
Rimsky-Korsakov. Ivan the Terrible.
in DAVIDSON. Stories from the Russian operas, p.118-37. illus.
"Ivan the Terrible" is another title for "The Maid of Pskov".

1396. **NEWMARCH, Rosa**
Rimsky-Korsakov. Overture, "Ivan the Terrible".
CL, 4, p.72-3.

1397. **ABRAHAM, Gerald**
Rimsky-Korsakov's first opera.
in ABRAHAM. Studies in Russian music, p.142-66. illus., mus.

1398. **ABRAHAM, Gerald**
Pskovityanka: the original version of Rimsky-Korsakov's first opera.
MQ, 54, Jan. 1968, p.58-73. mus.

May Night.

1399. **DAVIDSON, Gladys**
Rimsky-Korsakov. A Night in May.
in DAVIDSON. Stories from the Russian operas, p.97-117

1400. **ABRAHAM, Gerald**
Rimsky-Korsakov's Gogol operas.
ML, 12, July 1931, p.242-52. mus.
Also *in* ABRAHAM. Studies in Russian music, p.167-92. illus., mus.
On "May Night" and "Christmas Eve"

1401. **NEWMARCH, Rosa**
Rimsky-Korsakov. Overture, "Night in May"
CL, 5, p.70.

Mlada.

1402. **ABRAHAM, Gerald**
Rimsky-Korsakov's "Mlada", 1891.
MO, 58, Nov. 1934, p.118-19. mus.
Also *in* ABRAHAM. On Russian music, p.113-121. mus.
Not to be confused with the unfinished composite opera-ballet by Borodin, Cui, Mussorgsky, Rimsky-Korsakov and Minkus.

1403. **NEWMARCH, Rosa**
Rimsky-Korsakov. Ballet suite, "Mlada".
CL, 5, p.67-9.
Adapted from his opera.

1404. **ABRAHAM, Gerald**
Rimsky-Korsakov's "Mlada".
L, 71, 12 Mar. 1964, p.448.

Mlada, opera-ballet (with Borodin, Cui, Mussorgsky and Minkus).

see no. 119.

see no. 146.

Mozart and Salieri.

1405. **DAVIDSON, Gladys**
Rimsky-Korsakov. Mozart and Salieri.
in DAVIDSON. Stories from the Russian operas, p.138-48.

1406. **HADLAND, F. A.**
Mozart and Salieri.
MMR, 57, Oct. 1927, p.292.

1407. **PAYNE, Anthony**
Russian rarities.
MMu, 16, Mar. 1968, p.34-5.
On "Mozart and Salieri" and Tchaikovsky's "Iolanta".

Pskovityanka, opera – *see The Maid of Pskov.*

Sadko.

1408. **ABRAHAM, G.**
"Sadko" and "The Tsar's Bride".
MMR, 61, June 1931, p.168-9.

1409. **ABRAHAM, G.**
Music of "Sadko".
MS, n.i.s., 37, July 1931, p.183-4. mus.
Aug. 1931, p.197-8. mus.

1410. **ABRAHAM, Gerald**
"Sadko".
in ABRAHAM. Studies in Russian music, p.221-45. mus.

1411. **EVANS, Edward**
"Sadko".
Time and tide, 23, 28 Mar. 1942, p.267+.

The Snow Maiden.

1412. **TIDEBÖHL, Ellen von**
Rimsky-Korsakov and his opera "The Snow Maiden".
M, 17, Mar. 1912, p.156. illus.
Mostly devoted to the plot.

1413. **COOKE, J. F.**
The Snow Maiden, "Snegourotschka".
E, 42, June 1924, p.419.

1414. **ABRAHAM, Gerald**
"Snow Maiden".
in ABRAHAM. Studies in Russian music, p.193-220. mus.

The Tale of Tsar Saltan.

1415. **NEWMARCH, Rosa**
Rimsky-Korsakov. Suite from "The Legend of Tsar Saltan".
CL, 5, p.74-8.

1416. **ABRAHAM, Gerald**
"Tsar Saltan".
in ABRAHAM. On Russian music, p.122-37. mus.

1417. **GODDARD, Scott**
"The Legend of Tsar Saltan".
L, 33, 19 Apr. 1945, p.445.

The Tsar's Bride.

See no. 1408.

1418. **ABRAHAM, Gerald**
The Tsar's Bride.
in ABRAHAM. Studies in Russian music, p.246-60. illus., mus.

1419. **PAYNE, Anthony**
Wide-screen Rimsky.
MMu, 15, Mar. 1967, p.32-3. illus.
On the Soviet film of the opera.

ROSSLAVETZ, Nikolay (1881-1944)

1420. **SABANEYEFF, Leonid**
Nikolay Roslavets.
in SABANEYEFF. Modern Russian composers, p.201-7.

ROSTROPOVITCH, Mstislav (1927-)

1421. **THIS month's personality. Mstislav Rostropovich.**
MMu, 4, Mar. 1956, p.5. illus.

1422. **SABIN, Robert**
Rostropovich, Soviet cellist whose interests include mechanics and engineering.
MA, 76, Apr. 1956, p.9+. illus.

1423. **USVATOV, Alexander**
Soviet cellist in America.
News, 17, Sept. 1956, p.14. illus.

1424. **STANFIELD, M. B.**
Mstislav Rostropovich.
Strad, 70, May 1959, p.29+. illus.

1425. **ROSTROPOVICH, Mstislav**
Soviet composers and the interpreter. Tr. by S. Ostrofsky.
SR, 42, 14 Nov. 1959, p.52-3. illus.

1426. **THE YOUNG master of the cello.**
MMu, 9, July 1961, p.7+. illus.

1427. **UEBEL, Ruth**
... Mstislav Rostropovich.
MA, 84, Feb. 1964, p.20-1. illus.
An interview with him.

1428. **GINSBURG, Lev**
Mstislav Rostropovich. Tr. by Ralph Parker.
SL, June 1964, p. 153-6.

1429. **CHISLETT, Alicia**
Rostropovich master-class at Oxford.
Strad, 75, Aug. 1964, p.145+.

*1430. **SEAMAN, G.**
Rostropovich and Oistrakh in interview.
Canon, 17, no.7, 1966, p.5-7.

1431. **GINSBURG, Lev**
The world's leading cellist.
in LIPOVSKY. Lenin Prize winners, p.256-75. illus.
Excerpts from Ginsburg's book *Mstislav Rostropovich.*

1432. **SAAL, Hubert**
Master cellist.
Newsweek, 69, 13 Mar. 1967, p.62-3. illus.

*1433. **PEOPLE are talking about ...**
Vogue, 153, 15 Apr. 1969, p.82-3.

1434. **ROSTROPOVICH, Mstislav**
Rostropovitch appeals for Solzhenitsyn.
SR, 53, 28 Nov. 1970, p.28.
His outspoken letter was written to four leading Russian periodicals.

RUBINSTEIN, Anton (1829-94)

A. *General*

1435. **RUBINSTEIN and the Slavonians.**
Old and New, 6, Oct. 1872, p.477-81.

1436. **EICHBERG, Oscar**
Analytical and historical remarks on Anton Rubinstein's cycle of seven pianoforte recitals. [Tr. by G. E. Prince].
London. [n.p.]. [1886]. 8-44p. mus.
The first book published in English on any Russian composer, it is spattered with errors and misprints (Byrd becomes "Bird"). There is no index of the works discussed.

1437. **ANTON, Rubinstein.**
MMR, 16, June 1886, p.121-2.

1438. **ANTON Rubinstein, pianist.**
MT, 27, July 1886, p.385-7.

1439. **ANTON Rubinstein.**
MS, n.s., 31, 10 July 1886, p.28.
He says "I was born fifty-six years ago". In fact he was born in 1829.

1440. **RUBINSTEIN'S first visit to London.**
MMR, 16, Aug. 1886, p.174-5.
The date was 1842.

1441. **M'ARTHUR, Alexander,** ***pseud.***
Anton Rubinstein. A biographical sketch.
Edinburgh, Adam and Charles Black. 1889. 1-154p. 4pl.
A laudatory account by the composer's private secretary (real name Lillian McArthur), it contains a useful list of works but no index. The first biography of a Russian composer published in English.

1442. **RUBINSTEIN, Anton**
Autobiography. Tr. from the Russian by Aline Delano.
Boston, Little, Brown and Co.1890. vi-xii, 1-171p.
illus., 1pl.
Outspoken anecdotes and opinions taken down from the composer's own words. There is a concluding section: *Rubinstein as a composer,* but no index. Charles MacLean *(Proceedings of the Musical Association,* 39, 1912-13) states that Delano's commentary is "most untrustworthy".

1443. **SOME opinions of Anton Rubinstein.**
MT, 33, Mar. 1892, p.142-3.

1444. **HANSLICK, Edouard**
M. Rubinstein on music and musicians. Tr. by Benjamin Cutter.
MO, 15, May 1892, p.359-60. illus.

1445. **ANTON Rubinstein.**
Rev. of revs., 10, Dec. 1894, p.543-6. illus.

1446. **BENNETT, Joseph**
Anton Rubinstein.
MT, 35, Dec. 1894, p.801-4. illus.

1447. **FERRIS, G. T.**
Anton Rubinstein.
Harper's weekly, 38, 1 Dec. 1894, p.1132. illus.

*1448. **MASON, William**
Dr. Mason on Rubinstein's touch.
M, 7, 1894-5, p.390-2.

*1449. **STEINWAY, William**
Reminiscences of Rubinstein.
M, 7, 1894-5, p.394-400.
An excerpt appears in *Rev. of revs.,* 11, Mar. 1895, p.324-5.

*1450. **FINCK, H. T.**
Rubinstein's fate and future.
Music of the modern world, 1, 1895, p.67-70.

*1451. **RODENBURG, Julius**
My personal recollections of Antoine Rubinstein, together with letters.
M, 8, 1895, p.437-65.

*1452. **SAINT-SAENS, Camille**
Recollections of Antoine Rubinstein.
M, 8, 1895, p.423-30.

1453. **HAWEIS, H. R.**
Rubinstein.
FR, 57, Jan. 1895, p.27-36.
Also *in* LLA, 204, 23 Feb. 1895, p.451-7, and reported *in* *Eclectic mag.*, 124, 1894, p.229, and also reported *in* MS, i.s., 3, 12 Jan. 1895, p.31-2.

1454. **McARTHUR, Alexander,** *pseud.*
Rubinstein: the man and the musician.
Century, 28, May 1895, p.28-33. illus.

1455. **A LAST** look.
AM, 76, Aug. 1895, p.287.
Highly sentimental. The place was Cologne railway station.

1456. **McARTHUR, Alexander,** *pseud.*
Rubinstein: the man and his music.
MS, i.s., 4, 24 Aug. 1895, p.126-8.

*1457. **GANSS, H. G.**
Anton Rubinstein.
Catholic world, 64, Nov. 1896, p.193-201. illus.

*1458. **MARTINOFF, I.**
Incidents in the life of Anton Rubinstein.
M. 13, 1897, p.34.

1459. **RUBINSTEIN, Anton**
Guide to the proper use of the pianoforte pedals with examples out of the historical concerts of Anton Rubinstein. Tr. from the German by John A. Preston.
Bosworth. 1897. 4-44p. mus.
The musical examples are by Chopin, Beethoven, Liszt, Rubinstein, Schumann and Schubert, among others, some relating to the use of the pedal by Nicholas Rubinstein.

*1460. **McARTHUR, Alexander,** *pseud.*
Rubinstein as a teacher.
M, 13, 1897-8, p.365-9.

1461. **MERRY, Frank**
The real Rubinstein.
MO, 21, Dec. 1898, p.176. illus.

1462. McARTHUR, Alexander, *pseud.*
Rubinstein's theory of practice.
MS, i.s., 11, 1 Apr. 1899, p.196-7.

1463. RUBINSTEIN's works.
MS, i.s., 11, 29 Apr. 1899, p.265-6.

1464. ILIAS,?
Anton Rubinstein. Tr. by Mary J. Safford.
LLA, 222, 5 Aug. 1899, p.370-4.

1465. DAVIDOWA, N.
Reminiscences of Anton Rubinstein.
MMR, 29, Dec. 1899, p.268-70.

1466. MAZZUCATO, G.
Anton Rubinstein in Milan.
MS, i.s., 12, 30 Dec. 1899, p.418-19.

1467. CRONK, Cuthbert
The works of Anton Rubinstein (Nov. 1829-Nov. 1894). A study.
Novello. 1900. 6-24p. bib.
Useful if unscholarly sections on Rubinstein's style and method, individuality, invention and creation. There is a list of the major works and a biographical note. *See also* no. 1510.

1468. SAINT-SAENS, Camille
Anton Rubinstein.
MS, i.s., 14, 25 Aug. 1900, p.123-4.

*1469. RITTER, Hermann
Personal recollections of Anton Rubinstein.
M, 19, Apr. 1901, p.577-81.

1470. RUBINSTEIN on Bach and Handel.
MS, i.s., 18, 1 Nov. 1902, p.273-4.

1471. JOHNSTON, Vera
In old Peterhof.
Era, 11 Apr. 1903, p.374-80.

1472. SHERWOOD, Mrs. W. H.
Some reminiscences of Rubinstein.
MS, i.s., 21, 23 Jan. 1904, p.58.

1473. **KEETON, A. E.**
Anton Grigðrovitch Rubinstein.
MMR, 34, Dec. 1904, p.226-7.

1474. **KEETON, A. E.**
Anton Rubinstein. Born November 1830. Died November 1894.
FR, 77, Jan. 1905, p.111-23.
Also *in* LLA, 244, 25 Feb. 1905, p.493-503. illus.
It is now known that Rubinstein was born in November 1829.

1475. **OYLER, Edna**
Anton Rubinstein (told to children).
Musician, 1, Apr. 1906, p.163. illus.

1476. **DROUCKER, Sandra**
Notes on Rubinstein's teaching.
MS, i.s., 26, 14 July 1906, p.25.

1477. **SHEDLOCK, J. S.**
Anton Rubinstein.
MMR, 36, Aug. 1906, p.172-3.

*1478. **BAGBY, A. M.**
How Rubinstein played the piano.
E, 25, 1907, p.646-7.

*1479. **HIPPIUS, Adelaide**
Anton Rubinstein in his class-room.
E, 25, 1907, p.230+.

*1480. **RYAN, Thomas**
Personal recollections of Anton Rubinstein and Henri Wieniawski.
Musical observer, 1, no.12, 1907, p.25.

1481. **HOFMANN, Josef**
How Rubinstein taught me to play.
Ladies' home j., 24, Jan. 1907, p.11+. illus.

*1482. **TIDEBÖHL, Ellen von**
With Rubinstein in the class-room.
E, 26, 1908, p.765.

1483. **KITCHENER, Frederick**
A neglected colossus.
MS, i.s., 29, 18 Jan. 1908, p.39.

*1484. **GOLDMARK, Carl**
[Recollections of Anton Rubinstein].
MMR, 7, July 1908, p.461-2.

1485. **SCHLOESSER, Adolph**
Anton Rubinstein (1829-1894).
MMR, 38, Sept. 1908, p.198-9.

*1486. **TRACY, J. M.**
Central figure in Russian music.
Mu, 14, Aug. 1909, p.351.

1487. **GRAU, Robert**
Memories of musicians: Rubinstein and Wieniawski.
M, 15, July 1910, p.442. illus.

*1488. **MOORE, A. W.**
Rubinstein's meteoric tour of America. Personal recollections of the great Russian master.
E, 29, 1911, p.731-2.

1489. **A STUDY of Rubinstein's playing.**
M, 16, Aug. 1911, p.517. illus.

*1490. **NARODNY, Ivan**
What Rubinstein did for Russia.
MA, 16, no.5, 1912, p.27.

1491. **LESCHETIZKY, Eugenie**
Personal recollections of Anton Rubinstein.
M, 17, Aug. 1912, p.516.
Also in *Musical observer,* 2, Sept. 1912, p.228.
Says "He never played a composition twice in the same way".

1492. **NICHIA, Lillian,** *pseud.*
A girl's recollections of Rubinstein.
Harper's monthly, 65, Dec. 1912, p.39-47.

1493. **MACLEAN, Charles**
Rubinstein as a composer for the pianoforte.
PMA, 39, 1912-13, p.129-51. bib.
Also *in* QMIMS, 15, 1913-14, p.360-1. bib.

1494. **HERVEY, Arthur**
Rubinstein.
Jack. [1913]. 7-63p. illus., 1pl., mus.
Less than two dozen pages on the composer; the rest is given over to five of Rubinstein's compositions. An index is lacking.

1495. **MONTAGU-NATHAN, M.**
The story of Russian music. 10. The Rubinsteins.
MSt, 9, June 1917, p.clvi+.

1496. **WALTER, Victor**
Reminiscences of Anton Rubinstein. Tr. by D. A. Modell.
MQ, 5, Jan 1919, p.10-19.

1497. **HOFMANN, Josef**
What Rubinstein taught and told me.
Ladies' home j., 36, Oct. 1919, p.39. illus.

1498. **SILOTI, Alexander**
Memories of Rubinstein and Liszt.
E, 38, July 1920, p.447-8. illus.
Aug. 1920, p.523-4.

1499. **MOORE, Aubertine**
Rubinstein, master of tone.
E, 38, Dec. 1920, p.801-2. illus.

*1500. **MARTENS, Frederick H.**
Rubinstein.
New York, Breitkopf and Hartel. 1922. 28p. illus.
One of the *Little biographies* series.

See no. 1550.

1501. **STANISLAVSKY, Constantin**
My life in art. Part three - Rubinstein and Tolstoi.
Tr. from the Russian by J. J. Robbins.
Forum, 71, Apr. 1924, p.437-47.

1502. **HEINK, Felix**
Rubinstein's master methods in piano study.
E, 42, Dec. 1924, p.812-20. illus.

*1503. **UPTON, George P.**
Rubinstein, the master.
E, 44, Aug. 1926, p.574.

1504. **[WOLF, Hugo]**
Selected musical criticisms of Hugo Wolf. Tr. by Marie Boileau.
MMR, 58, Sept. 1928, p.262.
Nov. 1928, p.324.
On recitals given by Rubinstein on 17 Feb. 1884 and 20 Dec. 1885.

*1505. **ABELL, A. M.**
Impressions of Anton Rubinstein.
MC, 99, 1929, p.26+.

*1506. **GEIRINGER, Karl**
Pictorial biography of Anton Rubinstein.
MC, 99, no.21, 1929, p.27-34.

*1507. **SOHN, Joseph**
The centenary of Rubinstein.
E, 47, 1929, p.647-8. illus.

1508. **SOUTHERN, H.**
The Rubinstein centenary.
MO, 52, Sept. 1929, p.1107-9.
Lists 60 of his piano pieces.

1509. **SABANEEV, L.**
Anton Rubinstein (Born November 28, 1829). Tr. by S. W. Pring.
MT, 70, Nov. 1929, p.977-80.

1510. **SOUTHERN, H.**
The Rubinstein centenary. Some further considerations.
MO, 53, Dec. 1929, p.233-5.
On Cronk's book, no. 1467.

1511. **[HACKETT, Henry]**
Anton Rubinstein: a centenary sketch.
Choir, 21, Jan. 1930, p.5-7.

1512. **SOHN, Joseph**
The centenary of Rubinstein.
MS, n.i.s., 35, 8 Mar. 1930, p.79-80.
22 Mar. 1930, p.93-4.

*1513. **ARONSON, Maurice**
Lest we forget Anton Rubinstein.
MC, 109, 17 Nov. 1934, p.6+.

*1514. **PHILIPP, Isidor**
Personal recollections of Anton Rubinstein.
E, 56, 1938, p.493-4.

1515. **BOWEN, Catherine Drinker**
Free artist. The story of Anton and Nicholas Rubinstein.
New York, Random House. 1939. vii-xi, 3-412p. illus., 11pl., bib.
Chatty, vivid, semi-fictional account. Contains a useful catalogue of compositions, a massive, if not entirely accurate, bibliography and an unhelpful index.

1516. **BOWEN, Catherine D.**
Music comes to America.
AM, 163, May 1939, p.591-602.
On Rubinstein's tour of the United States, 1872-3.

1517. **BENNIGSEN, Olga**
The brothers Rubinstein and their circle.
MQ, 25, Oct. 1939, p.407-19. 2pl.

*1518. **CADMAN, D. M.**
The amazing Rubinsteins.
E, 58, Feb. 1940, p.86. illus.

*1519. **ERNEST, Gustav**
Kings of the keyboard: Liszt and Rubinstein.
E, 58, Sept. 1940, p.585-6+. illus.

1520. **RUBINSTEIN, Anton**
Music and its masters. A conversation by Anton Rubinstein.
Tr. for the author by Mrs. John P. Morgan.
Augener. [1943]. 4-108p.
Not to be confused with Rubinstein's autobiography, this was first published in New York in 1892. There is no index.

*1521. **ZAVADSKY, V.**
Anton Rubinstein: a study in perspective.
Mu, 50, June 1945, p.11-12. illus.

1522. **ABRAHAM, G.**
Anton Rubinstein: Russian composer.
MT, 86, Dec. 1945, p.361-5. mus.
Also *in* ABRAHAM. Slavonic and Romantic music, p.99-106. mus.

*1523. **ARONSON, M.**
A Christmas recollection.
E, 73, Dec. 1955, p.20+.

1524. **GOLDIN, Milton**
The great Rubinstein Road Show.
HF, 16, Sept. 1966, p.60-2.
The title refers to Rubinstein's concert tour of the United States in 1872-3.

B. *Works.*

Symphony no.2.

*1525. **PARSONS, Albert R.**
Rubinstein as pianist and how he composed his Ocean Symphony.
MC, 99, no.21, 1929, p.39.

1526. **SLONIMSKY, Nicolas**
Musical oddities.
E, 73, Oct. 1955, p.8-9.
Slonimsky is incorrect in stating that the "Ocean" is the longest symphony.

Symphony no.4.

See no. 1526.

Don Quixote.

1527. **ABRAHAM, Gerald**
Rubinstein's "Don Quixote".
L, 16, 409, 11 Nov. 1936, p.927.

Chamber music.

1528. **COBBETT, W. W.** , *and others.*
Rubinstein's best for strings and piano.
MS, n.i.s., 35, 25 Jan. 1930, p.26-9.

Piano works.

1529. **DUTORDOIT, Coralie**
A note on Anton Rubinstein's piano works.
MS, n.i.s., 28, 17 Aug. 1926, p.8.

1530. **EVANS, Edwin**
A neglected composer.
DT, no. 354, Mar. 1940, p.343-3.

1531. **JOHNSON, Thomas Arnold.**
The piano music of Anton Rubinstein.
MTe, 31, Aug. 1952, p.373+.

Kamennoy-Ostrov.

*1532. **GOODSON, K.**
Master-lesson on Rubinstein's Kamennoiostrow, op.10, no.22.
E, 43, Sept. 1925, p.623-4.

*1533. **GEHRKENS, K. W.**
What does Kamennoi Ostrow mean?
E, 58, Oct. 1940, p.672.

1534. **MELCHER, R. A.**
About Kammenoi-Ostrov.
E, 71, July 1953, p.22.

Melody in F.

1535. **WILKINSON, Charles W.**
Well known piano solos. Practical hints as to performances. 5. Rubinstein's "Melody in F".
MS, i.s., 27, 18 May 1907, p.310-11.

*1536. **BONNER, A. M.**
Rubinstein's Melody in F.
E, 50, Sept. 1932, p.662.

Souvenir de Dresde.

1537. **A SOUVENIR: Rubinstein.**
MT, 35, Dec. 1894, p.809-10. mus.

Songs.

1538. **NIECKS, Frederick**
Modern song-writers. 3. Anton Rubinstein.
MT, 26, Feb. 1885, p.67-9.

*1539. **SAUNDERS, C. E.**
Rubinstein's songs.
M, 10, 1896, p.112-16.

1540. **BOUGHTON, Rutland**
The songs of Rubinstein.
MO, 21, July 1898, p.684-5.

1541. **PROCTOR, Charles**
Rubinstein as a song-writer.
MO, 55, Dec. 1931, p.214-15. mus.
Jan. 1932, p.309-10. mus.

Der Asra.

*1542. **KEEFER, A. R.**
Der Asra, as arranged by Liszt.
E, 53, Nov. 1935, p.642. illus.
The arrangement (G554) was published in 1884.

Operas.

The Demon.

1543. **HERR Rubinstein's "Il Demonio".**
MS, n.s., 21, July 1881, p.6-8.

1544. **RUBINSTEIN'S grand opera - The Demon.**
MS, n.s., 36, 16 Mar. 1889, p.214-15.

1545. **DAVIDSON, Gladys**
Rubinstein. The Demon.
in DAVIDSON. Stories from the Russian operas, p.175-85. illus.

Feramors.

1546. **[FINCK, R. T.]**
Rubinstein's "Feramors".
Na, 28, 10 Apr. 1879, p.246-7.

1547. **NEWMARCH, Rosa**
Rubinstein. Ballet music and wedding march from "Feramors".
CL, 3, p.82-3.

Nero.

1548. **ANTON Rubinstein's "Nero".**
MMR, 10, Feb. 1880, p.20-2.

Paradise Lost.

1549. **RUBINSTEIN, Anton**
"Oratorio" or "Sacred opera"?
MO, 5, Aug. 1882, p.422-3.
On the designation of his "Paradise Lost" and "The Tower of Babel".

The Tower of Babel.

See no. 1549.

RUBINSTEIN, Nicholas (1835-81)

General.

See no. 1459.

See no. 1495.

1550. **SCOTT, George A.**
A forgotten salon.
ML, 4, Jan. 1923, p.42-53.
Recollections of the Rubinstein brothers by Sophie Bogdanoff, favourite pupil of Nicholas Rubinstein.

See no. 1515.

See no. 1517.

See no. 1518.

SABANEYEV, Leonid (1882-1967)

*1551. **SABANEYEV, Leonid**
To conquer new tonal regions.
MM, 4, May 1927, p.15-19.

1552. **SABANEEV, Leonid**
Two critiques. 1. Richard Strauss. Tr. by S. W. Pring.
ML, 8, July 1927, p.322-8.
The other was on Medtner.

1553. **L. SABANEEV. Tr. by S. W. Pring.**
MT, 68, Dec. 1927, p.1090.

*1554. **SABANEEF, Leonid**
The biometrical method in its application to [the] question of the study of style. Tr. by S. W. Pring.
Pro musica quarterly, Dec. 1927, p.7.

1555. **SABANEEV, Leonid**
The destinies of musical romanticism. Tr. by S. W. Pring.
MT, 69, Feb. 1928, p.113-15.

1556. **SABANEEV, Leonid**
A conductorless orchestra. Tr. by S. W. Pring.
MT, 69, Apr. 1928, p.307-9.
No one in particular.

1557. **SABANEEV, Leonid**
The destinies of music. Tr. by S. W. Pring.
MT, 69, June 1928, p.502-6.

1558. **SABANEEV, Leonid**
The limits of music. Tr. by S. W. Pring.
MT, 69, July 1928, p.602-4.

1559. **SABANEEV, Leonid**
The musical receptivity of the man in the street.
Tr. by S. W. Pring.
ML, 9, July 1928, p.226-39.

1560. **SABANEEV, Leonid**
The process of mechanisation in the musical art. Tr. by S.W. Pring.
Nineteenth century and after, 104, July 1928, p.108-17.

1561. **SABANEEV, Leonid**
The perspectives of musical style. Tr. by S. W. Pring.
MT, 69, Aug. 1928, p.694-6.

1562. **SABANEEV, Leonid**
The crisis in the teaching of theory. Tr. by S. W. Pring.
MT, 89, Nov. 1928, p.985-8.

1563. **SABANEEV, Leonid**
Gosta Nyström: a new Swedish composer. Tr. by S. W. Pring.
MT, 69, Dec. 1928, p.1084-5.

1564. **SABANEEV, Leonid**
The problem of the conductor: and a proposed mechanical solution. Tr. by S. W. Pring.
MT, 89, Dec. 1928, p.1073-5.

1565. **SABANEEV, Leonid**
The rhythm of music and the rhythm of the age. Tr. by S.W. Pring.
Dominant, 1, Dec. 1928, p.23-7.

1566. **SABANEEV, Leonid**
Claude Debussy. Tr. by S. W. Pring.
ML, 10, Jan. 1929, p.1-34.

1567. **SABANEEV, Leonid**
Music in the cinema. Tr. by S. W. Pring.
MT, 70, Feb. 1929, p.113-15.

*1568. **SABANEYEFF, Leonid**
Dawn in Sweden.
MM, 6, Mar. 1929, p.30-2.

1569. **SABANEEV, L.**
The evolution of the orchestra. Tr. by S. W. Pring.
Nineteenth century and after, 105, Mar. 1929, p.379-86.

1570. **SABANEEV, Leonid**
The possibility of quarter-tone and other new scales.
Tr. by S. W. Pring.
MT, 70, June 1929, p.501-4.

1571. **SABANEEV, Leonid**
The Jewish national school in music. Tr. by S. W. Pring.
MQ, 15, July 1929, p.448-68.
The article was written in 1924.

1572. **SABANEEV, Leonid**
The relation between sound and colour. Tr. by S. W. Pring.
ML, 10, July 1929, p.266-75.

1573. **SABANEEV, Leonid**
The organisation of musical science. Tr. by S. W. Pring.
MT, 70, Sept. 1929, p.785-7.

1574. **SABANEEV, Leonid**
Types of musical outlook. Tr. by S. W. Pring.
MT, 71, Jan. 1930, p.18-21.

1575. **GODDARD, Scott**
A Russian critic: Leonid Sabaneiev.
MMR, 60, Feb, 1930, p.42-3.

1576. **SABANEEV, Leonid**
Opera at the present day. Tr. by S. W. Pring.
MT, 71, July 1930, p.593-6.

1577. **SABANEEV, Leonid**
Some social causes of the present musical crisis. Tr. by
S.W. Pring.
ML, 13, Jan. 1932, p.75-9.

1578. **SABANEEV, Leonid**
Remarks on the leit-motif. Tr. by S. W. Pring.
ML, 13, Apr. 1932, p.200-6.

1579. **SABANEEV, Leonid**
Music and the sound film. Tr. by S.W. Pring.
ML, 15, Apr. 1934, p.147-52.

1580. **SABANEEV, Leonid**
Technical progress in the music of today. Tr. by S. W. Pring.
MT, 75, Oct. 1934, p.881-3.

1581. **SABANEEV, Leonid**
Music and the economic crisis. Tr. by S. W. Pring.
MT, 74, Dec. 1934, p.1075-7.

1582. **SABANEEV, Leonid**
Music for the films: a handbook for composers and conductors. Tr. by S. W. Pring.
Pitman. 1935. v-vii, 1-128p. illus.
A general handbook, aiming to provide practical and technical advice.

1583. **SABANEEV, Leonid**
The teaching of composition. Tr. by S. W. Pring.
MT, 76, Oct. 1935, p.849+.

1584. **SABANEEV, Leonid**
The musical ear: its various categories. Tr. by S. W. Pring.
MT, 76, Dec. 1935, p.1073-5.

1585. **SABANEEV, Leonid**
Light music. Tr. by S. W. Pring.
MT, 79, July 1938, p.496-8.

1586. **SABANEEV, Leonid**
Maurice Ravel. Tr. by S. W. Pring.
MO, 61, Aug. 1938, p.943-4.

1587. **SABANEEV, Leonid**
Opera and the cinema. Tr. by S. W. Pring.
MT, 81, Jan. 1940, p.9-11.

1588. **SABANEEV, Leonid**
The symphony in the service of ballet. Tr. by S. W. Pring.
MT, 81, July 1940, p.297-8.

1589. **SABANEEFF, Leonid**
Pavel Florensky - priest, scientist and mystic.
RR, 20, Oct. 1961, p.312-25.

SAMINSKY, Lazare (1882-1959)

*1590. **SAMINSKY, Lazare**
Schönberg and Bartok: path-breakers.
MM, 1, Feb. 1924, p.27-8.

1591. **SAMINSKY, Lazare**
Bēla Bártok and the graphic current in music.
MQ, 10, July 1924, p.400-4. illus.
By the "graphic current" Saminsky means clarity of linear development.

*1592. **SAMINSKY, Lazare**
The downfall of Strauss.
MM, 1, Nov. 1924, p.11-13.
Refers to Richard Strauss.

*1593. **SAMINSKY, Lazare**
East meets West.
MM, 4, Jan. 1927, p.21-3.

1594. **SAMINSKY, Lazare**
The musical year in New York. Season 1926-7.
MS, n.i.s., 30, 10 Sept. 1927, p.96.

*1595. **SAMINSKY, Lazare**
More about "Faustus".
MM, 6, Nov. 1927, p.38-9.

*1596. **SAMINSKY, Lazare**
Race and revolution.
MM, 6, Mar. 1929, p.26-9.

1597. **PAOLI, Domenico de,** *and others.*
Lazare Saminsky, composer and civic worker.
New York, Bloch Publishing Co. 1930. 1-65p. illus., 1pl., mus.
Some of the essays previously appeared in periodicals. There is a list of Saminsky's works but no index.
Contents: Lazare Saminsky by Domenico de Paoli. - The youth in Saminsky by Leigh Henry. - Saminsky, the contemporary by Leonid Sabaneyeff. - Saminsky as a symphonist by Josef Yasser. - The man and civic worker by Leon Vallas.

*1598. **SAMINSKY, Lazare**
Encounters stimulating and otherwise.
MM, 9, Nov. 1931, p.38-41.

1599. **SAMINSKY, Lazare**
Music of our day: essentials and prophecies.
New York, Thomas Cromwell Co. 1932. v,3-313p. mus.
Essays on various aspects of modern music. Marred by verbosity, overstatement and misprints, they have been described by Gerald Abraham (*Music and letters,* 2, July 1940, p.296) as not "entirely worthless". Probably the best section is that on conductors. *See also* no. 1611.

*1600. **SAMINSKY, Lazare**
A conductor on modern music.
MM, 9, Mar. 1932, p.138?

*1601. **SAMINSKY, Lazare**
New tonal horizons.
MM, 10, Nov. 1932, p.56-7.

*1602. **SAMINSKY, Lazare**
Europe and America in music today.
MM, 10, Jan. 1933, p.93-5.

1603. **SAMINSKY, Lazare**
Music of the Ghetto and the Bible.
New York, Bloch Publishing Co. 1934. vii,3-261p. mus.
Informative history of Jewish music, distorted by some gross exaggerations.

*1604. **SLONIMSKY, Nicolas**
Lazare Saminsky.
MM, 12, Jan.-Feb. 1935, p.69-72.

*1605. **SAMINSKY, Lazare**
The composer and the critic.
MM, 13, Jan. 1936, p.12-14.

*1606. **SAMINSKY, Lazare**
The work of Roger Sessions.
MM, 13, Jan. 1936, p.40-1.

1607. **FREED, Isadore**
Forum portraits: Saminsky, Josten, Finney.
MM, 14, Nov.-Dec. 1936, p.33-6.
The Forum refers to the Composer's Forum Laboratory of the Works Progress Administration. The article is mainly devoted to Saminsky.

1608. **SAMINSKY, Lazare**
Europe takes fresh bearings.
MM, 15, Nov.-Dec. 1937, p.27-32.
Deals with new European music.

1609. **SAMINSKY, Lazare**
Electric marvels in Pittsburgh.
MM, 15, Mar.-Apr. 1938, p.171-4.
Discusses electronic musical instruments.

1610. **PISK, Paul A.**
Lazare Saminsky.
Ch, 20, Jan.-Feb. 1939, p.74-8.

1611. **BROWN, Ray**
Saminsky revises *Music of our day.*
MM, 17, Oct.-Nov. 1939, p.65-6.
See also no.1599.

1612. **SAMINSKY, Lazare**
In the Argentine.
MM, 18, Nov.-Dec. 1940, p.31-6.
On music in Argentina.

1613. **SAMINSKY, Lazare**
Canadian youth.
MM, 19, Nov.-Dec. 1941, p.21-5. illus.
Young Canadian composers.

1614. **SAMINSKY, Lazare**
Composers of the Pacific.
MM, 20, Nov.-Dec. 1942, p.23-6.

*1615. **SAMINSKY, Lazare**
Living music of the Americas.
New York, Howell, Soskin. 1949. 284p. mus.

1616. **SAMINSKY, Lazare**
From Paris to Glendalough, music of Europe shows stirring contrasts.
MC, 146, 15 Oct. 1952, p.10. illus.

1617. **SAMINSKY, Lazare**
New music of the United States.
Ch, 27, Jan. 1953, p.68-71.

1618. **SAMINSKY, Lazare**
Physics and metaphysics of music and essays on the philosophy of mathematics.
The Hague, Martinus Nijhoff. 1957. 2-151p.
A highly technical and mystical amalgamation. Stimulating, but not easy reading.

1619. **SAMINSKY, Lazare**
Essentials of conducting.
Dobson. 1958. 9-64p. mus.
Informative, despite Saminsky's seeming inability to write good English. There is a selective list of his musical and literary output.

1620. **SAMINSKY, Lazare**
The twilight of chromatization.
Ch, 32, Spring 1958, p.124-5.

*1621. **WEISSER, A.**
On the death of Lazare Saminsky.
American organist, 42, Nov. 1959, p.373.

SCRIABIN, Alexander (1872-1915)

A. *General.*

See no. 534.

*1622. **RUSSIAN composer with a new message.**
Current literature, 42, Feb. 1907, p.182.

1623. **NEWMARCH, Rosa**
Scryabin and contemporary Russian music.
Russian rev., 2, Feb. 1913, p.153-69.

1624. **CLUTSAM, G. H.**
The harmonies of Scriabine.
MT, 54, Mar. 1913, p.156-8. mus.
Includes a tabulation of the colour-scheme for the score of "Prometheus".

1625. **RUNCIMAN, John F.**
Noises, smells and colours.
MQ, 1, Apr. 1915, p.142-61.
Discusses Scriabin's theories about combining the above.

1626. **SHEDLOCK, J. S.**
Alexandre Scriabin. 1871-1915.
MMR, 45, May 1915, p. 153-4.
Scriabin was born on December 25th. 1871 (Old Style).

1627. **EVANS, Edwin**
Scriabin.
FR, 97, June 1915, p.1071-80.

1628. **MONTAGU-NATHAN, M.**
Alexander Skryabin.
MSt, 7, June 1915, p.187-8.

1629. **NEWMARCH, Rosa**
Alexander Scriabin.
MT, 56, June 1915, p.329-30. 1pl.
Gives a list of his principal works.

1630. **SCRIABIN and "color music".**
Rev. of revs., 51, June 1915, p.747-9. illus.

1631. **TIDEBÖHL, Ellen von**
A further note on Alexandre Nikolaewitsch Scriabin.
MMR, 45, June 1915, p.154.

1632. **HULL, A. Eaglefield**
A great Russian tone-poet, Scriabin.
Kegan Paul. 1916. vi-viii, 2-304p. 4pl., mus.
The catalogue of works is arranged in "periods" of creative activity and there are annotated notes on the piano works. Despite many minor inaccuracies, a useful survey.

1633. **MITCHELL, Edward S.**
The psychology of Scriabin: an introductory article for pianists.
MSt, 9 Sept. 1916, p.19-20.

1634. **A REVOLUTIONARY musical genius.**
Rev. of revs., 54, Nov. 1916, p.563-4.

1635. **HULL, A. Eaglefield**
Scriabin's scientific derivation of harmony versus empirical methods.
PMA, 43, 1916-17, p.17-28. mus.
Grove says this article is untrustworthy.

1636. **MONTAGU-NATHAN, M.**
Skryabin.
in MONTAGU-NATHAN. Contemporary Russian composers, p.37-77. illus.

*1637. **ALEXANDER Scriabin, the student.**
Mu, 22, Nov. 1917, p.870.

See no. 1999.

1638. **MITCHELL, Edward S.**
Scriabin.
Musical news, 58, 10 Jan. 1920, p.27.

1639. **A NEW musical sense:** *The Times* discusses Scriabin.
MSt, 12, Mar. 1920, p.325.

1640. **NEWMAN, Ernest**
Scriabin's programmes and markings.
Musician, no.8, Apr. 1920, p.163-4.

1641. **HULL, A. Eaglefield**
Three musical innovators. 2. Alexander Scriabin.
Bookman, 60, Sept, 1921, p.262-4. illus.

1642. **MITCHELL, Edward**
Scriabin for pianists.
MSt, 13, Sept. 1921, p.681-3. mus.

1643. **SCRIABIN – the man and musician.**
Rev. of revs. 64, Dec. 1921, p.657. illus.

1644. **GILMAN, Lawrence**
... A mystical tone-poet.
North American rev., 215, June 1922, p.838-43.

1645. **SWAN, Alfred J.**
Scriabin.
Bodley Head. 1923. 1-119p. bib.
A short general survey, adulatory in tone, biographical and critical in scope, and containing a list of the composer's works.

1646. **HULL, A. Eaglefield**
The vogue of Scriabin.
MO, 47, Apr. 1924, p.702-3.

1647. **ANTCLIFFE, Herbert**
The significance of Scriabin.
MQ, 10, July 1924, p.333-45.
Reprinted *in* MO, 48, Jan. 1925, p.387-9+.
Feb. 1925, p.495-6.

1648. **LATHAM, Peter**
Scriabin.
G, 2, July 1924, p.3-5.

*1649. **SCHLOEZER, Boris de**
Scriabine.
MM, 1, Nov. 1924, p.14-18.

1650. **FOWLES, Ernest**
The value of Scriabin's music.
MTe, 4, June 1925, p.382.

1651. **FENNEY, William**
Scriabine.
MO, 49, Jan. 1926, p.382-3.

*1652. **LAVOIE-HERZ, S..**
Art of Scriabin.
E, 44, May 1926, p.345-6. illus.

1653. **TIDEBÖHL, Ellen von**
Memories of Scriabin's Volga tour (1910).
MMR, 56, May 1926, p.137-8.
June 1926, p.168-9.

1654. **BRENT-SMITH, Alexander**
Some reflections on the work of Scriabin.
1. MT, 67, July 1926, p.593-5
2. Aug. 1926, p.692-4.
The first article discusses the role of colour in Scriabin's music

1655. **SCHLOEZER, Boris de**
Alexander Scriabin. Tr. by Fred Rothwell.
Sackbut, 7, Nov. 1926, p.92-4.

1656. **HULL, Robert H.**
Alexander Scriabin.
FR, 124, Dec. 1928, p.812-21.

1657. **SABANEYEFF, Leonid**
Alyeksandr Skryabin.
in SABANEYEFF. Modern Russian composers, p.40-63.

*1658. **GALPIN, Alfred**
The development of Skryabin's harmonic technique.
M. Mus. thesis, Northwestern University, Illinois. 1930.

1659. **ABRAHAM, G.**
Scriabin reconsidered.
MS, n.i.s., 37, Sept. 1931, p.214-16.

1660. **SABANEEV, Leonid**
Scriabin and the idea of religious art. Tr. by S. W. Pring.
MT, 72, Sept. 1931, p.789-92.

1661. **WHITE, Terence**
Alexander Scriabin.
Ch, 13, July 1932, p.213-17.

*1662. **VODARSKY-SHIRAEFF, Alexandria**
Bibliography of Skryabin.
New York, New York School of Library Service, Columbia University. 1934. 23p.

1663. **HULL, Robert H.**
The orchestral method of Scriabin.
Ch, 16, Sept.-Oct. 1934, p.34-7.

*1664. **COOPER, M.**
Scriabin.
London mercury, 31, Dec. 1934, p.209-10.

1665. **COOPER, Martin**
Scriabin's mystical beliefs.
ML, 16, Mar. 1935, p.110-15.

1666. **ABRAHAM, Gerald**
Alexander Scriabin.
in CALVOCORESSI *and* ABRAHAM. Masters of Russian music, p.450-98. 1pl.

1667. **LYLE, Watson**
Alexander Scriabin, whose curtain descended before "The Act".
MO, 63, Apr. 1940, p.297-8.
Refers to Scriabin's crowning idea, his unfinished work "The Mystery" or "The Act".

*1668. **ROSENFELD, Paul**
Scriabin and his music; a quarter century since his death.
American music lover, 5, Apr. 1940, p.446-50. illus.

1669. **SABANEEV, Leonid**
Scriabin. On the twenty-fifth anniversary of his death.
Tr. by S. W. Pring.
MT, 81, June 1940, p.256-7.

*1670. **MURRAY, W.**
Song of the rainbow; do you see colors when you hear music?
E, 60, May 1942, p.312+.

1671. **POWELL, Lawrence**
Skryabin.
Gramophone record, Mar. 1943, p.2-3+.
Apr. 1943, p.2-3.

1672. **COOPER, Martin**
Alexander Skryabin: 1872-1915.
L, 31, 8 June 1944, p.645.

1673. **BROOK, Donald**
Scriabin.
in BROOK. Six great Russian composers, p.173-93.

1674. **BOELZA, Igor**
Alexander Scriabin.
SL, Feb. 1947, p.62-5. illus.

1675. **MYERS, Rollo**
A Russian musical mystic.
L, 40, 28 Oct. 1948, p.661.

1676. **STANLEY, Louis**
Scriabin in America.
MA, 74, 15 Feb. 1954, p.33+. illus.

1677. **WOOD, Ralph W.**
Skryabin and his critics.
MMR, 86, Nov.-Dec. 1956, p.222-5.
On Gray's essay on Scriabin in Gray's *A survey of contemporary music.* 1924.

1678. **MYERS, Rollo**
Scriabin: a reassessment.
MT, 98, Jan. 1957, p.17-18. illus.

1679. **COOPER, Martin**
Ecstasy for ecstasy's sake.
L, 48, 10 Oct. 1957, p.563. illus.

1680. **GRAY, Bryan**
Russia's musical mystic.
MMu, 8, Nov. 1959, p.17+. illus.

1681. **DALE, Kathleen**
Skryabin: composer, pianist and mystic.
L, 65, 13 Apr. 1961, p.677.

1682. **TRUSCOTT, Harold**
Alexander Scriabin.
Ch, 35, Winter 1961, p.81-9.

1683. **DICKINSON, Peter**
Skryabin's later music.
MR, 26, Feb. 1965, p.19-22. mus., bib.

1684. **LYLE, Wilson**
Alexander Scriabin – innovator of sound and colour.
MO, 88, Apr. 1965, p.401+.

1685. **RICHTER, Sviatoslav**
Richter on Scriabin. [Interview, ed. by Faubion Bowers].
SR, 48, 12 June 1965, p.58-9. illus.

1686. **ASHKENAZY, Vladimir**
Scriabin – musical philosopher.
MMu, 14, Dec. 1965, p.35. illus.

1687. **SABANEEFF, Leonid**
A. N. Scriabin – a memoir.
RR, 25, July 1966, p.257-67.

1688. **BOWERS, Faubion**
Scriabin. A biography of the Russian composer 1871-1915.
Tokyo and Palo Alto, San Francisco, Kodansha. 1969. 2v. 26pl.
The first seventy-four pages, called *Kaleidoscope of Russian music,* seem to be irrelevant, and the main part of the work is a series of snippets of information rather than a cohesive biography. According to the author, Bach was born in 1695, Shostakovitch in 1908, and Beethoven died in 1826 and Liszt in 1876. The discography lists the piano works by performer and not by title and the index is of limited value. A very informative but flawed first full-length English life of Scriabin.

1689. **CAVALLO, Diana** *and* **BOWERS, Faubion**
A 60-year old controversy flares up again.
HF, 19, June 1969, p.54-60+. illus.
On the relations between Koussevitzky and Scriabin, Bowers' part being from his biography.

1690. **GARVELMANN, Donald**
A talk with Faubion Bowers about Scriabin.
Clavier, 8, Nov. 1969, p.21-2+. illus., mus.

1691. **RUBBRA, Edmund**
The resurgence of Scriabin.
L, 83, 26 Feb. 1970, p.289.

1692. **BOWERS, Faubion**
How to play Scriabin.
Piano quarterly, no. 74, Winter 1970-1, p.12-18. mus.

B. *Works.*

Symphonies.

1693. **HULL, A. Eaglefield**
The five symphonies of Scriabin.
MMR, 46, Feb. 1916, p.36.
The "Poème de l'Extase" and "Prometheus" are here counted as nos. 4 and 5 respectively.

Symphony No. 3, The Divine Poem.

1694. **GILMAN, Lawrence**
Mr. Scriabine's "Divine Poem".
Harper's weekly, 51, 30 Mar. 1907, p.474.

Poème de l'Extase.

1695. **GOODWIN, Noel**
Torrent of feeling. Music.
DD, 21, May 1970, p.34+.

Prometheus: the Poem of Fire.

See no. 1624.

1696. **NEWMARCH, Rosa**
"Prometheus": the Poem of Fire.
MT, 55, Apr. 1914, p.227-31. mus.

*1697. **COLOR music: Scriabin's attempt to compose a rainbow symphony.**
Current opinion, 58, May 1915, p.332-3. illus.

1698. **SCRIABIN'S "Prometheus" and its keyboard of light.**
MSt, 7, June 1915, p.196.

1699. **TURNER, W. J.**
Prometheus.
NS, 16, 19 Mar. 1921, p.705.

1700. **NEWMARCH, Rosa**
Scriabin. Prometheus (the Poem of Fire).
CL, 2, p.61-5.
These notes were approved by Scriabin.

1701. **ABRAHAM, Gerald**
The poet of Fire.
L, 76, 18 Aug. 1966, p.252. illus.

Piano works.

1702. **TERRY, R. R.**
Impressions of Scriabin's pianoforte works.
MSt, 7, June 1915, p.193-4.
July 1915, p.221.

1703. **MONTAGU-NATHAN, M.**
Handbook to the piano works of Scriabin.
Chester. 1916. 2-16p. illus., 1pl.
A brief, annotated handbook. Still the best book in English on Scriabin's music.

1704. **HULL, A. Eaglefield**
A survey of the pianoforte works of Scriabin.
MQ, 2, Oct. 1916, p.601-14. mus.

1705. **MONTAGU-NATHAN, M.**
The piano music of Skryabin.
L, 50, 20 Aug. 1953, p.317. mus.

See no. 922.

*1706. **PINNIX, David Clemmons**
Evolution of stylistic elements in selected solo piano works by Scriabin.
D.M.A., Music Lit., thesis, Eastman School of Music, University of Rochester, New York. 1969. 142p. [typescript]. mus., bib.

*1707. **RANDLETT, Samuel L.**
The nature and development of Scriabin's pianistic vocabulary.
DA, 29, June 1969, p.286A.
D. Mus. thesis, Northwestern University, Illinois. 1966. 155p.

*1708. **CHEETHAM, John Everett**
Quasi-serial technique in the late piano works of Alexander Scriabin.
Part 1 of a PhD., mus., thesis, University of Washington. 1969. 105p.

1709. **RANDLETT, Samuel**
Elements of Scriabin's keyboard style.
Piano quarterly, no. 74, Winter 1970-1, p.20-1.

Preludes for piano.

*1710. **HUGHES, Matt Cordell**
Tonal orientation in Skriabin's preludes on the basis of information theory.
Unpublished Master's thesis, University of Texas. 1965.
Reviewed by Michael Kassler *in Current musicology,* no. 3, Spring 1966, p.82-6. Hughes replies *in* no. 5, 1967, p.143-4 and Kassler replies to Hughes *in* p.144-5. mus.

Sonatas for piano.

1711. **HULL, A. Eaglefield**
The pianoforte sonatas of Scriabin.
MT, 57, Nov. 1916, p.492-5. mus.
Dec. 1916, p.539-42. mus.

1712. **MITCHELL, Edward**
The sonatas of Scriabin.
MSt, 14, Oct. 1921, p.13-16. mus.
Nov. 1921, p.69-71. mus.
Dec. 1921, p.123-5. mus.

1713. **COOPER, Martin**
Scriabin and his pianoforte sonatas.
L, 27, 1 Jan. 1942, p.29

1714. **MELLERS, Wilfred**
Skryabin and the piano sonata.
L, 42, 6 Oct. 1949, p.600.

1715. **WEISSMANN, John S.**
Skryabin and his piano sonatas.
L, 46, 26 July 1951, p.156.

*1716. **STEGNER, G.**
Scriabin an experimentator [sic]. The resulting ten piano sonatas.
Chicago, Chicago Musical College. 1954.

1717. **CLUTSAM, G. H.**
More harmonies of Scriabine. (1).
MT, 54, July 1913, p.441-3. mus.
Deals with Sonatas nos. 5 and 6.

1718. **CLUTSAM, G. H.**
More harmonies of Scriabine. (2).
MT, 54, Aug. 1913, p.512-14. mus.
Deals with Sonata no. 7.

*1719. **TALLEY, H.**
Scriabine the inscrutable, or, making the complicated simple.
Clavier, 3, 1964, p.28-31. mus.
Analysis of the Poème fantasque, op. 45, no. 2.

1720. **BOWERS, F.**
Scriabin's opera.
ON, 31, 4 Mar. 1967, p.6-7. illus.
Scriabin worked intermittently on an opera for 4 years, parts being later used in other compositions.

SEROV, Alexander (1820-71)

1721. **NEWMARCH, Rosa**
Serov.
MJIMS, 4, Jan. 1903, p.173-80.

1722. **MONTAGU-NATHAN, M.**
... Seroff and Lvoff.
MS, n.i.s., 1, 21 June 1913, p.546-7.
28 June 1913, p.567-8.

1723. **MONTAGU-NATHAN, M.**
The story of Russian music. 9. Serof.
MSt, 9, May 1917, p.273+. illus.

1724. **RIESEMANN, O. von**
Alexander Seroff and his relations to Wagner and Liszt. Tr. by Theodore Baker.
MQ, 9, Oct. 1923, p.450-68.

1725. **ABRAHAM, Gerald**
Alexander Serof.
in CALVOCORESSI *and* ABRAHAM. Masters of Russian music p.74-96.

1726. **STEINPRESS, Boris**
Alexander Serov, critic and composer.
SL, 12, Jan. 1945, p.75-8. illus.

SHALIAPIN, Feodor (1873-1938)

A. *General.*

1727. **FINCK, Henry T.**
Chaliapine, The Russian "Mephistopheles".
Century, 81, Dec. 1910, p.230-7. illus.

1728. **THE GREATEST actor of our time.**
Literary digest, 49, 22 Aug. 1914, p.308-9. illus.

1729. **MIASNITSKY, Wladislaw**
Shaliapin.
Twentieth century Russia, 2, Oct. 1916, p.43-7.

*1730. **VAN VECHTEN, C.**
... Feodor Chaliapine.
Bellman, 22, 21 Apr. 1917, p.413-4. illus.

1731. **EVANS, Edwin**
Chaliapine.
Musical news, 61, 8 Oct. 1921, p.354-5.

1732. **KLEIN Herman**
The art of Chaliapin.
MT, 62, Nov. 1921, p.785-6.

*1733. **BAUGHAN, B. A.**
The art of Chaliapin.
LLA, 311, 31 Dec. 1921, p.24-5.

*1734. **CHALIAPIN, premier actor of the operatic stage.**
Current opinion, 72, Jan. 1922, p.66-9. illus.

*1735. **LYLE, W.**
Chaliapin. A personal sketch.
Musical news, 63, 7 Oct. 1922, p.310.

*1736. **INTERVIEWING Chaliapin.**
LLA, 315, 28 Oct. 1922, p.244-5.

*1737. **CHALIAPIN discusses himself.**
LLA, 318, 11 Aug. 1923, p.285-6.

1738. **NADEJIN, Nicolai**
Gramophone celebrities. 5. Fyodor Ivanovitch Chaliapin.
G, 2, Aug. 1924, p.83-5.

1739. **CHALIAPIN, Feodor**
Roles.
Ladies' home journal, 41, Oct. 1924, p.10+. illus., mus.
Nov. 1924, p.14+. illus.
42, Mar. 1925, p.28+. illus.
Apr. 1925, p.29+. illus.
May 1925, p.31+. illus.

*1740. **HENDERSON, W. J.**
Chaliapin, superman of song.
Mentor, 14, Feb. 1926, p.54-5. illus.

*1741. **DON Quixote comes to life in Chaliapin.**
Literary digest, 89, 1 May 1926, p.26-7.

1742. **WORTHAM, H. E.**
... Chaliapine's astral methods.
Apollo, 4, Aug. 1926, p.43.
On Shaliapin in Boito's "Mefistofele".

*1743. **[CHALIAPINE, Feodor]**
Pages from my life.
LLA, 331, 1 Nov. 1926, p.265-8.
See also no. 1744.

1744. **CHALIAPINE, Feodor Ivanovitch**
Pages from my life. An autobiography. Authorized translation by H. M. Buck. Rev., enlarged and ed. by Katharine Wright.
Harper, 1927. 1-345p. 18pl.
Chatty reminiscences and anecdotes covering the period up to the mid-twenties. There is a paucity of dates and no index.
See also nos. 1743 and 1771.

1745. **KENNEDY, John B.**
Against the wind.
Colliers, 79, 30 Apr. 1927, p.14+. illus.
Interview with Shaliapin.

1746. **CAN Chaliapin be degraded?**
Literary digest, 94, 10 Sept. 1927, p.28.
Deals with Shaliapin being deprived of the title of "National People's Artist".

1747. **CHALIAPIN, Feodor**
The Russian opera.
Saturday rev., 151, 20 June 1931, p.894.

1748. **CHALIAPIN, Feodor**
Man and mask. Forty years in the life of a singer. Tr. by Phyllis Megroz.
Gollancz. 1932. 6-413p. 16pl.
This volume of anecdotes, companion to the *Autobiography* and *Pages from my life,* only covers the period up to about 1920. There is a detailed contents list but no index. Some chapters in a different translation appear in the Chaliapin/Gorky autobiography (ed. Froud and Hanley), no. 1771.

1749. **WALTERS, H. L.**
Genius by destiny – Feodor Chaliapin.
Music lover, 1, 30, July 1932, p.1-2.

1750. **CHALIAPIN, Feodor**
Life behind art: a romantic in the making.
Bookman, 84, July 1933, p.186-7. illus.
Describes his early days.

1751. **MEADMORE, W. S.**
Feodor Ivanovitch Chaliapin (in an interview).
G, 11, Sept. 1933, p.135-7.

*1752. **CHALIAPIN, Feodor I.**
My friend Gorki.
LLA, 351, Sept. 1936, p.42-5.
The same article is abridged in *Current history,* 44, Sept. 1936, p.107-9, the title being *Shaliapin's eulogy of Gorky.*

1753. **HUSSEY, Dyneley**
Feodor Chaliapin.
Sp, 160, 22 Apr. 1938, p.706.

1754. **GAISBERG, F. W.**
Chaliapin as I knew him.
G, 15, May 1938, p.507-9. illus.

1755. **MCNAUGHT, W.**
Chaliapin.
MT, 79, May 1938, p.380-1. illus.

1756. **LA MAIN GAUCHE,** *pseud.*
... Chaliapin.
MO, 61, May 1938, p.683.

1757. **NADEJINE, Nicholas**
Chaliapin (In memoriam, 1873-1938).
G, 15, May 1938, p.509-10.

1758. **NEWMARCH, Rosa**
Obituary. Fedor Shalyapin.
Slavonic rev., 17, July 1938, p.209-11.

1759. **SEMEONOFF, Boris**
Feodor Chaliapine.
Record collector, 5, June 1950, p.125-41. illus., disc.
The discography is arranged in approximately chronological order (1901-36) and there is a separate sequence by composer.

1760. **BERNSTEIN, Hillel**
White hope of 102nd Street.
New Yorker, 26, 14 Oct. 1950, p.56+.

*1761. **CHALIAPINA, Irina**
Chaliapin and the Volga boatmen.
River transport, 20 Mar. 1951, p.?

1762. **SEMEONOFF, B.**
Chaliapine: a postscript.
Record collector, 6, Aug. 1951, p.189-90.

1763. **MONTAGU-NATHAN, M.**
Shalyapin in caricature.
O, 3, Feb. 1952, p.87-90. illus.

1764. **MONTAGU-NATHAN, M.**
Shaliapin's precursors.
ML, 33, July 1952, p.232-8.
On Russian opera singers, including Shaliapin.

*1765. **FAVIA-ARTSAY, A.**
Chaliapin.
Hobbies, 58, Apr. 1953, p.31-2.

1766. **HARVEY, Hugh H.**
Feodor Chaliapine.
G, 33, Jan. 1956, p.308-9. illus.

1767. **ILYIN, Eugen**
Chaliapin and Don Quixote.
MMu, 6, Jan. 1958, p.11. illus.

1768. **FORESTA, Genia**
Son of Russia.
ON, 23, 16 Mar. 1959, p.4-7+. illus.

1769. **NEWTON, Ivor**
Chaliapine as I knew him.
MT, 101, Feb. 1960, p.82-3. illus.

1770. **HOPKINSON, Cecil**
Diaghilev, Chaliapine and their contracts.
MR, 25, May 1964, p.149-53.
Contracts for 1909 and 1913.

See no. 994.

1771. **CHALIAPIN, Feodor Ivanovitch**
Chaliapin. An autobiography as told to Maxim Gorky. With supplementary correspondence and notes, tr. from the Russian, comp. and ed. by Nina Froud and James Hanley.
Macdonald. 1967. 7-320p. 59pl., bib.
A new version of Chaliapin's *Pages from my life* (no. 1744). The narration and the appendix listing the singer's 63 operatic roles stop at 1914. The last third of the book consists of letters (up to about 1930), notes and reminiscences by other people, and the appendices include some chapters of *Man and mask.* The outstanding illustrations do not compensate for the shoddy and romanticised translation and for the inaccuracies. *See also* no. 1748.

1772. **FROUD, Nina *and* HANLEY, James**
A visit to Tolstoy with Sergei Rachmaninov.
in CHALIAPIN. An autobiography as told to Maxim Gorky, p.277-9.

1773. **[STASSOV, Vladimir]**
Vladimir Stassov on Chaliapin.
in CHALIAPIN. An autobiography as told to Maxim Gorky, p.282-4.

1774. **CHALIAPIN, Marina**
I remember father.
HF, 17, June 1967, p.MA4-5.

SHAPORIN, Yuri (1887-)

A. *General.*

1775. **MOISENCO, Rena**
Yuri Shaporin.
in MOISENCO. Twenty Soviet composers, p.55-6.

1776. **ABRAHAM, G.**
Yury Shaporin.
MMR, 72, Sept. 1942, p.148-54.
Also *in* ABRAHAM. Eight Soviet composers, p.89-98. mus.

1777. **MOISENKO, Rena**
Yuri Shaporin.
in MOISENKO. Realist music, p.188-99. 1pl., mus.

1778. **SHAPORIN, Y.**
We shall defend peace.
SL, Oct. 1950, p.157.

*1779. **SHAPORIN, Y.**
Shaping a creative personality.
MJ, 27, Mar. 1969, p.34+.

1780. **KREBS, Stanley D.**
Jurii Shaporin.
in KREBS. Soviet composers and the development of Soviet music, p.168-84. mus.

B. *Works.*

Symphony in C minor.

1781. **CHEMODANOV, S.**
Yuri Shaporin and his symphony.
MMR, 65, Jan. 1935, p.11-12. mus.
Chemodanov says the work is op.11 in E minor, but it is very probably the Symphony in C minor.

1782. **HUSSEY, Dyneley**
... News from Russia.
Sp, 154, 1 Feb. 1935, p.163.
On Shaporin's Symphony in C minor and Shostakovitch's Symphony no. 1.

The Flea.

See no. 1862.

On the Field of Kulikovo.

1783. **CLARK, Edward**
Shaporin and his "Kulikovo".
L, 34, 1 Nov. 1945, p.505.
The symphony-cantata, op. 14.

The Story of the Battle for the Russian Land.

1784. **BOELZA, Igor**
A new Russian oratorio.
SL, 11, July 1944, p.70-2. illus.

SHCHEDRIN, Rodion (1932-)

1785. **VISIT** by Rodion Shchedrin.
C, 12, Autumn 1963, p.27-8. illus.

*1786. **LAGINA, N.**
Audacious composer.
Soviet life, no. 7, July 1966, p.14-15. illus.

1787. **KREBS, Stanley D.**
Rodion Shchedrin.
in KREBS. Soviet composers and the development of Soviet music, p.281-9. mus.

SHEBALIN, Vissarion (1902-63)

A. *General.*

1788. **ABRAHAM, G.**
Vissarion Shebalin.
MMR, 72, June 1942, p.99-104.
Also *in* ABRAHAM. Eight Soviet composers, p.61-78. mus.

1789. **BOELZA, Igor**
Vissarion Shebalin.
SL, June 1945, p.76-7.

1790. **KREBS, Stanley D.**
Vissarion Shebalin.
in KREBS. Soviet composers and the development of Soviet music, p.205-16. mus.

B. *Works.*

1791. **BOELZA, Igor**
Shebalin's overture, Glière's concerto.
MM, 20, Mar.-Apr. 1943, p.187-9. mus.
Shebalin's "Russian Overture" and Glière's "Concerto for Soprano."

SHOSTAKOVITCH, Dmitri (1906-75)

A. *General.*

1792. **EWEN, David**
Dmitri Shostakovich.
MT, 76, Oct. 1935, p.890-2.

1793. **FLETCHER, Stuart**
A Soviet composer faces the music.
Millgate, 31, May 1936, p,430-2. illus.

1794. **LA MAIN GAUCHE,** *pseud.*
... Dimitri Shostakovich.
MO, 59, May 1936, p,665-6.

1795. **CALVOCORESSI, M. D.**
A Soviet composer.
L, 17, 26 May 1937, p.1058.

1796. **SHOSTAKOVICH, Dmitri**
From a composer's notebook.
SL, Apr.-May 1939, p.195-8. illus.

1797. **CALVOCORESSI, M. D.**
A modern Russian master.
L, 26, 28 Aug. 1941, p.317.

1798. **BAYLISS, Stanley**
Dmitri Shostakovitch.
Choir, 32, Oct. 1941, p.154-5.

1799. **MOISENCO, Rena**
Dmitri Shostakovich.
in MOISENCO. Twenty Soviet composers, p.56-8.

1800. **ABRAHAM, Gerald**
Shostakovich: a study of music and politics.
Horizon, 6, Sept, 1942, p.196-210.

1801. **SLONIMSKY, Nicolas**
Dmitri Dmitrievitch Shostakovitch.
MQ, 28, Oct. 1942, p.415-44. 4pl., mus.
The list of works is the one by Shostakovitch used in Seroff's biography, no. 1804.

1802. **SEROFF, Victor I.**
Boy who didn't like music.
Collier's, 110, 3 Oct. 1942, p.44-5+. illus., mus.

1803. **ABRAHAM, Gerald**
Dmitry Shostakovitch.
in ABRAHAM. Eight Soviet composers, p.13-31.

1804. **SEROFF, Victor**
Dmitri Shostakovich. The life and background of a Soviet composer.
New York, Knopf. 1943. vii-x, 3-260, i-viip. illus., 8pl.
Written in collaboration with the composer's aunt, it includes a list of works (to op. 59) compiled by Shostakovitch for an article by Slominsky in *Musical quarterly,* no. 1801.

1805. **NABOKOV, Nicolas**
The case of Dmitri Shostakovitch.
Harper's mag., 186, Mar. 1943, p.422-31.

1806. **EVANS, Edwin**
Shostakovich: a dual personality.
L, 29, 4 Mar. 1943, p.281.
The duality refers to the half which incurred drastic criticism and the other half which never fell from grace.

*1807. **GEHRKENS, K. W.**
Is Shostakovich a satirist?
E, 63, Dec. 1945, p.686.

1808. **MARTYNOV, Ivan**
Dmitri Shostakovich. The man and his work. Tr. from the Russian by T. Guralsky.
New York, Philosophical Library. 1947. 1-197p. mus.
Martynov says the book was written in 1942, the manuscript having been reviewed by Shostakovitch, but the catalogue of compositions ends at op. 70 (1945). Despite its verbose style, a most valuable work until superseded by Rabinovich's biography.
See also no. 1844.

1809. **MOISENKO, Rena**
Dmitri Shostakovich.
in MOISENKO. Realist music, p.200-14. mus.

*1810. **SHOSTAKOVICH: real or formal music.**
Symphony, 2, Apr. 1949, p.5.

*1811. **MARX, H.**
Shostakovitch in New York.
Music news, 41, May 1949, p.4-5+.

1812. **SHOSTAKOVICH, D.**
Inestimable assistance.
SL, Apr. 1950, p.137.
Paean to Stalin.

1813. **SHOSTAKOVICH, D.**
Voices of America.
News, no.1, 15 July 1951, p.13-15. illus.
On the desire for peace in Korea.

1814. **SHOSTAKOVICH, Dmitri**
The duty of cultural workers.
News, no. 53, 15 Sept. 1953, p.4. illus.

1815. **KABALEVSKY, Dmitry**
A composer who fights for peace.
News, 14, 16 July 1954, p.17-18. illus.

1816. **SHOSTAKOVICH, D.**
The joy of seeking new ways.
SCR, 1, Aug. 1954, p.5-7.

1817. **SHOSTAKOVICH, Dmitry**
Music - a bond between nations and continents.
News, 23, 1 Dec. 1954, p.23-5.

1818. **RAYMENT, M.**
Shostakovitch.
LME, 10, Apr. 1955, p.22-4. illus.

1819. **SHOSTAKOVICH, Dmitri**
Music for children's concerts.
SCR, 2, Sept. 1955, p.10-13.

1820. **SHOSTAKOVICH, Dmitry**
Music a universal language.
News, 3, 1 Feb. 1956, p.23-5. illus.

1821. **SHOSTAKOVICH, Dmitri**
Chaikovsky Contest.
SL, Feb. 1957, p.153-4. illus.

1822. **GORODINSKY, Victor**
Dmitri Shostakovich.
SL, May 1957, p.132-9.

*1823. **At home with the Shostakovitchs.**
High-fi music at home, 8, Mar. 1958, p.42-3. illus.

1824. **RABINOVICH, David**
Dmitry Shostakovich. Tr. from the Russian by George Hanna.
Lawrence and Wishart. 1959. 3-166p. 15pl.
Written by a friend of the composer, the book is informative but rather brief, and lacks an index, bibliography and list of works.

1825. **SHOSTAKOVICH, Dmitri**
The artist of our times.
ASJ, 21, Winter 1960, p.3-6.

*1826. **SHOSTAKOVICH, D.**
Bourgeois culture is bankrupt.
MJ, 20, Jan. 1962, p.32-3+.

*1827. **SHOSTAKOVICH, D.**
Today's songs are vulgar!
MJ, 20, Mar. 1962, p.34-5+.

*1828. **SHOSTAKOVICH, D.**
Great fête of music.
Music and dance, 52, Apr. 1962, p.9+.

1829. **ANGLES, Robert**
The music of Shostakovich - a Western view.
MMu, 11, Sept. 1962, p.25. illus.

1830. **POPOV, Innokenty**
The music of Shostakovich - a Russian view.
MMu, 11, Sept. 1962, p.26-7. illus.

1831. **SHOSTAKOVICH, Dmitri**
Art must reflect reality!
MJ, 20, Sept. 1962, p.20-1+.

*1832. **TIOMKIN, D.**
In response to Shostakovich.
MJ, 21 Nov. 1963, p.29.

*1833. **SHOSTAKOVICH, D** *and* **VINOGRADOV, V.**
Signs of the times and the destinies of music.
MJ, 22, Jan. 1964, p.24+.

*1834. **SHOSTAKOVICH, D.** *and* **VINOGRADOV, V.**
Dodecaphony shatters creativity.
MJ, 22, Mar. 1964, p.46+.

1835. **SHOSTAKOVICH at press conference.**
LME, 19, May 1964, p.8-10.

*1836. **HEYWORTH, Peter**
Shostakovich without ideology.
HF, 14, Oct. 1964, p.96-100+. illus.

1837. **SHOSTAKOVICH, Dimitry**
Music and life.
LME, 19, Nov. 1964, p.8-9. illus.

*1838. **SHOSTAKOVICH, D.**
Music and the times.
MJ, 23, Jan. 1965, p.33+.

1839. **KAY, Norman**
The art of Shostakovich,
MMu, 13, Apr. 1965, p.20-3. illus, mus.

*1840. **SHOSTAKOVICH, D.**
The power of music.
MJ, 23, Sept. 1965, p.37+.

*1841. **[SHOSTAKOVICH, Dmitri]**
An open letter from Dmitri Shostakovich.
MJ, 23, Nov. 1965, p.31+.
On the International Tchaikovsky Contest.

See no. 2307.

*1842. **SHOSTAKOVICH, D.** *and* **VINOGRADOV, V.**
"Modernists" are anti-social acrobats.
MJ, 24, Mar. 1966, p.55+.

1843. **ASAFYEV, Boris**
A rare talent.
in LIPOVSKY. Lenin Prize winners, p.44-51. illus.

1844. **MARTYNOV, Ivan**
The majesty of sound and thought.
in LIPOVSKY. Lenin Prize winners, p.52-79.
Excerpts from Martynov's book, no.1808.

*1845. **KABALEVSKY, Dmitri**
A Soviet salute to Shostakovich.
MJ, 25, Mar. 1967, p.30-1+.

*1846. **SHOSTAKOVICH, D.**
A great artist of our time.
UU, Oct. 1968, p.9-10.
Tribute to David Oistrakh.

*1847. **LONGAZO, George**
The bassoon: its use in selected works of Shostakovich, Stravinsky and Schoenberg.
DA, 30, Dec. 1969, p.2561A-2A.
Thesis, University of Southern California. 1969. 278p.

1848. **KREBS, Stanley D.**
Dmitri Shostakovich.
in KREBS. Soviet composers and the development of Soviet music, p.185-204.

*1849. **SHOSTAKOVICH, D.**
Opera: music is all.
MJ, 28, Mar. 1970, p.35+.

*1850. **SHOSTAKOVICH, D.** *, and others.*
Lenin Prize winners speak.
UU, Apr. 1970, p.3.

1850a. **KAY, Norman**
Shostakovich.
O.U.P. 1971. 7-80p. mus.
One of the *Oxford studies of composers,* this is entirely devoted to the music. "A number of key works... have been chosen for discussion" (Introduction). There is a chronological list of

principal works (with dates) covering 1922-69, but no index. Not for the beginner.

B. *Works.*

Symphonies.

1851. **DIAMANT, A.**
The Shostakovitch symphonies.
G, 20, Feb. 1943, p.133.

1852. **LLOYD-JONES, David**
Shostakovich and the symphony.
L, 64, 15 Sept. 1960, p.445.

1853. **ABRAHAM, Gerald**
The worlds of Dmitry Shostakovich.
L, 68, 19 July 1962, p.115.

1854. **RAYMENT, Malcolm**
Shostakovitch the symphonist.
LME, 17, Nov. 1962, p.23.

1855. **SEAMAN, Gerald**
The symphonies of Shostakovich.
L, 70, 18 July 1963, p.108.

1856. **LAYTON, Robert**
Shostakovich and the symphony.
Making music, no, 62, Autumn 1966, p.10-12. illus.

1857. **BOBROWSKY, Victor**
The Shostakovich symphonies.
SL, Oct. 1966, p. 159-65.
Covers Symphonies 1-13.

1858. **BROWN, Royal S.**
Shostakovich's symphonies. An appraisal of the music and the recordings.
HF/MA, 19, Apr. 1969, p.43-7+. illus., disc.
Nos. 1-13.

1859. **OSBORNE, Charles**
Shostakovich: opera and symphony.
London mag., 3, Feb. 1964, p.72-7.
Mostly devoted to Symphonies 1-11, but with a small section on "Lady Macbeth".

1860. **HERBAGE, Julian**
The symphonies of Shostakovich.
L, 34, 19 Sept. 1945, p.305.
Discusses nos. 1-8.

1861. **BUSH, Alan**
Shostakovich and his symphonies.
L, 27, 4 June 1942, p.733.
Deals with nos. 1-7, with emphasis on no. 5.

Symphony no.1.

1862. **CALVOCORESSI, M. D.**
From my notebook.
MO, 58, May 1935, p.678-9.
There is also a section on Shaporin's "The Flea".

Symphony no.2.

1863. **LAWSON, Peter**
Shostakovich's Second Symphony.
T, 91, Winter 1969-70, p.14-17. mus.

Symphony no.3.

1864. **CALVOCORESSI, M. D.**
"The First of May".
L, 15, 19 Feb. 1936, p.373.

1865. **HUSSEY, Dyneley**
... The Communist symphony.
Sp, 156, 6 Mar. 1936, p. 396.

Symphony no.4.

1866. **LEONARD, Richard Anthony**
Case of the missing bridge.
Hi-fi and music rev., 1, Aug. 1958, p.23-5+. illus.
This symphony is here considered the bridge between early and later styles and was first performed only in 1961.

1867. **HALL, D.**
The not altogether lost bridge.
Hi-fi and music rev., 1, Oct. 1958, p.33.

1868. **MARTYNOV, Ivan**
Shostakovich's Fourth Symphony.
LME, 17, Sept. 1962, p.6-7+. illus.

See no. 1123.

1869. **BURN, John**
Shostakovich's Fourth Symphony.
C, 13, Spring 1964, p.19-21. mus.

1870. **SOUSTER, Tim**
Shostakovich at the crossroads.
T, 78, Autumn 1966, p.2-9. mus.
On Symphonies 4 and 5.

Symphony no.5.

1871. **SCHNEERSON, Grigori**
Shostakovitch rehabilitated.
MM, 15, Mar.-Apr. 1938, p.174-6.

See no. 1870.

Symphonies nos. 7-9.

1872. **GOW, David**
Shostakovich's "War" symphonies.
MT, 105, Mar. 1964, p.191-3. mus.

Symphony no.7.

*1873. **RABINOVICH, D.** *and* **SHLIFSTEIN, S.**
Shostakovich pens victory symphony during darkest hour.
Mu, 47, Apr. 1942, p.55+.

1874. **OISTRAKH, David**
A symphony of the great struggle.
ASJ, 3, July-Sept. 1942, p.180-1.

1875. **YAROSLAVSKY, Emelyan**
Shostakovich's Seventh Symphony.
ASJ, 3, July-Sept. 1942, p.177-9. illus.

1876. **NABOKOV, Nicolas**
Shostakovitch's Seventh.
NR, 107, 3 Aug. 1942, p.144.

1877. **HAGGIN, B. H.**
Music.
Na, 155, 15 Aug. 1942, p.138.

*1878. **HOVANESS, A.**
Shostakovitch and his Seventh Symphony.
Mu, 47, Sept. 1942, p.133.

*1879. **DE GRAZIA, Sebastian**
Shostakovich's Seventh Symphony: reactivity-speed and adaptiveness in musical symbols.
Psychiatry, 6, May 1943, p.117-22. illus.

1880. **OTTAWAY, Hugh**
Shostakovich's "Fascist" theme.
MT, 111, Mar. 1970, p.274.

Symphony no.8.

1881. **SHOSTAKOVICH sells symphony for $10,000.**
Life, 15, 22 Nov. 1943, p.43-4+. illus.
The title refers to the right to broadcast the first performance. The article consists almost entirely of photographs.

1882. **HERBAGE, Julian**
Shostakovich's Eighth Symphony.
MT, July 1944, p.201-3. mus.

Symphony no.9.

1883. **ZHITOMIRSKY, Daniel**
Dmitri Shostakovich's Ninth Symphony.
[Soviet] music chronicle, no. 9, Sept. 1945, p.1-4. mus.

1884. **SARKISIAN, Onik**
Audition of Shostakovich's new Symphony.
[Soviet] music chronicle, no. 10, Oct. 1945, p.13-15.

1885. **RABINOVICH, David**
The Ninth Symphony and its place among the works of Dmitri Shostakovich.
SL, 6, June 1946, p.66-71. illus.

Symphony no.10.

1886. **SHOSTAKOVICH'S Tenth Symphony.**
SCR, 1, Aug. 1954, p.12-16.

1887. **OISTRAKH, David**
Shostakovich's 10th Symphony.
SCR, 1, Oct. 1954, p.1-2.

1888. **SOKOLSKY, M.**
A new interpretation of Shostakovich's Tenth Symphony.
SCR, 2, May 1955, p.1-3.

1889. **OTTAWAY, Hugh**
Shostakovich's Tenth Symphony.
MT, 97, July 1956, p.350-2. mus.

1890. **OTTAWAY, Hugh**
Shostakovich: some later works.
T, 50, Winter 1958, p.2-14. illus.
Mostly on Symphonies 10 and 11, Piano Concerto no.2 and Violin Concerto no.1.

Symphony no.11.

1891. **MASON, Colin**
Shostakovich's new symphony.
Sp, 200, 31 Jan. 1958, p.135.

See no. 1890.

1892. **MATTHEWS, David**
Shostakovich's Eleventh Symphony.
L, 75, 24 Mar. 1966, p.448. illus.

Symphony no.12.

1893. **BOGDANOV-BEREZOVSKY, Valerian**
New Shostakovitch symphony.
MMu, 10, Nov. 1961, p.19. illus.

1894. **SEAMAN, Gerald**
Shostakovich's Twelfth.
LME, 17, Jan. 1962, p.9-10.

1895. **MARTYNOV, Ivan**
Shostakovich's Twelfth Symphony. Tr. by Maya Birman.
SL, Feb. 1962, p.149-52.

*1896. **VERSHININA, I.**
Dmitri Shostakovich and his Twelfth Symphony.
U.S.S.R. illus. monthly, no.2, Feb. 1962, p.38-41. illus.

Symphony no. 13.

*1897. **WOLINS, Leroy**
Shostakovich and Babii Yar.
Jewish currents, Sept. 1964, p.20-4.

Symphony no.14.

1898. **KAY, Norman**
Shostakovich's Fourteenth Symphony.
T, 92, Spring 1970, p.20-1. mus.

1899. **MARTYNOV, Ivan**
A new symphony by Dmitri Shostakovich.
SL, Apr. 1970, p.158-62.

1900. **LAYTON, Robert**
Shostakovich's new symphony.
L, 83, 11 June 1970, p.802-3.

The Golden Age.

'1901. **MAIER, G.**
Polka; a master lesson.
E, 68, Sept. 1950, p.26-8. mus.

Concerto for piano no.1.

1902. **CALVOCORESSI, M. D.**
Shostakovitch: Concerto no.1.
L, 14, 24 Dec. 1935, p.1184.

Concerto for piano no.2.

See no. 1890.

1903. **GOODWIN, Noel**
Concerto. Music.
DD, 18, July 1967, p.16-17. illus.

Concerto for violin no.1.

1904. **SABINA, M.**
New Shostakovich violin concerto.
SCR, 3, Mar. 1956, p.9-10.

See no. 1890.

Concerto for violin no.2.

1905. **KAY, Norman**
Shostakovich's Second Violin Concerto.
T, 83, Winter 1967-8, p.21-3. mus.

1906. **ORGA, Ates**
Shostakovich's new concerto.
MMu, 16, Jan. 1968, p.23-5+. illus., mus.

Concerto for 'cello no.1.

1907. **POPOV, Innokenti**
Violoncello concerto of Dmitri Shostakovich. Tr. by Jacob Guralsky.
SL, Apr. 1960, p.169-72.

Chamber music.

1908. **SEAMAN, Gerald**
The chamber music of Shostakovich.
L, 68, 30 Aug. 1962, p.332.

Pieces for string octet.

1909. **SLONIMSKY, Nicolas**
Shostakovich. Two Pieces for string octet.
in SLONIMSKY. Programme notes: 1947-1948, p.9-10.

Quartets.

1910. **MASON, Colin**
Shostakovich and the string quartet.
L, 62, 23 July 1959, p.152.

1911. **OTTAWAY, Hugh**
Shostakovich and the string quartet.
L, 76, 17 Nov. 1966, p.746. illus.

*1912. **WALSH, S.**
D-S-C-H and his string quartets.
MMu, 17, Sept. 1968, p.18.

1913. **O'LOUGHLIN, Niall**
Shostakovich's string quartets.
T, 87, Winter 1968-9, p.9-16. mus.
Discusses quartets nos. 1-11.

1914. **MASON, Colin**
Form in Shostakovich's quartets.
MT, 103, Aug. 1962, p.531-3. mus.
Includes a table of the (first 8) quartets.

Quartet for strings no.8.

1915. **KELDYSH, Yury**
An autobiographical quartet. Tr. by Alan Lumsden.
MT, 102, Apr. 1961, p.226-8. mus.

Quartet for strings no. 9.

1916. **MARTYNOV, Ivan**
New quartettes by Shostakovich.
SL, Apr. 1965, p.159-62.
Includes discussion of no. 10.

1917. **HOPKINS, G. W.**
Shostakovich's ninth string quartet.
T, 75, Winter 1965-6, p.23-5.

Quartet for strings no.10.

See no. 1916.

Quartet for strings no. 12.

*1918. **A NEW work by Dmitri Shostakovich.**
UU, July-Aug. 1968, p.4-5.

1919. **KELLER, Hans**
Shostakovich's twelfth quartet.
T, 94, Autumn 1970, p.6-15. mus.

1920. **KELLER, Hans**
Shostakovich discovers Schoenberg.
L, 84, 8 Oct. 1970, p.494. mus.

Quintet for piano.

1921. **[MARTYNOV, I.]**
A Russian critic on Shostakovich's Quintet.
MT, 82, Nov. 1941, p.395-6, mus.
An abridged translation by M. D. Calvocoressi of an article which appeared in *Sovietskaya Muzyka* in January 1941.

Fantastic Dances for piano.

1922. **BRYANT, Celia**
The music lesson.
Clavier, 8, Oct. 1969, p.24-8. mus.
Only deals with the first of the 3 dances. The opus number has been variously given as op. 5 or op.1.

Romances to Words of Alexander Blok.

1923. **WALSH, Stephen**
Shostakovich's "Seven Romances".
T, 85, Summer 1968, p.27-8. mus.

Katerina Ismailova, opera – *see Lady Macbeth of Mtzensk.*

Lady Macbeth of Mtzensk.

*1924. **SHOSTAKOVITCH, Dmitri Dmitrievich**
My opera, "Lady Macbeth of Mtzensk".
MM, 12, Nov. 1934, p.23-30.

1925. **ABRAHAM, Gerald**
Shostakovich's "Lady Macbeth of Mtsensk".
MMR, 65, July-Aug. 1935, p.121-3. mus.

1926. **CALVOCORESSI, M. D.**
From my notebook.
MO, 59, May 1936, p.670.

1927. **CHAOS instead of music.**
SL, June 1936, p.77-9.

1928. **SHUMSKAYA, Natalia**
Shostakovich's "Katerina Izmailova" Tr. by Hilda Perham.
SL, June 1963, p.167-72. illus.

1929. **COOPER, Martin**
Introduction to "Katerina Ismailova".
O, 14, Dec. 1963, p.794-7. illus.

1930. **DOWNES, Edward**
The opera that very nearly wasn't.
Music mag., no. 4, Dec. 1963, p.4-6. illus.

1931. **PORTER, Andrew**
Lady Macbeth of Mtsensk.
MT, 104, Dec. 1963, p.858-60. illus.

1932. **NOBLE, Jeremy**
Shostakovich's "Katerina Ismailova".
L, 70, 12 Dec, 1963, p.1005.

1933. **SHOSTAKOVICH, Dimitry**
About my opera Katerina Ismailova.
About the house, 1, Christmas 1963, p.18-21. illus.

See no. 1859.

*1934. **BUCHAU, S. von**
Music: Katerina Ismailova.
Contact, 5?, Feb.-Mar. 1965, p.76-8.

Moscow Cheryemushki.

1935. **SHNEYERSON, Grigori**
Shostakovitch turns to operetta in waltz-time.
MMu, 7, Mar. 1959, p.16-17. illus.

The Nose.

See no. 844.

1936. **DREW, David**
The Nose.
NS, 67, 12 June 1964, p.922-3.

SKRYABIN – *see* **SCRIABIN**

SLONIMSKY, Nicolas (1894-)

*1937. **SLONIMSKY, Nicolas**
Composers of New England.
MM, 7, Feb. 1930. p.24-7.

1938. **SLONIMSKY, Nicolas**
Absolute pitch.
American mercury, 21, Oct. 1930, p.244-7.

*1939. **SLONIMSKY, Nicolas**
Why modern music is modern. Ed. by L. R. Copp.
E, 49, June 1931, p.395-6.

*1940. **SLONIMSKY, Nicolas**
The gaiety and sadness of Harris.
MM, 10, Mar. 1933, p.162-3.
Roy Harris, American composer.

*1941. **SLONIMSKY, Nicolas**
Russia revisited.
MM, 13, Nov. 1935, p.20-5.

1942. **SLONIMSKY, Nicolas**
Music since 1900.
Dent. 1938. vii-xxii, 3-592p.
The descriptive chronology of musical events was extended in the third edition (1949) from 1937 to 1948, and the fourth edition (Cassell, 1972) brings the work up to 1970. Each edition also contains the text of important letters and documents. The concise biographical dictionary ot twentieth century musicians (1938) and the tabular view of stylistic trends in music (1949) were replaced in the 1595 page revision of 1972 by a dictionary of terms, including some of Slonimsky's own invention. Well-indexed, accurate and shrewdly presented by an emminent lexicographer, it is a mine of information and has become something of a standard work.

1943. **SLONIMSKY, Nicolas**
The plurality of melodic and harmonic systems.
PAMS, 1938, p.16-24. illus.

1944. **SLONIMSKY, Nicolas**
Caturla of Cuba.
MM, 17, Jan.-Feb. 1940, p.76-80. illus.
Alejandro Caturla, Cuban composer.

1945. **SLONIMSKY, Nicolas**
Composers of Peru.
MM, 18, Mar.-Apr. 1941, p.155-8. illus., mus.

1946. **SLONIMSKY, Nicolas**
Music of Latin America.
New York, Thomas Crowell. 1945. 1-374p. 16pl., mus.
The main section deals with the twenty republics in turn (alphabetically), and there is a dictionary of Latin American musicians, songs and dances, and musical instruments. Gilbert Chase, author of a book on the subject, calls part one of the book "a bureau of general misinformation" *(Musical quarterly,* 32, Jan. 1946, p.141).

*1947. **SLONIMSKY,Nicolas**
The road to music.
New York, Dodd, Mead and Co. 1947. ix, 178p. illus., mus.
The result of a series of articles on the children's page of *Christian Science monitor.* It was revised in 1960 and reprinted in 1970.

1948. **SLONIMSKY, Nicolas**
Thesaurus of scales and melodic patterns.
New York, Coleman-Ross. 1947. i-viii, 1-243p. mus.
Slonimsky equates the thesaurus with "phrasebooks and dictionaries of idiomatic expressions" (Introduction). "It includes a great number of melodically plausible patterns which are new". Arrangement is "in the form of piano scales and melodic studies", adaptable to use on various instruments. Slonimsky has coined new terms for intervals not in the system of historic scales, and there is an explanation of terms and a synopsis of chords.

1949. **SLONIMSKY, Nicolas**
Roy Harris.
MQ, 33, Jan. 1947, p.17-37. illus., mus.
Includes a list of Harris's compositions.

1950. **SLONIMSKY, Nicolas**
A thing or two about music. Illustrated by Maggi Fiedler.
New York, Allen, Towne and Heath. 1948. 3-340p. illus.
A miscellaneous hodge-podge collection from newspapers and magazines dating from 1784 and "intended for non-consecutive reading". There is no index.

1951. **SLONIMSKY, Nicolas**
Young music must have new tools.
E, 66, Jan. 1948, p.7+.
Also *in Canon,* 2, Feb. 1949, p.300-3. mus.

1952. **SLONIMSKY, Nicolas**
Bringing Ives alive.
SR, 31, 28 Aug. 1948, p.45. illus.

1953. **SLONIMSKY, Nicolas**
Chopiniana: some materials for a biography.
MQ, 34, Oct. 1948, p.467-86. Illus. 2pl.

*1954. **SLONIMSKY, Nicolas**
Musical children: prodigies or monsters?
E, 66, Oct. 1948, p.591-2. illus.

1955. **SLONIMSKY, Nicolas**
Programme notes: 1947-1948.
[Little Orchestra Society?] [1949?] 3-50p. illus.
Notes for eight programmes of the Little Orchestra Society, mostly neglected works for a chamber size orchestra from Bach to Dello Joio. There are three Russian works: Shostakovitch's Two Pieces for string octet, Stravinsky's Danses Concertantes and Tcherepnin's Chamber Concerto for flute, violin and chamber orchestra.

1956. **SLONIMSKY, Nicolas**
Unique American composer.
E, 67, Mar. 1949, p.138.
Ives.

1957. **SLONIMSKY, Nicolas**
The Koussevitzky mission.
SR, 34, 30 June 1951, p.41+. illus.

1958. **EWEN, David** *and* **SLONIMSKY, Nicolas**
Fun with musical games and quizzes.
New York, Prentice-Hall. 1952, v-vii, 2-168p. illus., mus.
Not confined solely to serious music. Answers are included.

1959. **SLONIMSKY, Nicolas**
Lexicon of musical invective. Critical assaults on composers since Beethoven's time.
New York, Coleman-Ross. 1953. 3-296p.
Arranged alphabetically by composer, this entertaining compilation includes indexes of deprecatory words and phrases, and of names and titles. The second edition came out in paperback in 1965.

1960. **SLONIMSKY, Nicolas**
Musical rebel.
Américas, 5, Sept. 1953, p.6-8+. illus., mus.
On Ives.

1961. **SLONIMSKY, Nicolas**
Charles Ives - America's musical prophet.
MA, 74, 15 Feb. 1954, p.18-19. illus.
Reprinted *in Pan pipes,* 47, Jan. 1955, p.20.

*1962. **SLONIMSKY, Nicolas**
The story of Roy Harris - American composer.
E, 74, Dec. 1956, p.11+. illus.
75, Jan. 1957, p.12+.

*1963. **GELATT, R.**
Music makers.
HF, 9, Mar. 1959, p.53. illus.
Slonimsky.

1964. **SLONIMSKY, Nicolas**
The weather at Mozart's funeral.
MQ, 46, Jan. 1960, p.12-21.
Despite some dubious meteorological reasoning, a fascinating article.

1965. **SLONIMSKY, Nicolas**
Chou Wen-Chung.
A.C.A. bull., 9, 1961, no. 4, p.2-9. illus., mus.
A Chinese composer, born in 1923. Includes a detailed catalogue of works.

*1966. **SLONIMSKY, N.**
Slonimsky on Cowell.
Music mag., 164, May 1962, p.12.
Reprinted from Cowell's book *American composers on American music* (NewYork, Ungar. 1962).

*1967. **SLONIMSKY, N.**
The flamboyant chanticleer.
Show, 2, Nov. 1962, p.76+.
Villa-Lobos.

*1968. **SLONIMSKY, Nicolas**
"Musique"; reminiscences of a vanished world and a great teacher.
Piano teacher, 6, no.1, 1963, p.2-4. illus.

1969. **SLONIMSKY, Nicolas**
Critics can be wrong.
About the house, 1, Christmas 1963, p.34-6.
Excerpts from the *Lexicon of musical invective,* no. 1959.
Reprinted from *Show,* Aug. 1963.

1970. **SLONIMSKY, Nicolas**
Modern composition in Rumania.
MQ, 51, Jan. 1965, p.236-43.

1971. **SLONIMSKY, Nicolas**
New music in Greece.
MQ, 51, Jan. 1965, p.225-35.

SMOLSKY, Dmitri

B. *Works.*

Symphony no.1.

See no. 498.

SOLOVYEV-SEDOY, Vassily (1907-)

1972. **ADIGEZALOVA, Lyudmila**
The song king.
in LIPOVSKY. Lenin Prize winners, p.121-9.

1973. **ZHIVOV, Leonid**
The song that goes straight to the heart.
in LIPOVSKY. Lenin Prize winners, p.116-20. illus.

SPENDIAROV, Alexander (1871-1928)

1974. **MOISENCO, Rena**
A. Spendiarov.
in MOISENCO. Twenty Soviet composers, p.59-62.

1975. **MOISENKO, Rena**
A. Spendiarov.
in MOISENKO. Realist music, p.215-23. mus.

STANCHINSKI, Alyeksey (1889-1913)

1976. **SABANEYEFF, Leonid**
Alyeksey Stanchinski.
in SABANEYEFF. Modern Russian composers, p.190-4.

STASOV, Vladimir (1824-1906)

1977. **SHEDLOCK, J.S.**
Wladimir Stassow. 1824-1906.
MMR, 37, Jan. 1907, p.5.

1978. **NEWMARCH, Rosa**
Stassov as musical critic.
MMR, 38, Feb. 1908, p.31-2.
Mar. 1908, p.51-2.

1979. **CALVOCORESSI, M. D.**
Stassov and Russian music.
MMR, 54, June 1924, p.166-8.

1980. **CALVOCORESSI, M. D.**
Stassof and Rimsky-Korsakof.
MMR, 54, July 1924, p.198-9.

See no. 874.

1981. **IVANOV, Vsevolod**
Vladimir Stassov, a motive force in Russian culture.
SL, Nov. 1945, p.66-9. illus.

See no. 208.

1982. **MONTAGU-NATHAN, M.**
Stasov in London.
MMR, 83, June 1953, p.126-8.

1983. **ZETLIN, Mikhail**
Stassov.
in ZETLIN. The Five, p.7-19.

1984. **ZETLIN, Mikhail**
Stassov and the "Mighty Handful".
in ZETLIN. The Five, p.176-93.

1985. **STASOV, Vladimir Vasilevich**
Selected essays on music. Tr. by Florence Jonas.
Barrie and Rockcliff. 1968. 1-202p. 1pl.
A major primary source on "The Five", this first translation into English spans 1847 to 1906. The smooth translation, excellent introduction and especially the valuable sections on Cui and Serov make this a notable contribution to the literature of Russian music.
Contents: Review of the musical events of the year 1847. Letters from abroad. - The letters of Berlioz. - A letter from Liszt. - Twenty-five years of Russian art: our music. - Liszt, Schumann and Berlioz in Russia. - A friendly commemoration.

*1986. **OLKHOVSKY, George**
Vladimir Stasov and his quest for Russian national music.
DA, 29, Feb. 1969, p.2653A-4A.
PhD, mus., thesis, Georgetown University, Washington, D.C. 1968. 278p.

STEINBERG, Maximilian (1883-1946)

1987. **MOISENCO, Rena**
Maximilian Steinberg.
in MOISENCO. Twenty Soviet composers, p.62-3.

1988. **MOISENKO, Rena**
Maximilian Steinberg.
in MOISENKO. Realist music, p.224-30. mus.

STRAVINSKY, Igor (1882-1971)

A. *General.*

1989. **CALVOCORESSI, M. D.**
A Russian composer of today: Igor Stravinsky.
MT, 52, Aug. 1911, p.511-12.
The first article in English on the composer, written when he was only 29.

1990. **MONTAGU-NATHAN, M.**
Igor Stravinsky.
MS, n.i.s., 1, 19 Apr. 1913, p.330-1.

*1991. **HILL, Edward B.**
A note on Stravinsky.
Harvard musical rev., 2, Apr. 1914, p.3-7+.

*1992. **THE DIONYSIAN** spirit which vitalises the music of Igor Stravinsky.
Current opinion, 57, Aug. 1914, p.108-9.

1993. **VAN VECHTEN, Carl**
A new principle in music: Stravinsky and his work.
Russian rev., 1, Apr. 1916, p.160-3.

1994. **WISE, C. Stanley**
Impressions of Igor Stravinsky.
MQ, 2, Apr. 1916, p.249-56. 1pl.

*1995. **FINCK, Henry T.**
Igor Stravinsky.
Mentor, 4, Nov. 1916, p.?. illus.

1996. **MONTAGU-NATHAN, M.**
Stravinsky.
in MONTAGU-NATHAN. Contemporary Russian composers, p.113-52. illus.

1997. **CHENNEVIÈRE, Rudhyar**
The two trends of modern music in Stravinsky's works.
Tr. by Frederick H. Martens.
MQ, 5, Apr. 1919, p.169-74.

1998. **HENRY, Leigh**
Igor Stravinsky.
MT, 60, June 1919, p.268-72. mus.

1999. **TURNER, W. J.**
Stravinsky and Scriabin.
NS, 14, 22 Nov. 1919, p.220-1.

2000. **HENRY, Leigh**
The humour of Stravinsky.
MT, 60, Dec. 1919, p.670-3. mus.

2001. **HENRY, Leigh**
Igor Stravinsky and the objective direction in contemporary music.
Ch, n.s., no.4, Jan. 1920, p.97-102.

2002. **HENRY, Leigh**
"Contemporaries": Igor Stravinsky.
MO, 43, Feb. 1920, p.371-2.

2003. **ROSENFELD, Paul**
Strawinsky.
NR, 22, 14 Apr. 1920, p.207-10.

2004. **MORRIS, R. O.**
The later Stravinsky.
Nation, 27, 31 July 1920, p.553-4.

2005. **SOUND for sound's sake.**
Sackbut, 1, Aug. 1920, p.153-6.
A very scathing appraisal.

2006. **EVANS, Edwin**
The Stravinsky debate.
MSt, 13, Dec. 1920, p.139-45. illus.

*2007. **EVANS, Edwin**
Igor Stravinsky: contrapuntal titan.
MA, 33, 1921, no.16, p.9.

2008. **IGOR Stravinsky.**
Chester. [1921]. 3-13p. mus.
Very brief survey (six pages) in English and French.

2009. **HARTY, Hamilton**
The Stravinsky dispute.
Musician, no. 23, July 1921, p.225.
Discusses the lack of extremes in the criticism of Stravinsky's music.

2010. **HENRY, Leigh**
Stravinsky and the pragmatic criterion in contemporary music.
English rev., 33, July 1921, p.67-73.

2011. **BLISS, Arthur**
A short note on Stravinsky's orchestration.
MS, n.i.s., 18, 30 July 1921, p.43.

2012. **HENRY, Leigh**
Stravinsky and the enfranchisement of sound.
MS, n.i.s., 18, 30 July 1921, p.41-2. illus.

2013. **MELTZER, Charles**
Stravinsky - the enigma.
Forum, 66, Sept. 1921, p.241-8.

2014. **HULL, A. Eaglefield**
Three musical innovators. 3. Igor Stravinsky.
Bookman, 61, Nov. 1921, p.110-12.
"Le Sacre du Printemps" becomes "The Rite of Springtime".

2015. **GILMAN, Lawrence**
... From Stravinsky to Sibelius.
North American rev., 215, Jan. 1922, p.117-21.

2016. **KALISCH, Alfred**
Stravinsky day by day.
MT, 18, Jan. 1922, p.27-8.
On his recent pronouncements on music.

2017. **MITCHELL, Edward**
The Stravinsky theories.
MT, 63, Mar. 1922, p.162-4.

*2018. **JADE, Ely**
Igor Stravinski.
Franco-American Musical Society quarterly bull., 3, 1924, p.4-7
Lists his works with dates of first performances.

*2019. **WHITHORNE, Emerson**
And after Stravinsky?
MM, 1, Feb. 1924, p.24-5.

*2020. **BAUER, Marion**
Igor Stravinsky.
Musical leader, 47, 20 Mar. 1924, p.277.

2021. **STRAUSS, Henrietta**
On the giving of Stravinsky.
Na, 118, 30 Apr. 1924, p.512.
Discusses various conductors' interpretations of his works.

*2022. **WIBORG, Mary**
Igor Stravinsky, one of the great Russians.
Arts and decoration, 22, Jan. 1925, p.36. illus.

*2023. **MALKIEL, Henrietta**
Modernists have ruined modern music, says Stravinsky.
MA, 41, 10 Jan. 1925, p.9.

*2024. **OSGOOD, H. O.**
Stravinsky conducts an interview and a concert.
MC, 90, 15 Jan. 1925, p.7.

2025. **ROSENFELD, Paul**
Musical chronicle.
Dial, 78, Mar. 1925, p.259-64.

*2026. **[STRAVINSKY, Igor]**
Stravinsky previsions a new music.
Current opinion, 78, Mar. 1925, p.329-30. illus.
Statement on music in general and on the merits of the player-piano.

2027. **SANBORN, Pitts**
Koussevitzky and Stravinsky.
Na, 120, 18 Mar. 1925, p.298-9.

2028. **WILSON, Edmund**
Stravinsky.
NR, 42, 1 Apr. 1925, p.156-7.

2029. **KOLISCH, Mitzi**
Stravinsky - Russian of the Russians.
Independent, 114, 16 May 1925, p.559. illus.

*2030. **BAYFIELD, Stanley**
Igor Stravinsky.
NMR, 24, Oct. 1925, p.396-8.

2031. **BOULANGER, Nadia**
Lectures on modern music. 3. Stravinsky.
Houston, Texas, The Rice Institute. 1926. [Pamphlet].
178-195p. mus.
One of three lectures delivered in January 1925.

*2032. **STRAVINSKY, Igor**
Chronological progress in musical art.
E, 44, Aug. 1926, p.559-60.
Also *in* COOKE, James, *ed. Great men and famous musicians on the art of music,* p. 266, published in Philadelphia in 1925.
An interview with Stravinsky.

2033. **MAINE, Basil**
Schönberg and Stravinsky.
Apollo, 4, Sept. 1926, p.99-100.

2034. **WEISSMANN, Adolf**
The influence of Schönberg and Stravinsky in Germany.
Music bull., 9, Feb. 1927, p.45-51. illus.

*2035. **EXIT Stravinski.**
LLA, 322, 15 Apr. 1927, p.737-8.
Extract from a critique of Ernest Newman.

2036. **STRAVINSKY, Igor**
Avertissement ... A warning.
Dominant, 1, Dec. 1927, p.13-14.
His statement on classicism and neo-classicism (French and English text). *See also* no. 2039.

*2037. **COEUROY, André**
Picasso and Stravinsky.
MM, 5, Jan.-Feb. 1928, p.3-8. illus.

*2038. **LOURIÉ, Arthur**
"Neogothic and neoclassic".
MM, 5, Mar. 1928, p.3-8.
Compares Stravinsky and Schoenberg.

2039. **MYERS, Rollo**
Some thoughts suggested by Stravinsky's "Avertissement".
Dominant, 1, Mar. 1928, p.32-4.
See also no. 2036.

2040. **SABANEEV, L.**
The Stravinsky legends. Tr. by S. W. Pring.
MT, 69, Sept. 1928, p.785-7.
Demolishes the legend of Stravinsky as a composer of pure music.

2041. **SCHLOEZER, Boris de**
Igor Stravinsky. Tr. from the French by Ezra Pound.
Dial, 85, Oct. 1928, p.271-83.
See also nos. 2068, 2073 and 2134.

2042. **SABANEYEFF, Leonid**
Igor Stravinski.
in SABANEYEFF. Modern Russian composers, p.64-86.

2043. **SCHLOEZER, Boris de**
Stravinsky: his technique. Tr. from the French by Ezra Pound.
Dial, 86, Jan. 1929, p.9-26.
Feb. 1929, p.105-15.
See also nos. 2068, 2673 and 2134.

2044. **SCHLOEZER, Boris de**
The problem of style. Tr. from the French by Ezra Pound.
Dial, 86, Apr. 1929, p.298-303.
See also nos. 2068, 2073 and 2134.

*2045. **COPLAND, Aaron**
From a composer's notebook: Stravinsky.
MM, 6, May 1929, p.15-19.

2046. **SCHLOEZER, Boris de**
A classic art. Tr. from the French by Ezra Pound.
Dial, 86, June 1929, p.463-74.
See also nos. 2068, 2073 and 2134.

2047. **HULL, Robert M.**
The wheel comes full circle.
Sackbut, 10, Nov. 1929, p.100-2.

2048. **WHITE, Eric Walter**
Stravinsky's sacrifice to Apollo.
Hogarth Press. 1930. v-vii, 9-150p. mus., disc.

A general outline of Stravinsky's life and career up to 1930, White's first book on the composer. There is an appendix listing twenty-one major works and also some details of the minor ones. A reliable early survey.

*2049. **STRAVINSKY, Igor**
Why people dislike my music.
Musical forecast, 17, Feb. 1930, p.1+.

2050. **FERROUD, P. O.**
The role of the abstract in Igor Stravinsky's work.
Ch, 11, Mar. 1930, p.141-7.

2051. **BROWNE, Andrew J.**
Aspects of Stravinsky's work.
ML, 11, Oct. 1930, p.360-6. illus.

2052. **ROSENFELD, Paul**
The two Stravinskys.
NR, 66, 18 Feb. 1931, p.20-1.
The two are "an important Stravinsky and a secondary one".

2053. **ROSENFELD, Paul**
European music in decay.
Scribner's mag., 89, Mar. 1931, p.277-83.
With especial reference to Stravinsky and his leadership in the world of music.

2054. **MENDEL, Arthur**
Stravinsky.
Na, 132, 11 Mar. 1931, p.279-80.

*2055. **PILKINGTON, V.**
Stravinsky and Walton.
London mercury, 25, Jan. 1932, p.300-1.

2056. **TERPANDER,** *pseud.*
Stravinsky, 1932.
G. 9, Feb. 1932, p.373-4. illus.

*2057. **SCHLOEZER, Boris de**
The enigma of Stravinsky.
MM, 10, Nov. 1932, p.10-17.

2058. **MURRILL, Herbert**
Stravinsky and Sorabji: a rejoinder.
MMR, 63, Feb. 1933, p.36.
On the criticism of Stravinsky in Sorabji's book *Around music.*

2059. **EWEN, David**
The decline of Stravinsky.
MMR, 63, Oct. 1933, p.179-80.

2060. **STRAVINSKY, Igor**
As I see myself. (In an interview with Norman Cameron).
G, 12, Aug. 1934, p.85-6. illus.

2061. **BOYS, Henry**
Stravinsky.
MMR, 64, Sept. 1934, p.152-4.
Nov. 1934, p.195-6.
Dec. 1934, p.226-8.
See also nos. 2068, 2069 and 2134.

*2062. **SCHAEFFNER, André**
On Stravinsky, early and late.
MM, 12, Nov. 1934, p.3-7, illus.

2063. **CALVOCORESSI, M. D.**
From my notebook.
MO, 58, June 1935, p.756-7.
Discusses Stravinsky's *Chroniques de ma vie,* no. 2074.

2064. **GODDARD, Scott**
Stravinsky's autobiography.
MMR, 65, June 1935, p.106-7.

2065. **HOGARTH, Basil**
Igor Stravinsky, the stormy petrel of music.
G, 13, June 1935, p.5-8. illus.

2066. **BLITZSTEIN, Marc**
The phenomenon of Stravinsky.
MQ, 21, July 1935, p.330-47. mus.

*2067. **JACOBI, Frederick**
Stravinsky begins his *Chronicles.*
MM, 13, Nov. 1935, p.51-3.
See also no. 2074.

2068. **ARMITAGE, Merle,** *ed.*
Igor Stravinsky.
New York, Schirmer. 1936. iii-v, 1-156p. illus., 24pl., disc.
Eleven untitled articles and critiques by Armitage, Boys*, Cocteau*, Danz, Olin Downes, Eugene Goossens*, Manuel Komroff, Jose Rodriguez, Satie*, de Schloezer* and Vuillermoz, those asterisked appearing in Corle's 1949 symposium.

There is a short biography of Stravinsky and a list of his principal compositions, but no index. *See also* no. 2134.

2069. **BOYS, Henry**
Organic continuity.
in ARMITAGE, *ed.* Igor Stravinsky, p.35-40.
Also *in* CORLE, *ed.* Igor Stravinsky, p.93-8.
Reprinted from *Monthly musical record,* no. 2061.

2070. **COCTEAU, Jean**
Critics and the comic spirit.
in ARMITAGE, *ed.* Igor Stravinsky, p.15-18.
Also *in* CORLE, *ed.* Igor Stravinsky, p.21-4.

2071. **GOOSENS, Eugene**
Whole-hearted champion.
in ARMITAGE, *ed.* Igor Stravinsky, p.9-14.
Also *in* CORLE, *ed.* Igor Stravinsky, p.99-104.

2072. **SATIE, Erik**
A composer's conviction.
in ARMITAGE, *ed.* Igor Stravinsky, p.26-34.
Also *in* CORLE, *ed.* Igor Stravinsky, p.25-32.
First appeared *in Vanity fair,* 19, Feb. 1923.

2073. **SCHLOEZER, Boris de**
An abridged analysis. Tr. by Ezra Pound.
in ARMITAGE, *ed.* Igor Stravinsky, p.69-137.
Also *in* CORLE, *ed.* Igor Stravinsky, p.33-91.
Abridged from *Dial,* nos. 2041, 2043, 2044 and 2056.

2074. **STRAVINSKY, Igor**
Chronicle of my life.
Gollancz. 1936. 8-286p. 6pl.
Originally published as *Chroniques de ma vie* (two volumes, Paris, 1935-6), it was written in collaboration with Walter Nouvel "to present to the reader a true picture of myself". Forthright and entertaining, but the lack of an index is a serious omission. The American title is *An autobiography,* the 1958 edition being much curtailed. Calder and Boyars issued a 180p. edition in 1975.
See also nos. 2063, 2067 and 2076.

*2075. **THOMSON, Virgil**
The official Stravinsky.
MM, 13, May 1936, p.57-8.

2076. **EDITORIAL. Igor Stravinsky.**
G, 14, June 1936, p.2-3.
On *Chronicle of my life,* no. 2074.

2077. **MYERS, Rollo**
Igor Stravinsky in retrospect.
L, 16, 11 Nov. 1936, p.925-6. illus.

*2078. **EATON, Quaintance**
Stravinsky: apostle of today.
MA, 57, 10 Jan. 1937, p.11.

*2079. **STRAVINSKY, Igor**
Early musical influences in my life.
E, 55, Mar. 1937, p.155-6. illus.
An extract from his autobiography, no. 2074.

*2080. **KIRSTEIN, Lincoln**
Homage to Stravinsky.
Arts and decoration, 46, May 1937, p.14-15+. illus.

2081. **CALVOCORESSI, M. D.**
Debussy and Stravinsky, a comparison.
L, 18, 15 Sept. 1937, p.584.

2082. **MELLERS, W. H.**
Stravinsky at Dumbarton Oaks.
L, 20, 3 Nov. 1938, p.972.
This article in fact has little about the concerto, which was commissioned by Mr. and Mrs. Robert Bliss, with whom Stravinsky stayed at Dumbarton Oaks, Washington, D.C.

2083. **MYERS, Rollo**
Stravinsky and the violin.
L, 21, 5 Jan. 1939, p.48.

2084. **JACOBI, Frederick,** *jnr.*
Harvard soirée.
MM, 17, Oct.-Nov. 1939, p.47-8.
On Stravinsky's opening lecture at Harvard. *See also* no.2113.

*2085. **STRAVINSKY, Igor**
... Pushkin: poetry and music ...
A very rare pamphlet printed in the U.S.A. from the French manuscript by Gregory Golubeff in 1940.

2086. **MAGRIEL, Paul**
Igor Stravinsky: a bibliography comprising critical writings on his life, music and influence.
Bull. of bibliography, 17, Jan.-Apr. 1940, p.8-9.
May-Aug. 1940, p.31-3.
Over 600 items which have appeared in books and periodicals, including foreign language material. Later published in revised and enlarged form in Lederman's symposium, no. 2153.

2087. **CARTER, Elliott**
... Stravinsky and other moderns in 1940.
MM, 17, Mar.-Apr. 1940, p.164-70.

2088. **KALL, Alexis**
Stravinsky in the chair of poetry.
MQ, 26, July 1940, p.283-96.
On his Harvard lectures 1939-40. *See also* no.2113.

*2089. **GASSMAN, Remi**
The new Stravinsky.
MM, 18, Jan. 1941, p.114-16.

2090. **BAYLISS, Stanley**
The ideas of Igor Stravinsky.
Choir, 32, Mar. 1941, p.40-1.

*2091. **HILL, Edward B.**
Russian nationalist composers. Igor Stravinsky.
E, 59, Dec. 1941, p.815+. illus.

2092. **CHANDLER, Theodore**
Stravinsky's apologia.
MM, 20, Nov.-Dec. 1942, p.17-22. illus.
On *Poetics of music,* no.2113.

2093. **BLOM, Eric**
Stravinsky's theory and practice.
L, 29, 7 Jan. 1943, p.29.
Deals with Stravinsky's statue as a composer.

*2094. **BERGER, Arthur**
Igor Stravinsky.
Listen, 3, Aug. 1943, p.3-8. illus.

2095. **EVANS, Edwin**
Stravinsky then and now.
L, 30, 11 Nov. 1943, p.565.

2096. **NABOKOV, Nicolas**
Stravinsky now.
Partisan rev., 11, Summer 1944, p.324-34.
Discusses his ideas on tempo and rhythm.

*2097. **COLEMAN, Francis**
A talk with Igor Stravinsky.
Dance, Apr. 1945, p.14+.

*2098. **SOUVTCHINSKY, Pierre**
Igor Stravinsky.
Current opinion, 2, 1946, p.19-31.

2099. **MASON, Colin**
The two Stravinskys.
L, 35, 3 Jan. 1946, p.29.
The two aspects of his character: one engaging and poised; the other the restless searcher for new ideals.

2100. **DAHL, Ingolf**
Stravinsky in 1946.
MM, 23, Summer 1946, p.159-65. mus.
Based on an interview with the composer.

2101. **ANSERMET, Ernest**
Strawinsky's gift to the West. Tr. by Frani Musser.
DI, 6, 1947, p.235-6.
Also *in* LEDERMAN, *ed.* Stravinsky in the theatre, p.119-21. mus.

2102. **BALANCHINE, George**
The dance element in Stravinsky's music.
DI, 6, 1947, p.250-6.
Also *in* LEDERMAN, *ed.* Stravinsky in the theatre, p.75-84, illus., mus.

2103. **BERNSTEIN, Leonard**
A note on variety.
DI, 6, 1947, p.283.
Also *in* LEDERMAN, *ed.* Stravinsky in the theatre, p.132-3.

2104. **CHÁVEZ, Carlos**
DI, 6, 1947, p.243-4.
The surprise and the scandal.
Also *in* LEDERMAN, *ed.* Stravinsky in the theatre, p.126-8. illus.
The title here is *Perpetual renewal.*

2105. **COPLAND, Aaron**
Influence, problem, tone.
DI, 6, 1947, p.249.
Also *in* LEDERMAN, *ed.* Stravinsky in the theatre, p.121-2.

2106. **HAIEFF, Alexei**
The artist and the man.
DI, 6, 1947, p.237.
Also *in* LEDERMAN, *ed.* Stravinsky in the theatre, p.123-4.

2107. **LEDERMAN, Minna**
DI, 6, 1947, p.229-33.
Stravinsky's theatre.
Also *in* LEDERMAN, *ed.* Stravinsky in the theatre, p.3-10.
illus.
The title here is *The Theatre of Stravinsky.*

2108. **MILHAUD, Darius**
Thirty-seven years.
DI, 6, 1947, p.257.
Also *in* LEDERMAN, *ed.* Stravinsky in the theatre, p.131-2.
illus.

2109. **MONTEUX, Pierre**
Early years.
DI, 6, 1947, p.242-3.
Also *in* LEDERMAN, *ed.* Stravinsky in the theatre, p.128-9.

2110. **PISTON, Walter**
Stravinsky's rediscoveries.
DI, 6, 1947, p.256-7.
Also *in* LEDERMAN, *ed.* Stravinsky in the theatre, p.130-1.

2111. **RIETI, Vittorio**
The composer's debt.
DI, 6, 1947, p.278.
Also *in* LEDERMAN, *ed.* Stravinsky in the theatre, p.134.

2112. **SCHUMAN, William**
The final triumph.
DI, 6, 1947, p.282-3.
Also *in* LEDERMAN, *ed.* Stravinsky in the theatre, p.134-5.

2113. **STRAVINSKY, Igor**
Poetics of music: in the form of six lessons. Tr. by Arthur Knodel and Ingolf Dahl.
O.U.P. 1947, ix-xi, 3-142p, illus.
The text of the Charles Eliot Norton lectures at Harvard, 1939-40,

were first published as *Poetique musicale* in 1942 with one lecture *(The avatars of Russian music)* omitted. An important work, written in collaboration with Roland Manuel, but the translation is dull and sometimes careless. The 1970 edition (Harvard University Press) is bilingual (French and English).
See also nos. 2084, 2088, 2092 and 2117.

2114. **WHITE, Eric Walter**
Stravinsky. A critical survey.
John Lehmann. 1947. 7-192p. 7pl., disc., bib.
Aims to survey and comment on the evolution of Stravinsky's work. An excellent, well-documented, readable account, containing a list of seventy-two compositions. Much expanded in *Stravinsky: the composer and his works,* no. 2311.
See also no. 2119.

2115. **HUNT, Reginald**
Stravinsky and others.
MO, 70, May 1947, p.253.

2116. **LANG, Paul Henry**
Stravinsky - the enigma.
SH, 30, 3 May 1947, p.36-7.

2117. **GAIR, Sidney**
Notes on a text by Strawinsky.
Sewanee rev., 55, July 1947, p.447-59.
Analysis of a statement made by Stravinsky in *Poetics of music,* no.2113.

2118. **STRAVINSKY, Igor**
Recorded by the composer...
Musical digest, 1, August 1947, p.26-7. illus.
Extract from *Chronicle of my life,* no. 2074.

2119. **GISHFORD, Anthony**
A book about Stravinsky.
T, n.s., no.5, Autumn, 1947, p.23-4. illus.
White's *Stravinsky. A critical survey,* no. 2114.

2120. **ONNEN, Frank**
Stravinsky, Tr. from the Dutch by M. M. Kessler-Button.
Sidgwick and Jackson. [1948?] . 1-58p. illus., 1pl., mus., bib., disc.
Aims to be objective and decsriptive, Contains a list of compositions, but lacks an index and suffers from inconsistent spelling of proper names.

2121. **LEIBOWITZ, Rene**
... Schönberg and Stravinsky.
Partisan rev., 15, Mar. 1948, p.361-5.
See also no. 2122.

2122. **NABOKOV, Nicolas**
The atonal trail: a communication.
Partisan rev., 15, May 1948, p.580-5.
Stravinsky's position as a composer defended against Leibowitz's criticism (no.2121); the latter replies in the issue for August, p.943, and Nabokov counters in October, p.1048-51.

2123. **BEAUMONT, Cyril**
Some memorable occasions.
T, n.s., no.8, Summer 1948, p.9-14.
Eyewitness accounts of the world and London premières of some of Stravinsky's works.

2124. **CLOUGH, Francis *and* CUMING, Geoffrey**
Igor Strawinsky on records.
T, n.s., no.8, Summer 1948, p.29-30.
Arranged alphabetically by title of work, it covers approximately 1922-48.
See also no. 2145.

2125. **STRAWINSKY.**
T, n.s., no.8, Summer 1948, p.6.

2126. **STUART, Charles**
Recent works examined.
T, n.s., no.8, Summer 1948, p.20-8. mus.
Discusses the Symphony in Three Movements, Concerto in D for Strings, "Scènes de Ballet", the Capriccio, Concerto for Two pianos and the Sonata for Two Pianos.

2127. **WHITE, Eric Walter**
Stravinsky as a writer.
T, n.s., no.8, Summer 1948, p.18-20.

2128. **MASTER mechanic.**
Time, 52, 26 July 1948, p.26-9. illus.

2129. **STRAVINSKY and Stravinsky.**
Newsweek, 32, 2 Aug. 1948, p.72. illus.
The composer and his son, Soulima.

*2130. **SANTOLIQUIDO, F.**
Igor Stravinsky and the Greek tragedy.
E, 66, Dec. 1948, p.736. illus.

2131. **ARMITAGE, Merle**
The age of Stravinsky.
in CORLE, *ed.* Igor Stravinsky, p.169-78.

2132. **BERGER, Arthur**
The Stravinsky panorama.
in CORLE, *ed.* Igor Stravinsky, p.105-14.

2133. **COPLAND, Aaron**
The personality of Stravinsky.
in CORLE, *ed.* Igor Stravinsky, p.121-2.

2134. **CORLE, Edwin,** *ed.*
Igor Stravinsky.
New York, Duell, Sloan and Pearce. 1949. 17-245p. illus., 8pl., mus., bub., disc.
An enlarged second edition of Armitage's 1936 symposium (no. 2068), the essays by Boys, Cocteau, Goossens, Satie and de Schloezer being the only ones common to both books. There is a catalogue of works, and reproductions of paintings by Picasso, Chagall and others, but no index.
Contents: Critics and the comic spirit by Jean Cocteau. - A composer's conviction by Erik Satie. - An abridged analysis by Boris de Schloezer. - Organic continuity by Henry Boys. - Wholehearted champion by Eugene Goossens. - The Stravinsky panorama by Arthur Berger. - English discernment by Osbert Sitwell. - The personality of Stravinsky by Aaron Copland. - Christmas with Stravinsky by Nicolas Nabokoff. - The age of Stravinsky by Merle Armitage. - Working with Stravinsky by Samuel Dushkin. - Incongruity and faith by Lawrence Norton. - Stravinsky's Mass: a notebook by Robert Craft. - Stravinsky and classicism by Cecil Smith. - Brief note and discography by David Hall.

2135. **DUSHKIN, Samuel**
Working with Stravinsky.
in CORLE, *ed.* Igor Stravinsky, p.179-92. illus.

2136. **MORTON, Lawrence**
Incongruity and faith.
in CORLE, *ed.* Igor Stravinsky, p.193-200.

2137. **NABOKOV, Nicolas**
Christmas with Stravinsky.
in NABOKOV. Old friends and new music, p. 139-56.
Also *in* CORLE, *ed.* Igor Stravinsky, p.123-68, the chapter here including an additional section written for *Atlantic monthly* (no.2144).

2138. **SITWELL, Osbert**
English discernment.
in CORLE, *ed.* Igor Stravinsky, p.115-20.
From Sitwell's book *Great morning* (1947).

2139. **SMITH, Cecil**
Stravinsky and classicism.
in CORLE, *ed.* Igor Stravinsky, p.207-15.

2140. **TANSMAN, Alexandre**
Igor Stravinsky. The man and his music. Tr. by Thérèse and Charles Bleefield.
New York, Putnam. 1949. v-xv, 3-295p. mus.
A worthwhile, if too eulogistic study, by a friend of the composer. There is a catalogue of compositions up to 1948.

2141. **MURRILL, Herbert**
Stravinsky today.
Ch, 23, Apr. 1949, p.85-91.
Also *in Musical digest,* 1949, p.140-3.

2142. **BABITZ, Sol**
The violin ...
International musician, 47, May 1949, p.22+. mus.
On Stravinsky's rhythmic innovations in violin writing.

2143. **BOYS, Henry**
Stravinsky. (1). Critical categories needed for a study of his music.
S, no.1, Aug. 1949, p.3-12. illus., 1pl.

2144. **NABOKOV, Nicolas**
Igor Stravinsky.
AM, 184, Nov. 1949, p.21-7.
Later appeared *in* Nabokov's *Old friends and new music,* p.157-37 (no. 1022).
See also no. 2137.

2145. **MYERS, Rollo**
Introduction to the music of Stravinsky.
Dobson. 1950. 5-59p. mus., disc.
A clear and useful survey. The discography was first published *in Tempo,* no. 2124. There is no index.

2146. **BOYS, Henry**
Stravinsky. (2) A propos his aesthetic.
S, no. 2, Jan. 1950, p.61-4.

2147. **KERMAN, Joseph**
... Progress report on Stravinsky.
Hudson rev., 3, Spring 1950, p.124-31.

2148. **STRAVINSKY, Igor**
Stravinsky on music reproduction.
MTe, 29, May 1950, p.243.

2149. **SENIOR, Evan**
... Stravinsky - Firebird to Orpheus.
DD, 1, Aug. 1950, p.15. illus.
A general article.

2150. **STUART, Charles**
Stravinsky: the dialectics of dislike.
Music survey, 2, Winter 1950, p.142-8.

2151. **CRAFT, Robert**
Music and words.
in LEDERMAN, *ed.* Stravinsky in the theatre, p.85-103. illus., mus.

2152. **KIRSTEIN, Lincoln**
Working with Stravinsky.
in LEDERMAN, *ed.* Stravinsky in the theatre, p.136-40. illus.

2153. **LEDERMAN, Minna,** ***ed.***
Stravinsky in the theatre.
Peter Owen. 1951. 3-228p. 1pl., mus., bib., disc.
Twenty-six essays, sixteen of which appeared in *Dance index* (Vol. 6, nos. 10-12, 1947). There is a chronology of his life, a catalogue of the stage productions and a four page discography. Magriel's massive bibliography was first published in *Bulletin of bibliography,* no. 2086, and is here revised and enlarged. The appendices are now very out of date and there is no index, but this still holds a notable place in the literature of Stravinsky.

Contents: The theatre of Stravinsky by Minna Lederman. - Le Sacre du Printemps by Jean Cocteau. - An irresistable force by Emile Vuillermoz. - Nijinsky's innovation by Jacques Rivière. - Interpretation by Massine by Igor Stravinsky. - The two Sacres by André Levinson. - The triumph of the orchestra by Emile Vuillermoz. - Souvenir of Switzerland, 1917 by C.F. Ramuz. - Music for the ballet by Arthur Berger. - The new Orpheus by Ingolf Dahl. - The dance element in Stravinsky's music by George Balanchine. - Music and words by Robert Craft. - Stravinsky and the drama by Nicolas Nabokov. - Stravinsky's gift to the West by Ernest Ansermet. - Influence, problem, tone by Aaron Copland. - The artist and the man by Alexei Haieff. - Stravinsky's work table by C. F. Ramuz. - Perpetual renewal by Carlos Chávez. - Early years by Pierre Monteux. - Stravinsky's rediscoveries by Walter Piston. - Thirty-seven years by Darius Milhaud. - A note on variety by Leonard Bernstein. - The composer's debt by Vittorio Rieti. - The final triumph by William Schuman. - Working with Stravinsky by Lincoln Kirstein. - Stravinsky's own story by Igor Stravinsky.

2154. **NABOKOV, Nicolas**
Stravinsky and the drama.
in LEDERMAN, *ed.* Stravinsky in the theatre, p.104-16. illus.

2155. **RAMUZ, C. F.**
Stravinsky's work table.
in LEDERMAN, *ed.* Stravinsky in the theatre, p.124-5. illus.

2156. **STRAVINSKY, Igor**
Igor Stravinsky's own story.
in LEDERMAN, *ed.* Stravinsky in the theatre, p.143-66. illus.

2157. **BOYS, Henry**
Stravinsky. (3). The musical materials.
S, no.4, Jan. 1951, p.11-18. mus.

2158. **MURRILL, Herbert**
Aspects of Stravinsky.
ML, 32, Apr. 1951, p.118-24. mus.

*2159. **CRAFT, Robert**
The working habits of Stravinsky.
Opera and concert, 16, July 1951, p.14-15.

2160. **SKULSKY, A.**
Igor Stravinsky: sound in the defining element.
MA, 72, Feb. 1952, p.27+. illus.

2161. **FRANK, Alan**
Stravinsky the classicist.
L, 47, 20 Mar. 1952, p.489.

2162. **WHITE, Eric Walter**
Homage to Stravinsky.
Adelphi, 28, no.3, 1952, p.594-6.

2163. **CRAFT, Robert**
Stravinsky at seventy.
MC, 146, Oct. 1952, p.6-7. illus.

2164. **RAYNOR, Henry**
Britten, Stravinsky and the future of opera.
MO, 76, Oct. 1952, p.19+.
Nov. 1952, p.83+.

2165. **STRAVINSKY, Theodore**
The message of Igor Strawinsky. Tr. from the original French text by Robert Craft and André Marion.
Boosey and Hawkes. 1953. 1-57p. 7pl.
Written by Stravinsky's elder son, it aims to show the underlying unity in his work. It does not follow the French text of 1948, but the text was revised by the author for the 1952 German edition. There is no index.

*2166. **CRAFT, Robert**
Strawinsky's revisions.
Counterpoint, 18, Jan. 1953, p.14-16. illus.

2167. **KOZMA, Tibor**
Stravinsky's musical language.
ON, 17, 9 Feb. 1953, p.28-31. illus., mus.

2168. **HUXLEY, Aldous**
Conversation with Stravinsky.
Vogue, 121, 15 Feb. 1953, p.94-5+. illus.

2169. **TAYLOR, Ronald**
Stravinsky and the problems of twentieth century music.
Cambridge j., 6, Mar. 1953, p.363-73.

2170. **MITCHELL, D.**
Bartok, Strawinsky and Schoenberg. Periods: early, middle and late.
Ch, 28, July 1953, p.9-16.

2171. **STRAVINSKY, Igor**
The Diaghilev I knew. Tr. by Mercedes de Acosta.
AM, 192, Nov. 1953, p.33-6.

2172. **THE "BAD Boy" of music has now become the old master.**
MMu, 2, May 1954, p.9. illus.

2173. **GRAY, Bryan**
How he wants us to hear his music.
MMu, 2, June 1954, p.14. illus.

2174. **... Igor Stravinsky.**
DD, 5, June 1954, p.5. illus.

2175. **REES, C. B.**
Stravinsky.
LME, 9, June 1954, p.20-1. illus.

2176. **COOK, J. Douglas**
The composer tells how.
SR, 37, 26 June 1954, p.41+. illus.
Stravinsky is one of six interviewed about composing.

2177. **WOOD, Ralph W.**
The rickety bar.
MT, 95, Aug. 1954, p.412-15. mus.
On Stravinsky's time signatures.

*2178. **WILLIAMS, R.**
Stravinsky: from enfant terrible to old master.
House beautiful, 96, Sept. 1954, p.162+.

*2179. **CITKOWITZ, Israel**
Stravinsky and Schoenberg; a note on syntax and sensibility.
Juilliard rev., 1, Fall 1954, p.17-20.

2180. **FRANKENSTEIN, Alfred**
Stravinsky on microgroove.
HF, 4, Nov. 1954, p.73-85. illus., disc.
Arranged chronologically by date of composition, 1908-52.

2181. **KELLER, Hans**
First performances. Schönberg and Stravinsky: Schönbergians and Stravinskyans.
MR, 15, Nov. 1954, p.307-10.

2182. **CAZDEN, Norman**
Humor in the music of Stravinsky and Prokofiev.
Science and society, 18, Winter 1954, p.52-74.

2183. **STROBEL, Heinrich**
Stravinsky: classic humanist. Tr. from the German by Hans Rosenwald.
New York, Merlin Press. 1955. 5-184p.
A very general book which discusses a large number of compositions. There is no index.

2184. **BERGER, Arthur**
Stravinsky and the younger American composers.
S, no,12, June 1955, p.38-46.

2185. **RAYNOR, Henry**
Stravinsky the teacher.
Ch, 31, Autumn 1956, p.34-41.
Winter 1957 [i.e. 1956-7], p.69-75.

2186. **KELLER, Hans**
Towards the psychology of Stravinsky's genius.
L. 56, 29 Nov. 1956, p.897.

2187. **BURT, Francis**
An antithesis. 1. The technical aspect.
S, no.18, Dec. 1956, p.7-17. mus.
On Schoenberg and Stravinsky.

2188. **DREW, D.**
Stravinsky.
LME, 11, Dec. 1956, p.37+.

2189. **GRAY, Bryan**
Stravinsky's quarter-century of cold and classic music.
MMu, 5, Dec. 1956, p.23. illus.

2190. **IGOR Strawinsky. A complete catalogue of his published works.**
Boosey and Hawkes. 1957. 9-39p. 4pl.
The English, French and German text details eighty-six published works from 1905 to 1956 in chronological order. There is also a classified list with an alphabetical title index in three languages. The second edition has addenda covering the period to 1962. A more detailed listing is to be found in White's *Stravinsky. The composer and his works*, no. 2311.

*2191. **DRUCKMAN, Jacob**
Stravinsky's orchestral style.
Juilliard rev., 4, Spring 1957, p.10-19. mus.

*2192. **MENASCE, Jacques de**
Anniversary of Igor Stravinsky.
Juilliard rev., 4, Spring 1957, p.3-9.

2193. **BERMAN, Harvey**
Colossus of modern music.
E, 75, May-June 1957, p.11+. illus.

*2194. **CRAFT, Robert**
The composer and the phonograph.
HF, 7, June 1957, p.34-5+.
Surveys Stravinsky's use of recordings 1915 onwards.

2195. **CRAFT, Robert**
A personal preface.
S, 20, June 1957, p.7-13.
Stravinsky and his working habits 1947-55.

2196. **DREW, David**
Stravinsky's revisions.
S, 20, June 1957, p.47-58. mus.

*2197. **FRANKENSTEIN, Alfred**
The record of a self-interpreter.
HF, 7, June 1957, p.42-3+. illus.

2198. **GERHARD, Roberto**
Twelve-note technique in Stravinsky.
S, 20, June 1957, p.38-43. mus.

2199. **KELLER, Hans**
Rhythm: Gershwin and Stravinsky.
S, 20, June 1957, p.19-31. mus.

*2200. **KIRSTEIN, Lincoln**
Pictures from an album.
HF, 7, June 1957, p.36-41. illus.

2201. **MYERS, Rollo**
Stravinsky at seventy-five.
MT, 98, June 1957, p.313-14. illus.

*2202. **NABOKOV, Nicolas**
Stravinsky - fifteen and three-score.
HF, 7, June 1957, p.33. illus.

2203. **PERRIN, Maurice**
Stravinsky in a composition class.
S, 20, June 1957, p.44-6.

2204. **SESSIONS, Roger**
Thoughts on Stravinsky.
S, 20, June 1957, p.32-7.

2205. **STRAVINSKY, Igor** *and* **CRAFT, Robert**
Composing.
AM, 199, June 1957, p.46-50.
Later *in Conversations with Igor Stravinsky,* no.2221.

2206. **WHITE, Eric Walter**
Stravinsky and the concertante style.
L, 57, 6 June 1957, p.937.

2207. **KIRSTEIN, Lincoln**
Igor Stravinsky.
Na, 184, 15 June 1957, p.530-3.

2208. **THE MASTER'S work.**
Newsweek, 49, 24 June 1957, p.96. illus.

2209. **OLD revolutionary.**
Time, 69, 24 June 1957, p.48. illus.

2210. **MILNER, Anthony**
Melody in Stravinsky's music.
MT, 98, July 1957, p.370-1. mus.

2211. **STRAVINSKY, Igor**
Answers to 34 questions; an interview with Igor Stravinsky.
Encounter, 9, July 1957, p.3-7.
A translation of an article in *Melos,* 24, June 1957, p.161-7, illus.

2212. **STRAVINSKY, Igor**
An interview with Igor Stravinsky.
World of music, no.2, Oct. 1957, p.1-2. illus.

*2213. **STRAVINSKY at seventy-five and Agon.**
Dance mag., 31, Oct. 1957, p.22. illus.

2214. **STRAVINSKY, Igor *and* CRAFT, Robert**
Stravinsky on Schoenberg, "genius", Verdi, etc.
SR, 40, 9 Nov. 1957, p.36-7. illus.
Questions by Craft; answers by Stravinsky.

*2215. **THE FANTASTIC world of Stravinsky.**
Life, 23, 25 Nov. 1957, p.94-103, illus.

2216. **WILLIAMS, Richard**
The man who made dissonance respectable.
House beautiful, 100, June 1958, p.78+. illus.

2217. **STRAVINSKY, Igor *and* CRAFT, Robert**
Some painters of the Russian ballet.
AM, 202, Aug. 1958, p.65-8.
Excerpts from *Conversations with Igor Stravinsky,* no. 2221.

*2218. **STRAVINSKY as seen by Giacometti - Giacometti as seen by Stravinsky.**
Vogue, 132, 15 Aug. 1958, p.82-3.

2219. **STRAVINSKY will conduct his own works.**
MMu, 7, Sept. 1958, p.17. illus.

2220. **NEARLY half a century of Stravinsky.**
Mmu, 7, Dec. 1958, p.9. illus.

2221. **STRAVINSKY, Igor *and* CRAFT, Robert**
Conversations with Igor Stravinsky.
Faber. 1959. 9-140p. 15pl., mus.
The first in the series comprises questions by Craft and answers by Stravinsky, shrewd, fascinating and self-conscious.
Doubleday's 1959 edition was slightly longer than Faber's, but longer than either is the French edition *Avec Stravinsky* (Monaco, Editions du Rocher, 1958).
See also nos. 2226, 2231, 2242 and 2261.

2222. **LOCKSPEISER, E.**
... Stravinsky in London.
Twentieth century, 165, Jan. 1959, p.57-60.

2223. **BURKE, J. F.**
The "heart" of Stravinsky.
MMu, 8, Sept. 1959, p.11.

*2224. **CRAFT, Robert *and* STRAVINSKY, Igor**
Music and the church.
Caecilia, 86, Autumn 1959, p.99-102.
Reprinted from *Conversations with Igor Stravinsky*, no. 2221.

2225. **KELLER, Hans**
Conversations with Igor Stravinsky.
T, 52, Autumn 1959, p.16-25.
A review of the book, no.2221.

2226. **STRAVINSKY, Igor *and* CRAFT, Robert**
Memories and commentaries.
Faber. 1960. 11-183p. 22pl., mus.
Mostly a series of questions by Craft and answers by Stravinsky. This second book in the series includes a section on Russian composers, a genealogical tree of Stravinsky and the first scenario of "The Rake's Progress". The American edition is not indexed. *See also* nos. 2242 and 2261.

2227. **VLAD, Roman**
Stravinsky. Tr., with new material, by Frederick and Ann Fuller.
O.U.P. 1960. 2-232p. illus., 1pl., mus., bib.
Originating in a series of talks on Italian Radio, this detailed analysis is arranged chronologically, concentrating on the later works. There is very little biographical content. The analyses are illuminating but too laudatory. Stravinsky has written: "This is the best study of my music that has yet appeared in any country in the world". The 1967 edition has a new chapter dealing with works written from 1959 to 1966.

2228. **STRAVINSKY, Igor**
Stravinsky replies to Walt Disney.
SR, 43, 12 Mar. 1960, p.81.
On the preparation of *Fantasia.*

2229. **GOLDMAN, Richard F.**
Current chronicle. New York.
MQ, 46, Apr. 1960, p.260-4.
On "Movements", the "Double Canon" and "Epitaphium".

2230. **STRAVINSKY, Igor**
A St. Petersburg childhood.
New Yorker, 36, 24 Sept. 1960, p.146-9.

2231. **MYERS, Rollo**
Stravinsky on music.
Ch, 34, Winter 1960, p.85-8.
On *Conversations with Igor Stravinsky,* no. 2221.

*2232. **WARD-STEINMAN, David**
Serial techniques in the recent music of Igor Stravinsky.
D.M.A. dissertation, University of Illinois. 1961.

*2233. **THE DOYEN of modern composers.**
Philips music herald, Spring 1961, p.4.

2234. **EVANS, Peter**
Stravinsky: information and illusion.
T, 57, Spring 1961, p.2-5.

2235. **STRAVINSKY, Igor**
Images of myself.
AM, 207, May 1961, p.73-6. illus.
Excerpts from *Expositions and developments,* no. 2241.

*2236. **FREDRICKSON, Lawrence**
Stravinsky's instrumentation: a study of his orchestral techniques.
DA, 21, June 1961, p.3808-9.
Dissertation, University of Illinois. 1960. 220p.

2237. **ARDOIN, John**
Conversation with Robert Craft.
MA, 81, July 1961, p.27-8. illus.
Discussion of Stravinsky's new projects, Ives, Varèse etc.

*2238. **RAYNOR, H.**
The best organized language.
Music and dance, 52, July 1961, p.17-19+.
On Stravinsky.

2239. **COOKE, Deryck**
Strauss, Stravinsky and Mozart.
L, 66, 9 Nov. 1961, p.789.

2240. **COSMAN, Milein** *and* **Keller, Hans**
Stravinsky at rehearsal. A sketchbook ...
Dobson. 1962. 15p. [text only]. illus.
All Cosman's drawings (fifty pages) were done at rehearsals for B.B.C. concerts between 1958 and 1961. Keller's text adds little to the drawings; he is interviewed about the text in *Music and musicians,* no. 2258.

2241. **STRAVINSKY, Igor *and* CRAFT, Robert**
Expositions and developments.
Faber. 1962. 9-168p. 17pl.
Entertaining and egotistical reminiscences, the third in the set by Stravinsky and Craft. The American edition (Doubleday, 1962) excludes the appendices (the hitherto unpublished "Berceuse" of 1917 and "Anthem" of 1962, and the checklist of Tchaikovsky sources for "Le Baiser de la Fée") which appear in the English edition, but includes *Slightly more of a plague on one of their houses,* a brief extract of which appears in the Faber edition.
See also no.2260.

2242. **STRAVINSKY, Igor *and* CRAFT, Robert**
Stravinsky in conversation with Robert Craft.
Penguin. 1962. [2v.in 1] 11-145p. mus. 151-301p. 8pl.
A reprint of the English editions of the first two of the six conversation books, *Conversations with Igor Stravinsky* and *Memories and commentaries.* There is no index.
See also nos. 2221 and 2226.

2243. **THOMSON, J. M.**
Talking with Robert T. Craft.
Canon, 15, Jan.-Feb. 1962, p.6-8.
Mostly about Stravinsky.

2244. **STRAVINSKY, Igor**
In re Walter.
SR, 45, 31 Mar. 1962, p.39. illus.
Tribute to Bruno Walter.

2245. **MITCHELL, Donald**
Stravinsky and neo-classicism.
T, no. 61-2, Spring-Summer 1962, p.9-13.
An excerpt from Mitchell's *The language of modern music.*

2246. **READ, Herbert**
Stravinsky and the muses.
T, no. 61-2, Spring-Summer 1962, p.13-16.

2247. **WHITE, Eric Walter**
Stravinsky and Debussy.
T, no.61-2, Spring-Summer 1962, p.2-5.

2248. **ALLATT, Ann D.**
Stravinsky and the dance.
Dance mag., 36, May 1962, p.39-41. illus.
On New York Public Library's two exhibitions
See also nos. 2277 and 2386.

*2249. **IGOR Stravinsky talks to Robert Craft.**
Mademoiselle, 55, May 1962, p.182-3+.
Later *in Dialogues and a diary,* no. 2278.

2250. **KOLODIN, Irving**
A Stravinsky discography: performances with, or by, the composer.
SR, 45, 12 May 1962, p.58-9. disc.
Fifty-two works arranged by musical form.

2251. **STRAVINSKY at 80: some say the greatest.**
Newsweek, 59, 21 May 1962, p.38-42. illus.

2252. **BOONIN, Joseph**
Stravinsky records Stravinsky; Stravinsky in print.
MA, 82, June 1962, p.12-13. illus., bib., disc.
Lists books by Stravinsky and records of sixty-three of his works in which he took part.

2253. **DAVIS, Colin**
Stravinsky and the conductor.
MMu, 10, June 1962, p.24-5. illus.
Davis is interviewed about Stravinsky.

*2254. **[DISCOGRAPHY of works, 1908-1962].**
MC, 164, June 1962, p.42-7. disc.

*2255. **HARRISON, J. S.**
Fourscore for Stravinsky.
Show, 2, June 1962, p.38-9.

2256. **HART, Philip**
Stravinsky - just for the record.
Music mag./MC, 164, June 1962, p.42-7. illus., disc.
A discography arranged by date of composition.

2257. **HELM, Everett**
Stravinsky - a tribute.
MA, 82, June 1962, p.5.

2258. **KELLER, Hans**
Me about us and Stravinsky.
MMu, 10, June 1962. p.23. illus.
Interview with Keller about Cosman/Keller's *Stravinsky at rehearsal,* no. 2240.

2259. **McCLURE, John**
Igor Stravinsky at eighty.
G, 40, June 1962, p.1-3. illus.

2260. **NOBLE, Jeremy**
The self-exposed Stravinsky.
MMu, 10, June 1962, p.20-1. illus.
On *Expositions and developments,* no. 2241.

2261. **STRAVINSKY, Igor**
Conversations with Stravinsky.
MMu, 10, June 1962, p.16-19. illus.
Extracts from *Conversations with Igor Stravinsky* and *Memories and commentaries,* nos. 2221 and 2226.

2262. **STRAVINSKY, Igor *and* CRAFT, Robert**
Some composers.
MA, 82, June 1962, p.6-13. illus., disc.
Discussion of Carter, Gershwin, Hindemith, Schoenberg and Varèse, among others.

*2263. **GRUNFELD, F.**
Rebel at eighty.
Reporter, 26, 21 June 1962, p.38-40.

2264. **BECKWITH, John**
A Stravinsky triptych.
Canadian music j., 6, Summer 1962, p.5-22. mus.
Comprises *The vocal works in English,* no. 2494; *Stravinsky visits Toronto* (January and April 1962); and *New Stravinsky literature.*

2265. **CONE, Edward**
The uses of convention: Stravinsky and his models.
MQ, 48, July 1962, p.287-99. 2pl.
Also *in* LANG, *ed.* Stravinsky, p.21.

2266. **LANG, Paul Henry**
Editorial.
MQ, 48, July 1962, p.362-71.

2267. **NELSON, Robert**
Stravinsky's concept of variations.
MQ, 48, July 1962, p.327-39. 4pl., mus.
Also *in* LANG, *ed.* Stravinsky, p.61-73.

2268. **REES, C. B.**
... Igor Stravinsky.
LME, 17, July 1962, p.8-9.

2269. **SCHWARZ, Boris**
Stravinsky in Soviet Russian criticism.
MQ, 48, July 1962, p.340-61.
Also *in* LANG, *ed.* Stravinsky, p.74-95.

2270. **STRAVINSKY, Igor**
Thoughts on contemporary music and recording.
Hi-fi/stereo rev., 9, July 1962, p.29-33. illus.

2271. **WADE, Carroll D.** , *comp.*
A selected bibliography of Igor Stravinsky.
MQ, 48, July 1962, p.372-84.
Also *in* LANG, *ed.* Stravinsky, p.97-109.
Lists 359 articles and books, including foreign material but lacks some items in Austin's *Music in the twentieth century.* Should be used in conjunction with Magriel's list in Lederman's symposium, no. 2153. Although now very incomplete, this is still valuable, despite a few errors.

2272. **CONE, Edward T.**
Stravinsky: the progress of a method.
PNM, 1, Fall 1962, p.18-26. mus.
Also *in* BORETZ *and* CONE. Perspectives on Schoenberg and Stravinsky, p. 156-64.

2273. **STRAVINSKY, Igor** *and* **CRAFT, Robert**
A quintet of dialogues.
PNM, 1, Fall 1962, p.7-17.
On "Apollo Musagètes", the Octet, "Persěphone," "Scènes de Ballet" and the Symphony of Psalms.

2274. **SABANEEFF, Leonid**
Igor Stravinsky (in honor of his eightieth birthday).
RR, 21, Oct. 1962, p.370-6.

2275. **PARKER, Ralph**
Stravinsky in Russia.
NS, 64, 2 Nov. 1962, p.613+.

2276. **LANG, Paul Henry**, *ed.*
Stravinsky. A new appraisal of his work.
New York, Norton. 1963. 9-121p. mus., bib.
The essays, classified list of compositions and Wade's twelve page bibliography all appeared in the special Stravinsky issue of *Musical quarterly* (July 1962).
Contents: The uses of convention: Stravinsky and his models by Edward T. Cone. - Stravinsky's Oedipus as twentieth century hero by Wilfred Mellers. - Stravinsky and Tchaikovsky: Le Baiser de la Fée by Lawrence Morton. - Stravinsky's concept of variations by Robert Nelson. - Stravinsky in Soviet Russian criticism by Boris Schwarz.

2277. **NEW YORK PUBLIC LIBRARY.**
Stravinsky and the theatre. A catalogue of decor and costume designs for stage productions of his works, 1910-1962.
New York, New York Public Library. 1963. 4-57p. 1pl.
Detailed catalogue of the 1962 exhibition, with the works arranged chronologically. The index also covers the companion volume *Stravinsky and the dance,* no. 2386.

2278. **STRAVINSKY, Igor** *and* **CRAFT, Robert**
Dialogues and a diary.
New York, Doubleday. 1963. 9-328p. 10pl., mus.
The fourth in the series is controversial, witty and well-indexed and places special emphasis on the stage works. Part two comprises Craft's diary of Stravinsky's travels, 1948-62. The 1968 Faber edition has some material not in the American edition, including the famous comparative review of three recordings (Boulez's first recording, Craft and Karajan) of "The Rite of Spring", first published in *Hi-fi/stereo review,* no. 2458.
See also nos. 2345 and 2352.

2279. **BORETZ, Benjamin**
Stravinsky: a flood of genius.
London mag., 2, Jan. 1963, p.67-71.

2280. **FLEURET, Maurice**
Debussy speaks of Stravinsky, Stravinsky speaks of Debussy ...
Tr. by Dr. F. Harling-Comyns.
MO, 86, Jan. 1963, p.211+.
Originally appeared in the Debussy Memorial number of the *Journal musical français.*

2281. **STRAVINSKY, Vera**
Stravinsky at home.
MA, 83, Jan. 1963, p.10-11. illus.
Later *in Themes and episodes,* no. 2310.

2282. **A STRAVINSKY scrapbook.**
MA, 83, Jan. 1963, p.12-13. illus.

*2283. **STRAVINSKY, Igor**
Schoenberg and I.
Show, 3, Feb. 1963, p.30-1.

2284. **FRANK, Jonathan**
Tantalising octogenarian.
MO, 86, Mar. 1963, p.337+.

2285. **SHATTUCK, Roger**
Making time: a study of Stravinsky, Proust and Sartre.
Kenyon rev., 25, Spring 1963, p.248-63.

*2286. **STRAVINSKY, Igor**
Thoughts of an octogenarian.
Show, 3, Apr. 1963, p.74-5+. illus.

2287. **CRAFT, Robert**
Stravinsky's return, a Russian diary.
Encounter, 20, June 1963, p.33-48.
His return to Russia, September-October 1962.

2288. **STRAVINSKY, Igor**
Stravinsky off the cuff.
MMu, 11, July 1963, p.13. illus.

2289. **[STRAVINSKY, Igor]**
Interview with Stravinsky.
America, 109, 31 Aug. 1963, p.219-20.
Edited by C.J. McNaspy.

2290. **BERGER, Arthur**
Problems of pitch organization in Stravinsky.
PNM, 2, Fall-Winter 1963, p.11-42. mus.
Also *in* BORETZ *and* CONE. Perspectives on Schoenberg and Stravinsky, p.123-54.

*2291. **STRAVINSKY, Igor**
Speculations.
Show, 4, Feb. 1964, p.42-3+.
Later *in Themes and episodes,* no. 2310.

2292. **BABBIT, Milton**
Remarks on the recent Stravinsky.
PNM, 2, Spring-Summer 1964, p.35-55. mus.
Also *in* BORETZ *and* CONE. Perspectives on Schoenberg and Stravinsky, p.165-85.

*2293. **STRAVINSKY, Igor**
Music: a dialogue.
Show, 4, Apr. 1964, p.42.
Later *in Themes and episodes,* no. 2310.

*2294. **DUKE, V.**
The deification of Stravinsky.
Listen, 1, May-June 1964, p.1-5.
Sept.-Oct. 1964, p.1+.
Reprinted from Duke's book *Listen here!*

2295. **SZIGETI, Joseph**
Stravinsky at work.
MMu, 12, June 1964, p.23. illus.

2296. **REID, Charles**
Working with Stravinsky.
Sp, 213, 3 July 1964, p.14-15.

*2297. **STRAVINSKY, Igor**
On conductors and conducting.
Show, 4, July-Aug. 1964, p.28+.
Later *in Theme and episodes,* no. 2310.

*2298. **STRAVINSKY, Igor**
A cure for V.D.
Listen, 1, Sept.-Oct. 1964, p.1-2.
Refers to Vernon Duke. Later *in Themes and episodes,* no. 2310.

*2299. **SIOHAN, Robert**
Stravinsky.
Calder and Boyars. 1965. 7-192p. illus., 1pl., bib., disc.
A clearly written, well-illustrated survey, first published in Paris in 1959, and mostly devoted to the period up to 1930. There is a useful chronology covering 1943-1962.

*2300. **RASKIN, J.**
Diary of a recording artist.
MJ, 23, Feb. 1965, p.35+.

2301. **EVANS, Peter**
Stravinsky's Elegies.
L, 73, 11 Feb. 1965, p.241.
His memorial pieces.

*2302. **STRAVINSKY, Igor**
Schoenberg's letters.
HF/MA, 15, May 1965, p.136.
First published in *The Observer,* 18 Oct. 1964 and later *in Themes and episodes,* no. 2310.

2303. **STRAVINSKY, Igor**
An interview with Igor Stravinsky.
New York rev. of books, 4, 3 June 1965, p.4.
Mostly on critics and criticism, and is decidedly waspish.

2304. **STRAVINSKY, Igor**
Memories of T. S. Eliot.
Esquire, 64, Aug. 1965, p.92-3. illus.
Later *in Themes and episodes,* no. 2310.

2305. **CRAFT, Robert**
With Aldous Huxley.
Encounter, 25, Nov. 1965, p.10-16.
On Huxley, Craft and Stravinsky. Later *in Themes and episodes,* no. 2310.

*2306. **COLEMAN, Jack**
The trumpet: its use in selected works of Stravinsky, Hindemith, Shostakovich and Copland.
DA, 26, Dec. 1965, p.3389.
Thesis, University of Southern California. 1965. 268p.

*2307. **HUFF, J. A.**
Linear structures and their relation to style in selected compositions by Igor Stravinsky.
DA, 26, Dec. 1965, p.3393.
PhD, Music Theory, dissertation, Northwestern University, Illinois. 1965. 279p.
The six works selected: the Concerto for Piano and Wind Instruments, "The Flood," "Movements", "The Soldier's Tale", the Symphony of Psalms and "Threni".

*2308. **MASTER musician, Stravinsky.**
Music educator's j., 52, no.6, 1966, p.49-51.

2309. **STRAVINSKY, Igor**
A decade later ...
in IRVINE, *ed.* Anton von Webern: perspectives, p.xx-xxvii.
Later *in Themes and episodes,* no. 2310.

2310. **STRAVINSKY, Igor** *and* **CRAFT, Robert**
Themes and episodes.
New York, Knopf. 1966. viii-x, 4-352, i-xvip. mus.
The fifth volume in the series of fascinating and amusing jottings and essays, many of which have previously appeared in American periodicals. There are programme notes to seventeen of his works. Part two is called *From the diaries of Robert Craft 1949-66.*
See also nos. 2318 and 2360e.

2311. **WHITE, Eric Walter**
Stravinsky. The composer and his works.
Faber. 1966. ix-xv, 3-608p. illus., 12pl., mus., bib.
The register of works alone runs to 381 pages and is practically complete (except for the "Requiem Canticles"), with sixteen pages on "The Rake's Progress". There is some repetition of material, and the writing is occasionally trivial and naive, but by and large this is an admirably painstaking, self-effacing and splendidly laid-out survey containing 200 musical examples. The standard reference book on Stravinsky's music.
See also no. 2322.

2312. **CRAFT, Robert**
With Stravinsky in Warsaw.
Harper's mag. 232, Feb. 1966, p.66-70+.
Also *in Themes and episodes,* no. 2310.

2313. **HOPKINS, G. W.**
Stravinsky's chords (1).
T, 76, Spring 1966, p.6-12. mus.
(2).
77, Summer 1966, p.2-9. mus.

2314. **MODI, Sorab**
Salute to Stravinsky.
Philips music herald, Spring 1966, p.14-15. illus.

2315. **[STRAVINSKY, Igor]**
Stravinsky on the musical scene and other matters.
New York rev. of books, 6, 12 May 1966, p.10-12. illus.
Also *in Dialogues and a diary* no. 2278 (Faber edition), and *in Retrospectives and conclusions,* no. 2347.

*2316. **STRAVINSKY, Igor** *and* **CRAFT, Robert**
Perfect total.
Seventeen, 25, Aug. 1966, p.304+.
Also *in Themes and episodes,* no. 2310.

2317. **STRAVINSKY, Igor**
Music and the statistical age. An interview.
Commentary, 42, Sept. 1966, p.49-52.
Also *in Dialogues and a diary,* no. 2278 (Faber edition), and *in Retrospectives and conclusions,* no. 2347.

2318. **SOLLBERGER, Harvey**
Footnote to Stravinsky.
PNM, 5, Fall-Winter 1966, p.148-52.
Questions some of the statements in *Themes and episodes,* no. 2310.

*2319. **IGOR Stravinsky, how he lives and works.**
ASCAP today, 1, no. 2, 1967, p.2-4. illus.
Extract from *Themes and episodes,* no. 2310.

2320. **NEWMAN, Arnold**
Bravo Stravinsky. Photographs by Arnold Newman. Text by Robert Craft. Foreword by Francis Steegmuller.
Cleveland, World Publishing Co. 1967. 4-127p. illus.
Stravinsky portrayed between October 1966 and January 1967: in the process of composing, at concerts, at home etc. The photographs are outstanding, and the book includes a facsimile of the complete manuscript of the song "The Owl and the Pussycat", but there is no index. One of the most important and revealing books on the composer.
See also no. 2323.

2321. **NOBLE, Jeremy**
Portraits of Debussy. 1. Debussy and Stravinsky.
MT, 108, Jan. 1967, p.22-5. illus.

2322. **GOODWIN, Noël**
Stravinsky in detail.
MMu, 15, Feb. 1967, p.22-3. illus.
Review of White's *Stravinsky. The composer and his works,* no. 2311.

*2323. **SCULLY, J.**
World's greatest pictures: Stravinsky by Newman.
Modern photography, 31, May 1967, p.70-1+. illus.
See also no. 2320.

2324. **WHITE, Eric W.**
Igor Stravinsky.
L, 77, 18 May 1967, p.647-8. illus.

2325. **HAMILTON, David**
Stravinsky and the microphone.
HF, 17, June 1967, p.56-60. illus.

2326. **STRAVINSKY, Igor**
Stravinsky at eighty-five: an interview.
New York rev. of books, 8, 1 June 1967, p.12-15. illus.
Later *in Retrospectives and conclusions,* no. 2347.

2327. **HOMAGE to Stravinsky.**
T, 81, Summer 1967 [unpaged].
Short compositions to commemorate his eighty-fifth birthday by R. R. Bennett, Birtwistle, Crosse, Brian Dennis, Michael Finnissy, Maw, Maxwell Davies, Ogdon, Smalley, Souster, Tavener and Malcolm Williamson.

2328. **MELLERS, Wilfred**
Stravinsky and jazz.
T, 81 Summer 1967, p.29-31.

2329. **OGDON, John**
Stravinsky and the piano.
T, 81, Summer 1967, p.36-41. mus.

2330. **ROTH, Ernst**
A great mind and a great spirit.
T, 81, Summer 1967, p.4-5.

2331. **SMALLEY, Roger,** *and others.*
Personal viewpoints.
T, 81, Summer 1967, p.19-29.
Notes on Stravinsky by Crosse, Ginastera, Goehr, Smalley and Tavener.

2332. **SOUVCHINSKY, Pierre**
Stravinsky as a Russian [1].
T, 81, Summer 1967, p.5-6.

2333. **WARRACK, John**
Stravinsky as a Russian. [2].
T, 81, Summer 1967, p.7-9.

2334. **WHITE, Eric Walter**
Listening to Stravinsky's music in the 1920s.
T, 81, Summer 1967, p.32-6.

2335. **KELLER, Hans**
Stravinsky the downbeater.
L, 78, 19 Oct. 1967, p.509. mus.

2336. **SUTTON, Wadham**
Stravinsky and synthetic melody.
MO, 91, Nov. 1967, p.81+.

2337. **EVETT, Robert**
Stravinsky at 85.
NR, 157, 16 Dec. 1967, p.27-8.

*2338. **CRAFT, Robert**
Stravinsky.
Look, 31, 26 Dec. 1967, p.50-4+.

2339. **BORETZ Benjamin** *and* **CONE, Edward T.** , *editors.*
Perspectives on Schoenberg and Stravinsky.
New Jersey, Princeton University Press. 1968. v-x, 3-284p. mus., disc.
Six essays on Stravinsky (and nine on Schoenberg); all have previously appeared in the American periodical *Perspectives of new music.* The comprehensive Stravinsky discography was corrected and amended by Stravinsky and Craft. Complex but excellent.
Contents: Problems of pitch organisation in Stravinsky by Arthur Berger. -Stravinsky: the progress of a method by Edward T. Cone. - Remarks on the recent Stravinsky by Milton Babbitt. - Notes on Stravinsky's "Abraham and Isaac" by Claudio Spies. - Notes on Stravinsky's variations by Claudio Spies. - Some notes on Stravinsky's Requiem settings by Claudio Spies.

2340. **STRAVINSKY, Igor**
On manners, music and morality: an interview with Igor Stravinsky.
Harper's mag., 236, Feb. 1968, p.41-7.
Later *in Retrospectives and conclusions,* no. 2347. The interview was edited by Robert Craft.

2341. **STRAVINSKY, Igor**
Side effects: an interview with Stravinsky.
New York rev. of books, 10, 14 Mar. 1968, p.3-4+. illus.
Later *in Retrospectives and conclusions,* no. 2347.

2342. **ASENJO, F. G.**
The aesthetics of Igor Stravinsky.
J. of aesthetics and art criticism, 26, Spring 1968, p.297-305.

2343. **DAVIES, Laurence.**
Stravinsky as Littérateur.
ML, 49, Apr. 1968, p.135-44.
Discusses his writings.

2344. **STRAVINSKY, Igor**
A realm of truth.
New York rev. of books, 11, 26 Sept. 1968, p.3-4. illus.
Review of Joseph Kerman's book *The Beethoven quartets.* Later *in Retrospectives and conclusions,* no. 2347.

2345. **BUSH, Geoffrey**
Hear near Tiflis.
C, no.29, Autumn 1968, p.28-30.
Correction of a statement made by Stravinsky in *Dialogues and a diary,* no. 2278.
See also nos. 2351 and 2352.

2346. **CRAFT, Robert**
Stravinsky and some writers.
Harper's mag., 237, Dec. 1968, p.101-2+.
Excerpts from Craft's 1948 diary: on Auden, Aldous Huxley, Isherwood and Evelyn Waugh. Later *in Retrospectives and conclusions,* no. 2347.

2347. **STRAVINSKY, Igor** *and* **CRAFT, Robert**
Retrospectives and conclusions.
New York, Knopf. 1969. 4-350, vi-xip. mus.
Sixth of the series, all of it having appeared before in (mostly American) periodicals and in *Dialogues and a diary,* no. 2278. The miscellanea consist of interviews, prefaces and reviews; Craft's notes on "Lulu" are first-rate; but the highlight of the book is Craft's diaries, particularly the last years (up to 1968) which movingly tell of Stravinsky's fight for life. The exact extent of Craft's contribution is difficult to ascertain, but it is probably more than it seems. *See also* no. 2360e.

2348. **YOUNG, Percy M.**
Stravinsky. Illustrated by Richard Shirley Smith.
Ernest Benn. 1969. 5-7p. illus., mus.
Brief and sometimes careless biography for younger readers. One of the *Masters of music* series.

2349. **WHITTALL, Arnold**
Stravinsky and the music drama.
ML, 50, Jan. 1969, p.63-7.

2350. **STRAVINSKY, Igor**
Where is thy sting?
New York rev. of books, 12, 24 Apr. 1969, p.3+. illus.
Interview with Stravinsky, probably the last published before his death. Reprinted *in Retrospectives and conclusions,* no. 2347.

2351. **BUSH, Geoffrey**
[Heard near Tiflis].
C, no. 32, Summer 1969, p.7.
See also nos. 2345 and 2352.

2352. **STRAVINSKY, Igor**
Heard near Tiflis: a letter from Stravinsky.
C, no. 32, Summer 1969, p.5-6.
A reply to Bush's article, no.2345. Bush replies in equally scathing terms, no. 2351. Also *in Retrospectives and conclusions,* no. 2347.

2353. **DAWNEY, Michael**
Stravinsky.
Church music, 2, Aug. 1969, p.6-7.

*2354. **CRAFT, Robert**
[Excerpts from his diaries].
Harper's mag., 239, Oct. 1969, p?.
Also *in Retrospectives and conclusions,* no. 2347.

2355. **CRAFT, Robert**
Igor Stravinsky: on illness and death.
Harper's mag., 239, Nov. 1969, p.111-16+. illus.
Also *in Retrospectives and conclusions,* no. 2347.

See no. 1847.

*2356. **DOBRIN, A.**
Stravinsky, his life and times.
New York, Crowell. 1970. 197p. illus.

*2357. **STRAVINSKY, Igor**
The composer in academia; reflections on a theme of Stravinsky.
College music symposium, 10, 1970, p.57-9+.

2358. **EVETT, Robert**
Marriage of Craft and art.
NR, 162, 10 Jan. 1970, p.25-7.
On Stravinsky and Craft.

2359. **SAAL, Hubert**
Stravinsky's alter ego.
Newsweek, 75, 19 Jan. 1970, p.54-5. illus.
On his relationship with Craft.

2360. **MATTHEWS, David**
Copland and Stravinsky.
T, 95, Winter 1970-1, p.10-14. 2pl., mus.

2360a. **CRAFT, Robert**
Stravinsky: chronicle of a friendship, 1948-1971.
Gollancz. 1972. xv-xvi, 3-424, iii-xvip. 24pl., mus.
Excerpts from Craft's diaries, the book not being exclusively about Stravinsky. Each chapter is headed by an itinerary which includes dates of premières and recordings: these are useful but sometimes very incomplete. There is practically nothing on Stravinsky's concerts, and the illustrations are mostly different to those previously published. Craft's approach is cool and clinical compared with Lillian Libman's (no. 2360c).

2360b. **HORGAN, Paul**
Encounters with Stravinsky. A personal record.
The Bodley Head. 1972. 9-224p. illus., 10pl.
An affectionate portrait of Stravinsky by the novelist who was his friend and colleague from 1957 to 1971. Covers a similar period to that in Libman's book (no. 2360c) but is more anecdotal and less searching. The New York edition, also published in 1972 (by Farrar, Straus and Giroux), runs to 300 pages, part one of the American edition being more than double the length of the English.

2360c. **LIBMAN, Lillian**
And music at the close: Stravinsky's last years. A personal memoir.
Macmillan. 1972. 11-400p. 8pl.
Describes her tenure (1959-71) as the composer's personal manager, secretary and companion. Throws revealing light on his relations with Craft and on the responsibility for the Stravinsky recordings and writings. A fascinating and moving picture of the composer at home, behind the scenes at concerts etc., and particularly of his illnesses, death and funeral. Miss Libman's narrative brings us closer to Stravinsky the man than any other book on him in English.

2360d. **McCALDIN, Denis**
Stravinsky.
Novello. 1972. 3-22p. bib.

One of the *Novello short biographies,* it contains a list of his principal works (wrongly printed) which omits "The Nightingale" but includes "Ragtime". There is constant reference to "Petruska" (sic) and no index.

2360e. **STRAVINSKY, Igor**
Themes and conclusions.
Faber. 1972. 9-328p. illus., 16pl., mus.
A combination of the revised *Themes and episodes* (no. 2310) and the expanded *Retrospectives and conclusions* (no. 2347), the book was seen through the press by Robert Craft. It collects together Stravinsky's programme notes on seventeen of his works, interviews, letters to the press, reviews and miscellaneous "Squibs". There is a review of three more versions of "The Rite", Boulez's second (with the Cleveland Orchestra), Mehta's and the composer's own (1960). If we are to believe Lillian Libman's moving account of his last year of life, Stravinsky could hardly have been responsible for the foreword and six pages of interviews all dated March-April 1971, the last five days before he died. One suspects considerable doctoring of the text by Craft.

2360f. **STRAVINSKY, Theodore**
Catherine and Igor Stravinsky: a family album.
Boosey and Hawkes. 1973. [unpaged]. 79pl.
Well-produced album covering 1874-1920, very largely of family photographs (Catherine was the composer's first wife). The last five photographs are in colour and are of Stravinsky in 1970. The text and captions, by his eldest son, are in English, French and German.

B. *Works.*

Symphonies.

2361. **WHITE, Eric Walter**
Stravinsky latter-day symphonist.
Horizon, 16, Nov. 1947, p.290-7.

Symphony in C.

2362. **BABITZ, Sol**
Stravinsky's Symphony in C (1940). A short analysis and commentary.
MQ, 27, Jan. 1941, p.20-5. mus.

2363. **STRAVINSKY, Igor**
Programme notes. Symphony in C.
London mag., 5, Feb. 1966, p.38-9+.

Symphony in Three Movements.

2364. **FULLER, Donald**
... Stravinsky full-length portrait.
MM, 23, Winter 1945, p.45-6.

See no. 2126.

Concerto in D for Strings.

See no. 2126.

Concerto in E flat ("Dumbarton Oaks").

2365. **THYBO, Leif**
A Stravinsky organ work?
MT, 94, Aug. 1953, p.353-4. mus.
Thybo's organ transcription of "Dumbarton Oaks".

2366. **STRAVINSKY, Igor**
Programme notes. Dumbarton Oaks concerto.
London mag., 5, Feb. 1966, p.37-8.

"Dumbarton Oaks" concerto — *see Concerto in E flat.*

Greeting prelude.

2367. **STRAVINSKY, Igor**
Programme notes. Greeting prelude.
London mag., 5, Feb. 1966, p.44.

Monumentum pro Gesualdo.

2368. **CRAFT, Robert**
A note on Gesualdo's "Sacrae Cantiones" and on Gesualdo and Stravinsky.
T, 45, Autumn 1957, p.5-7.

2369. **MASON, Colin**
Stravinsky and Gesualdo.
T, nos. 55-6, Autumn-Winter 1960, p.39-48. mus.

Four Studies for Orchestra.

2370. **DEL MAR, N.**
Confusion and error.
S, no. 21, Oct. 1957, p. 26-9. mus.
Highlights mistakes in printed editions of orchestral works.

Symphonies for Wind Instruments.

2371. [MYERS, Rollo]
"Symphonies d'instruments à vent".
L, 15, 18, Mar. 1936, p. 561-2.

*2372. WHITWELL, D.
Stravinsky - his music for winds.
Instrument, 20, June 1966, p.50-3. illus.

Variations (Aldous Huxley in Memoriam).

2373. STRAVINSKY, Igor
Variations.
LME, 20, Sept. 1965, p.5-6. illus.

2374. WHITE, Eric Walter
... Two new memorial works by Stravinsky.
T, 74, Autumn 1965, p.18-21. mus.
The Huxley Variations and "Introitus".

2375. SPIES, Claudio
Notes on Stravinsky's Variations.
PNM, 4, Fall-Winter 1965, p.62-74. mus.
Also *in* BORETZ *and* CONE. Perspectives on Schoenberg and Stravinsky, p.210-22.

Ballets.

2376. HENRY, Leigh
Igor Stravinsky and the ballet.
Musical news, 57, 5 July 1919, p.4.
19 July 1919, p.22.
16 Aug. 1919, p.50+.

*2377. LEVINSON, André
Stravinsky and the dance.
Theatre arts, 8, Nov. 1924, p.741-54. illus.

*2378. WATKINS, Mary F.
Who's who among ballet composers.
Dance mag., 12, May 1929, p.17+. illus.

*2379. SELTSAM, W. H.
The ballets of Igor Strawinski.
Phonograph monthly rev., 4, Sept. 1930, p.402-3.

2380. **BERGER, Arthur**
Music for the ballet.
DI, 6, 1947, p.258-77.
Also *in* LEDERMAN, *ed.* Stravinsky in the theatre, p.41-69.
illus., mus.

2381. **MOORE, Lillian**
Stravinsky on music for the ballet.
DT, no. 437, Feb. 1947, p.243-4.

2382. **KARSAVINA, Tamara**
A recollection of Strawinsky.
T, n.s., no.8, Summer 1948, p.7-9.

2383. **YANTCHEVSKY, Nicolas**
Historical extracts from the biography of Stravinsky bearing on his work with Diaghileff. Tr. by Nadine Nicolaeva-Legat.
Ballet world, 1, Mar. 1949, p.4-7. illus.

*2384. **HASTINGS, Baird**
Stravinsky and his choreographers.
Chrysalis, 4, no. 11-12, 1951, p.5.

*2385. **DONINGTON, R.**
Stravinsky: ballet music.
1952.
One of the *Decca music guides.*

2386. **NEW YORK PUBLIC LIBRARY.**
Stravinsky and the dance. A survey of ballet productions 1910-1962.
New York, New York Public Library. 1962. 4-60p. illus.
Well-illustrated catalogue of the 1962 exhibition of decor and costume designs. Indexed *in Stravinsky and the theatre,* no. 2277.

Agon.

2387. **MORTON, Lawrence**
Current chronicle. Los Angeles.
MQ, 43, Oct. 1957, p.535-41. mus.

See no. 2213.

2388. **GLOCK, William**
Stravinsky's "Agon".
LME, 13, July 1958, p.20-2.

2389. **HUNT, David**
Agon. Music.
DD, 9, Oct. 1958, p.10-11+.

2390. **KELLER, Hans**
Strawinsky's performance of "Agon": a report.
T, 50, Winter 1958, p.22-5. illus.

*2391. **TWO ballets by George Balanchine and Igor Stravinsky.**
Dance perspectives, no. 1, Winter 1959, p.35-46.
"Agon" and "Apollo".

Apollo Musagètes.

2392. **TURNER, W. J.**
Apollon Musagètes.
NS, 31, 30 June 1928, p.388-9.

2393. **LOURIÉ, Arthur**
Stravinsky's "Apollo".
Dominant, 1, Aug.-Sept. 1928, p.20-1.

2394. **SABANEEV, L.**
Dawn or dusk? Stravinsky's new ballets: "Apollo" and "The Fairy's Kiss". Tr. by S. W. Pring.
MT, 70, May 1929, p. 403-6.

*2395. **SELTSAM, William**
The ballets of Igor Strawinski.
Phonograph monthly rev., 5, Oct. 1930, p.12-13.
On "Apollo".

See no. 2391.

See no. 2273.

2396. **BARNES, Clive**
Apollo, Balanchine and Stravinsky.
About the house, 2, Christmas 1966, p.16-19. illus.

2397. **GOODWIN, Noel**
Apollo. Music.
DD, 18, Jan. 1967, p.15-16. illus.

Le Baiser de la Fee, ballet – *see The Fairy's Kiss.*

The Card Party.

2398. **KIRSTEIN, Lincoln**
Working with Stravinsky.
MM, 14, Mar.-Apr. 1937, p. 143-6.
Describes their collaboration on the ballet.

*2399. **THE CARD Party by Stravinsky.**
Cue, 5, 24 Apr. 1937, p.9. illus.

2400. **GODDARD, Scott**
Stravinsky's latest ballet: "Jeu de Cartes".
L, 19, 4 May 1938, p.981.

2401. **STRAVINSKY, Igor**
Programme notes. Jeu de Cartes.
London mag., 5, Feb. 1966, p.33-5+.

2402. **GOODWIN, Noel**
Card Game. Music.
DD, 17, Apr. 1966, p.24.

Danses Concertantes.

2403. **FRANKENSTEIN, Alfred**
Stravinsky in Beverly Hills.
MM, 19, 1941-2 [i.e. Mar. 1942?], p.178-81.
Mostly on "Dantes Concertantes".

2404. **SLONIMSKY, Nicolas**
Stravinsky. Danses Concertantes.
in SLONIMSKY. Programme notes: 1947-1948. p.31-2.

2405. **GOODWIN, Noël**
Danses Concertantes. Music.
DD, 10, May 1959, p.12-13.

The Fairy's Kiss.

See no. 2394.

2406. **GOODWIN, Noël**
"Le Baiser de la Fée". Music.
DD, 11, June 1960, p.11+.

2407. **MORTON, Lawrence**
Stravinsky and Tchaikovsky: Le Baiser de la Fée.
MQ, 48, July 1962, p.313-26. 4pl., mus.
Also *in* LANG, *ed.* Stravinsky, p.47-60.

The Firebird.

*2408. **BEAUMONT, Cyril W.**
L'Oiseau de Feu. Decorated by Ethelbert White.
Beaumont. 1919. 16p. illus.

2409. **EVANS, Edwin**
Stravinsky. The Firebird and Petrushka.
O.U.P. 1933. 4-44p. mus.
Clear and informative coverage of the two ballets.

2410. **HOGARTH, Basil**
... The Firebird and Petroushka (Stravinsky).
G, 14, June 1936, p.5-6. illus.

2411. **EVANS, Edwin**
The music of "L'Oiseau de Feu".
DT, no,346, July 1939, p.400-1. illus.

See no. 1374.

*2412. **SARGEANT, W.**
Firebird's progress.
Life, 14, 23 Mar. 1953, p.151-2+. illus.

*2413. **STRAVINSKY, Igor**
"Firebird's " first flight.
HF, 10, June 1960, p.34-6. illus.

2414. **DENNINGTON, A.**
The three orchestrations of Stravinsky's "Firebird".
Ch, 34, Winter 1960, p.89-94.

2415. **THE FIREBIRD.** Illustrated by Ludek Manasek. Tr. from the Czech by I. Kuthanova.

Dent. 1970. illus.

Jeu de Cartes, ballet – *see The Card Party.*

L'Oiseau de Feu, ballet – *see The Firebird.*

Orpheus.

2416. **DAHL, Ingolf**
The new Orpheus.
DI, 6, 1947, p.285-6.
Also *in* LEDERMAN, *ed.* Stravinsky in the theatre, p.70-4.
illus., mus.

2417. **BALLO, Ferdinando**
Introduction to Strawinsky's "Orpheus".
T, n.s., no.10, Winter 1948-9, p.13-15.

2418. **SHAWE-TAYLOR, Desmond**
New Stravinsky.
NS, 37, 26 Feb. 1949, p.201-2.
"Orpheus" and the Mass.

Petrushka.

*2419. **BEAUMONT, Cyril W.**
Petrouchka. Decorated by Michel Sevier.
Beaumont. 1919. 16p. illus.

2420. **SCHOLES, Percy A.**
... The ballet music of Stravinsky's "Petrouchka", as played by the Royal Albert Hall Orchestra conducted by Eugene Goossens.
G, 2, Jan. 1925, p.283-7.
Gives a synopsis of the ballet and a detailed description of it in the words of Stravinsky and Benois.

*2421. **EDGERTON, Giles**
Petroushka, Igor Strawinsky's famous ballet.
Arts and decoration, 22, Feb. 1925, p.17-18+. illus.

*2422. **BARNETT, David**
Petrouchka, an analysis.
FR, 1, Feb. 1928, p.31-5.

2423. **SCHAEFFNER, André**
Petroushka.
MMR, 62, Mar.-Apr. 1932, p.55-8.

See no. 2409.

See no. 2410.

*2424. **LAWRENCE, Robert**
Petrouchka, a ballet by Igor Stravinsky. Designed by Alexandre Benois. Illustrated by Alexander Serebriakoff. Authorized by the Ballets Russes.
New York, Random House, 1940. 39p. illus., mus.

2425. **POSNER, Sandy**
Petrouchka. The story of the ballet. With decorations by Joyce Millen.
Newman Wolsey. 1945. 9-96p. illus.
Largely a history of the ballet, but also includes a detailed synopsis.

2426. **STERNFELD, Frederick W.**
Some Russian folk-songs in Stravinsky's "Petrouchka".
N, s.s., 2, Mar. 1945, p.95-107. mus.

2427. **ANDERSON, W. R.**
Stravinsky's perfection "Petroushka".
G, 22, Apr. 1945, p.128-9.

2428. **HUSSEY, Dyneley**
The tragedy of Stravinsky.
DT, no. 432, Sept. 1946, p.617-18. illus.
Mostly on "Petrushka".

2429. **BOYS, Henry**
Note on the new "Petrouchka".
T, n.s., no.8, Summer 1948, p.15-18. mus.
Deals with the different versions.

2430. **SENIOR, Evan**
Stravinsky and Petrouchka.
DD, 1, Nov. 1950, p.17. illus.

2431. **BENOIS, Alexandre**
The story behind Petrouchka.
DD, 8, Mar. 1957, p.7-11. illus.
Reprinted from Benois's *Reminiscences of the Russian ballet* (Putnam, 1941).

2432. **HUNT, David**
Petrushka. Music.
DD, 8, May 1957, p.11.

*2433. **HAMM, Charles,** *ed.*
Stravinsky: Petrushka.
New York, Norton. 1967. 218p. mus., bib.
Contributors include Cyril Beaumont and Edith Sitwell.

Pulcinella.

2434. **ROUSSY DE SALES, Raoul de**
Igor Stravinsky's "Pulcinella".
Ch, n.s., no.8, June 1920, p.234-6.

2435. **SALAZAR, Adolfo.**
Pulcinella and Maese Pedro.
Ch, 6, Jan.-Feb. 1925, p.112-25.
Part of the article is on Falla's "Master Peter's Puppet Show".

2436. **MYERS, Rollo**
Stravinsky's "Pulcinella".
L, 17, 23 June 1937, p. 1278.

2437. **LIEBERMAN, William**
Picasso and the ballet. Pulcinella, 1919-1920.
DI, 5, Nov.-Dec. 1946, p.286-91. illus.

*2438. **ROSS, G.**
Pergolesi via Stravinsky.
Repertoire, 1, Jan. 1952, p.160-2.

2439. **STRAVINSKY, Igor** *and* **CRAFT, Robert**
Two for the theater
ON, 25, 10 Dec. 1960, p.8-11. illus.
An excerpt from *Expositions and developments* (no. 2241) on the composition of "Pulcinella" and "The Wedding".

The Rite of Spring.

*2440. **LALO, Pierre**
Remarks on the ballet "Le Sacre du Printemps".
NMR, 12, Oct, 1913, p.440-2.
From *Le Temps* and translated by Mrs. Daniel Gregory Mason.

2441. **"LE SACRE" in 1913.**
Musical news, 60, 11 June 1921, p.749-50.

2442. **TURNER, W. J.**
The Rite of Spring.
NS, 17, 2 July 1921, p.358.

2443. **MAINE, Basil**
Stravinsky and pure music.
MT, 63, Feb. 1922, p.93-4.
Mainly deals with "The Rite of Spring".

*2444. **RHODES, William**
Stravinsky's "Le Sacre du Printemps", a critical analysis.
M.A. thesis, Columbia University. 1926? 56p.
[typewritten].

2445. **GRAY, Cecil**
The "Sacre" reheard.
Nation and Athenaeum, 44, 2 Feb. 1929, p.616-17.

*2446. **STRAVINSKY, Igor,** *and others.*
Le Sacre du Printemps.
MC, 100, 29 Mar. 1930, p.7+. illus.
Comments by Stravinsky, Stokowski and Boris de Schloezer.

2447. **BLOM, Eric**
... Stravinsky. "The Rite of Spring".
MTe, 10, Jan. 1931, p.25-6. illus., mus.

*2448. **HOGARTH, Basil**
The masterpiece of the ballet. 5. Le Sacre du Printemps (Stravinsky).
G, 14, Aug. 1936, p.129-30.

2449. **HILL, Ralph**
"The Rite of Spring".
RT, 78, 8 Jan. 1943, p.4. illus.

2450. **COCTEAU, Jean**
Parisian memoir.
DI, 6, 1947, p.238-40. illus.
Also *in* LEDERMAN, *ed.* Stravinsky in the theatre, p.13-20. illus.
The title here is *Le Sacre du Printemps.*

2451. **LEVINSON, André**
The two Sacres.
in LEDERMAN, *ed.* Stravinsky in the theatre, p.26-9. illus.

2452. **RIVIÈRE, Jacques**
Nijinsky's innovation.
in LEDERMAN, *ed.* Stravinsky in the theatre, p.22-3.

2453. **STRAVINSKY, Igor**
Interpretation by Massine.
in LEDERMAN, *ed.* Stravinsky in the theatre, p.24-6.
illus.

2454. **VUILLERMOZ, Emile**
An irresistible force.
in LEDERMAN, *ed.* Stravinsky in the theatre, p.21-22.

2455. **VUILLERMOZ, Emile**
The triumph of the orchestra.
in LEDERMAN, *ed.* Stravinsky in the theatre. p.30-1. illus.

2456. **STRAVINSKY, Igor**
Apropos "Le Sacre du Printemps".
SR, 42, 26 Dec. 1959, p.29-31+. illus.

2457. **GOODWIN, Noel**
... The Rite of Spring. Music.
DD, 13, June 1962, p.16-17.

2458. **STRAVINSKY, Igor**
Stravinsky reviews three Rites of Spring.
Hi-fi/stereo rev., 14, Feb. 1965, p.66-3. illus.
The versions are those of Boulez (his first), Craft and Karajan.
The article is corrected *in Dialogues and a diary*, no. 2278.

*2459. **SACRE de Diaghilev.**
Vogue, 145, 15 Apr. 1965, p.124-5+.

2460. **CRAFT, Robert**
The Rite of Spring: genesis of a masterpiece.
PNM, 5, Fall-Winter 1966, p.20-37. mus.
Text of a lecture given at Ohio State University, November 1966.
Also *in* Stravinsky. The Rite of Spring..., p.xv-xxxvii. mus.

2461. **STRAVINSKY, Igor**
The Rite of Spring... Sketches 1911-1913. Facsimile reproductions from the autographs. Foreword by François Lesure.
Boosey and Hawkes. 1969. vii-x1vii, 1-139p. mus.
Colour facsimile of the autograph manuscript. The appendix, which includes *Commentary to the sketches*, is bound separately and contained in a pocket at the back of the book. Craft's introductory essay in three languages: *Genesis of a masterpiece* and his advice to conductors on the performance of "The Rite" enhance this beautifully produced work. Obligatory reading for all students of Stravinsky. *See also* no. 2460.

2462. **SMALLEY, Roger**
The sketchbook of the Rite of Spring.
T, 91, Winter 1969-70, p.2-13. 1pl., mus.
See also no. 2461.

2463. **KARLINSKY, Simon**
The composer's workshop.
Nation, 210, 15 June 1970, p.730-3.
Book reviews of *Retrospectives and conclusions,* no. 2347, and of *The Rite of Spring ...,* no. 2461. Stravinsky's reply: 211, 3 Aug. 1970, p.66+.

Le Sacre du Printemps, ballet – *see The Rite of Spring.*

Scènes de Ballet.

See no. 2126.

See no. 2273.

The Soldier's Tale.

2464. **ANSERMET, Ernest**
L'Histoire du Soldat.
Ch, n.s., no. 10, Oct. 1920, p.280-93.

2465. **MEADMORE, W. S.**
Stravinsky's "The Soldier's Tale".
MS, n.i.s., 30, 30 July 1927, p.38-9.

See no. 2307.

2466. **WARBURTON, A. O.**
Set works for O Level G.C.E. Stravinsky: The Soldier's Tale.
MTe, 46, Apr. 1967, p.12+.

*2467. **LEESON, D.**
The clarinettist's repertoire.
Instrument, 23, Oct. 1968, p.36.
On the septet and trio from "The Soldier's Tale".

Concertante works.

*2468. **STEVENS, Willis,** ***jnr.***
The concerted piano music of Stravinsky.
Thesis, University of Rochester, New York. 1960.

Capriccio.

*2469. **SCHAEFFNER, A.**
[Stravinsky's "Capriccio"].
MM, 7, Feb.-Mar. 1930, p.31-4.

*2470. **POWELL, Laurence**
Strawinsky's Capriccio.
Disques, 1, Jan. 1931, p.452-3.

See no. 2126.

Concerto for Piano and Wind Instruments.

*2471. **SILBER, Sidney**
The Stravinsky concerto.
Music news, 21, 26 July 1929, p.25.

See no. 2307.

Ebony Concerto.

2472. **GOODWIN, Noel**
Stravinsky with others.
DD, 18, Oct. 1967, p.28+. illus.
Mostly on the "Ebony Concerto".

Movements.

See no. 2229.

2473. **MASON, Colin**
Stravinsky's newest works.
T, nos. 53-4, Spring-Summer 1960, p.2-10. mus.
"Movements", the "Double Canon", and "Epitaphium".

2474. **KELLER, Hans**
No bridge to nowhere: an introduction to Stravinsky's Movements and Schoenberg's Violin Concerto.
MT, 102, Mar. 1961, p.156-8.

2475. **BOYKAN, Martin**
"Neoclassicism" and late Stravinsky.
PNM, 1, Spring 1963, p.158-69. mus.
Mostly on "Movements".

See no. 2307.

Chamber music.

2476. **TANGEMAN, Robert**
Stravinsky's two-piano works.
MM, 22, Jan.-Feb. 1945, p.93-8. mus.

2477. **MASON, Colin**
Stravinsky's contribution to chamber music.
T, 43, Spring 1957, p.6-16. mus.
Lists the chamber music. Also *in Musik der Zeit,* 1, 1958, p.72, and *in* Cobbett's *Cyclopedic survey of chamber music,* III, p.123-30. mus.

2478. **DONAT, Misha**
Stravinsky's chamber music.
L, 81, 29 May 1969, p.763.

Octet.

*2479. **STRAVINSKY, Igor**
Some ideas about my Octuor.
Arts, 5, Jan. 1924, p.5-6. illus.

2480. **STRAVINSKY the extremist.**
British musician, 10, Aug. 1934, p.181-2.

See no. 2273.

Septet.

2481. **EVETT, Robert**
Quo vadis, Igor?
NR, 130, 8 Feb. 1954, p.21.

2482. **STEIN, Erwin**
Strawinsky's Septet (1953) ... an analysis.
T, 31, Spring 1954, p.7-10. 1pl., mus.

2483. **PARSONS, Michael**
Stravinsky's "Septet".
L, 77, 4 May 1967, p.600. illus.

Concertino for String Quartet.

*2484. **ANSERMET, Ernest**
Igor Stravinsky, the man and his work: his first string quartet.
MC, 71, 25 Nov. 1915, p.41. illus.

Double Canon for String Quartet.

See no. 2229.

See no. 2473.

Three Pieces for String Quartet.

2485. **TERPANDER,** *pseud.*
Stravinsky's Three Pieces for String Quartet (1914).
G, 12, May 1935, p.469.

Epitaphium.

See no. 2229.

See no. 2473.

Concerto for Two Solo Pianos.

See no. 2126.

Duo Concertant.

2486. **TERPANDER,** *pseud.*
A note of the Duo Concertant.
G, 11, May 1934, p.469-70. illus.

Five Easy Pieces for Piano Duet.

*2487. **CHADABE, J.**
Stravinsky and his "Easy Duets" for piano.
Piano quarterly, no. 42, Winter 1962-3, p.14-17. illus., mus.

Sonata for Two Pianos.

See no. 2126.

2488. **JOHNS, Donald C.**
An early serial idea of Stravinsky.
MR, 23, Nov. 1962, p.305-13. mus.

2489. **BURKHART, Charles**
Stravinsky's revolving canon.
MR, 29, Aug. 1968, p.161-4. mus.
The canon comes in the second movement.

Instrumental solos.

2490. **RAJNA, Thomas**
Stravinsky's piano works.
C, no.29, Autumn 1968, p.5-9. mus.

Three Pieces for Clarinet Solo.

*2491. **GEE, H.**
Notes on Stravinsky's "Three Pieces".
Woodwind world, 3, 1960, no.10, p.18.

Serenade for Piano.

2492. **TERPANDER,** *pseud.*
Stravinsky's Serenade for pianoforte (1925).
G, 13, May 1936, p.504.

Vocal works.

2493. **CRAFT, Robert**
Stravinsky's pieces for voice ... a forty year development.
MA, 69, Feb. 1949, p.16-17+. illus., mus.

2494. **BECKWITH, John**
The vocal works in English.
Canadian music j., 6, Summer 1962, p.5-12. mus.

*2495. **FRIEDBERG, R.**
The solo vocal works of Igor Stravinsky: a review.
N.A.T.S. bull., 23, no. 1, 1966, p.6-8+.
Includes a complete chronological list.

In Memoriam Dylan Thomas.

2496. **KELLER, Hans**
In Memoriam Dylan Thomas: Strawinsky's Schoenbergian technique.
T, 35, Spring 1955, p.13-20. mus.
See also no. 2497.

2497. **SHAWE-TAYLOR, Desmond**
Stravinsky as serialist.
NS, 50, 2 July 1955, p.12-13.
An answer to the article by Keller (no. 2496) who replies: 50, 16 July 1955, p.72.

2498. **GOLDMAN, Richard F.**
Current chronicle. New York.
MQ, 42, Apr. 1956, p.236-9. mus.

The Owl and the Pussycat.

See no. 2320.

Three Songs from William Shakespeare.

2499. **MORTON, Lawrence**
Current chronicle. Los Angeles.
MQ, 40, Oct. 1954, p.572-5. mus.

Choral works.

*2500. **SHEERE, Richard**
The sacred music of Stravinsky.
S.M.M. thesis, Union Theological Seminary, New York. 1955.

2501. **SPIES, Claudio**
Some notes on Stravinsky's Requiem settings.
PNM, 5, Spring-Summer 1967, p.98-123. illus., mus.
Also *in* BORETZ *and* CONE. Perspectives on Schoenberg and Stravinsky, p.223-49.

2502. **BOYS, Henry**
A note on Stravinsky's settings of English.
S, 20, June 1957, p.14-18. mus.

2503. **WALSH, Stephen**
Stravinsky's choral music.
T, 81, Summer 1967, p.41-51. mus.
Also *in American choral rev.,* 10, no.3, 1968, p.99-112.

Abraham and Isaac.

2504. **STRAVINSKY, Igor**
"Abraham and Isaac": original notes by Igor Stravinsky.
LME, 19 Aug. 1964, p.8.

2505. **HELM, Everett**
Stravinsky's "Abraham and Isaac".
T, 71, Winter 1964-5, p.27.

2506. **BORETZ, Benjamin**
Stravinsky's Abraham and Isaac.
Na, 200, 11 Jan. 1965, p. 39-40.

2507. **SPIES, Claudio**
Notes on Stravinsky's "Abraham and Isaac".
PNM, 3, Spring-Summer 1965, p.104-26.
Also *in* BORETZ *and* CONE. Perspectives on Schoenberg and Stravinsky, p.186-209.

2508. **PAYNE, Anthony**
Stravinsky's "Abraham and Isaac" and "Elegy for J.F.K."
T, 73, Summer 1965, p.12-15. mus.

2509. **STRAVINSKY, Igor**
Programme notes. Abraham and Isaac.
London mag., 5, Feb. 1966, p.44-5.

2510. **WHITTALL, Arnold**
Thematicism in Stravinsky's "Abraham and Isaac".
T, 89, Summer 1969, p.12-16. mus.

Ave Maria.

2511. **STRAVINSKY, Igor**
Programme notes. 3 sacred choruses.
London mag., 5, Feb. 1966, p.32-3.
"Ave Maria", "Credo" and "Pater Noster".

Cantata.

2512. **LINDLAR, Heinrich**
Igor Strawinsky: "Cantata". Tr. by Graeme Chivers.
T, 27, Spring 1953, p.29-33. 1pl., mus.

2513. **COWELL, Henry**
Current chronicle.
MQ, 39, Apr. 1953, p.251-4. mus.

2514. **GARBUTT, John** *and* **PATTERSON, Matthew**
An approach to Stravinsky's "Cantata" and "The Wedding".
ML, 38, Jan. 1957, p.28-31.

2515. **MASON, Colin**
Serial procedures in the Ricercar II of Strawinsky's "Cantata".
T, nos. 61-2, Spring-Summer 1962, p.6-9. mus.

Canticum Sacrum.

2516. **STEIN, Erwin**
Igor Strawinsky: Canticum sacrum ad honorem sancti marci nominis.
T, 40, Summer 1956, p.3-5.

2517. **CRAFT, Robert**
A concert for Saint Mark.
S, 18, Dec. 1956, p.35-51. 1pl., mus.
Analysis of the "Canticum Sacrum" and the "Vom Himmel Hoch" variations.

2518. **WEISSMANN, John S.**
Current chronicle. Italy.
MQ, 43, Jan. 1957, p.104-10. mus.

2519. **STEINITZ, Paul**
On rehearsing a choir for the "Canticum Sacrum".
S, 19, Mar. 1957, p.56-9. mus.

Chorale Variations on "Vom Himmel Hoch".

See no. 2517.

Credo.

See no. 2511.

The Dove Descending, anthem – *see Anthem.*

Elegy for J. F. K.

See no. 2508.

The Flood.

2520. **STRAVINSKY, Igor**
"The Flood", the bomb and religion.
SR, 44, 29 July 1961, p.39-41+. illus.
Stravinsky talks to Craft. Later *in Expositions and developments,* no. 2241.

2521. **TODD, Arthur**
Noah and the Flood. Background.
DD, 13, July 1962, p.10-14. illus.

2522. **GOLDMAN, Richard F.**
Current chronicle. United States.
MQ, 48, Oct. 1962, p.514-17.

*2523. **COLEMAN, E.**
"Noah": TV versus composer and public.
Dance perspectives, Jan. 1963, p.15-16.

2524. **PAYNE, Anthony**
Stravinsky's "The Flood".
T, 70, Autumn 1964, p.2-8. mus.

2525. **McCREDIE, Andrew D.**
Igor Stravinsky ... The Flood.
Canon, 17, Apr. 1965, p.15-16.

See no. 2307.

Introitus (T.S. Eliot in Memoriam).

See no. 2374.

Mass.

2526. **ANSERMET, Ernest**
Strawinsky's newest work.
T, n.s., no.10, Winter 1948-9, p.6-7.

2527. **CRAFT, Robert**
Stravinsky's Mass: a notebook.
in CORLE, *ed.* Igor Stravinsky, p.201-6.

See no. 2418.

2528. **RUBBRA, Edmund**
Stravinsky's Mass.
The Month, n.s., 1, Apr. 1949, p.250-4.

2529. **GOLDMAN, Richard F.**
Current chronicle. New York.
MQ, 35, July 1949, p.451-8. mus.

2530. **RUBSAMEN, Walter H.**
Current chronicle.
MQ, 36, Oct. 1950, p.581-4. mus.
Includes Stravinsky's comments on the music.

2531. **GOLDMAN, Richard F.**
Stravinsky's Mass of 1948.
Perspectives, no. 3, Spring 1953, p.110-17. mus.

Les Noces, dance-cantata – *see The Wedding.*

Pater Noster.

See no. 2511.

Perséphone.

*2532. **SCHWERKÉ, Irving**
Stravinsky's Perséphone.
MC, 108, 26 May 1934, p.5+.

2533. **CALVOCORESSI, M. D.**
... A Stravinsky manifesto.
MT, 75, Sept. 1934, p.814.
Extract from Stravinsky's statement on "Perséphone".
Published in full in *Le Monde musical,* 31 May 1934.

2534. **CALVOCORESSI, M. D.**
Stravinsky on "Perséphone".
L, 12, 28 Nov. 1934, p.896.

2535. **ROSENFELD, Paul**
The mystery of Perséphone.
NR, 82, 3 Apr. 1955, p.213-14.

2536. **GLOCK, W.**
Stravinsky's "Perséphone".
LME, 12, June 1957, p.21-3.

2537. **GOODWIN, Noel**
Perséphone. Music.
DD, 13, Jan. 1962, p.10-12.

See no. 2273.

Requiem Canticles.

2538. **WHITE, Eric Walter**
Stravinsky's "Requiem Canticles".
T, 79, Winter 1966-7, p.14-15.

2539. **PAYNE, Anthony**
Requiem Canticles.
T, 81, Summer 1967, p.10-19. illus., mus.

2540. **SMALLEY, Roger**
Stravinsky's "Requiem Canticles".
L, 78, 31 Aug. 1967, p. 282.

2541. **ROSEBERRY, Eric**
Stravinsky's "Requiem Canticles".
L, 80, 1 Aug. 1968, p.153.

2542. **SOUVTCHINSKY, Pierre**
Thoughts on Stravinsky's "Requiem Canticles".
T, 86, Autumn 1968, p.6-7.

A Sermon, a Narrative and a Prayer.

2543. **MASON, Colin**
Stravinsky's new work.
T, 59, Autumn 1961, p.5-14. mus.

2544. **MORTON, Lawrence**
Current chronicle. Ojai, California.
MQ, 48, July 1962, p.392-6.

*2545. **WILKEY, J. W.**
Igor Stravinsky's cantata "A Sermon, A Narrative and a Prayer": a conductor's introduction.
Choral j., 10, no.2, 1969, p.14-19.

2546. **CLIFTON, Thomas**
Types of symmetrical relations in Stravinsky's A Sermon, a Narrative and a Prayer.
PNM, Fall-Winter 1970, p.96-112. illus., mus.

Symphony of Psalms.

*2547. **PISTON, Walter**
Stravinsky as psalmist - 1931.
MM, 8, Jan. 1931, p.42-5.

*2548. **COTTLER, Joseph**
Stravinsky's testament.
Disques, 2, Oct. 1931, p.334-6.

2549. **SACRED themes in the modern idiom: the spirit of a new world: Stravinsky's "A Symphony of psalms".**
British musician, 7, Dec. 1931, p.257-61. illus.
8, Jan. 1932, p.16-18.

*2550. **MATTEI, Otto A.**
Igor Stravinsky's Symphony of Psalms: an analytical study.
Master of Music thesis, Eastman School of Music, University of Rochester, New York. 1948.

*2551. **GREW, S.**
Symphony of the psalms.
American record guide, 15, Apr. 1949, p.229-32.

See no. 2273.

See no. 2307.

*2552. **BURNAU, J.**
Stravinsky's "Symphony of psalms."
Instrument, 23, Dec. 1968, p.60-2.

2553. **CHITTUM, Donald**
Compositional similarities in Beethoven and Stravinsky.
MR, 30, Nov. 1969, p.285-90. mus.
A comparison of Beethoven's Symphony no.9 and the "Symphony of Psalms".

Threni.

2554. **PAULI, Hansjörg**
On Stravinsky's "Threni".
T, 49, Autumn 1958, p.16-33. 1pl., mus.

2555. **GLOCK, William**
Stravinsky's Threni.
NS, 56, 22 Nov. 1958, p.723-4.

2556. **WEISSMANN, John S.**
Current chronicle. Italy.
MQ, 45, Jan. 1959, p.104-10. mus.

*2557. **BALL, James William**
The sacred choral works of Igor Stravinsky: Threni id est Lamentationes Jeremiae Prophetae.
S.M.M. thesis, Union Theological Seminary, New York. 1961.

See no. 2307.

The Wedding.

2558. **MANUEL, Roland**
Igor Stravinsky's "Les Noces".
Ch, n.s., no.33, Sept. 1923, p.1-4.

*2559. **CASELLA, A.**
Stravinsky's "Noces villageoises".
Arts, 9, Feb. 1926, p.73-5. illus.

2560. **GRAY, Cecil**
The music of "Les Noces".
Nation, 39, 10 July 1926, p.416.

2561. **WORTHAM, H. E.**
Music of the month.
Apollo, 4, Aug. 1926, p.88-9.
Deals largely with "The Wedding".
Contents: Stravinsky and his critics. - What Mr. Wells thought. - Stravinsky's convention.

See no. 2033.

2562. **BELAIEV, Victor**
Igor Stravinsky's Les Noces. An outline ... Tr. from the Russian by S. W. Pring.
O.U.P. 1928. 1-37p. mus.
The first book on Stravinsky's music to appear in English.

*2563. **HAMMOND, Richard**
Viewing "Les Noces" in 1929.
MM, 6, Mar. 1929, p.19-24.

*2564. **STOKOWSKI, Leopold**
Concerning Stravinsky's "Les Noces".
MC, 98, 20 Apr. 1929, p.24.

2565. **[STRAVINSKY, Igor]**
Stravinsky's Les Noces (The Wedding).
G, 12, Aug. 1934, p.86.

2566. **RAMUZ, C. F.**
Souvenir of Switzerland - 1917.
DI, 6, 1947, p.245-8.
Also *in* LEDERMAN, *ed.* Stravinsky in the theatre, p.32-8. illus.

See no. 2514.

See no. 2439.

2567. **GOODWIN, Noel**
Les Noces. Music.
DD, 17, May 1966, p.20-1+. illus.

2568. **LANCHBERY, John**
Stravinsky, peasants and pianos.
About the house, 2, June 1966, p.40-2. illus., mus.
Mostly about "The Wedding".

Operas.

2569. **RENNERT, Gunther**
Strawinsky's conception of opera.
O, 7, Aug. 1956, p.473-4. illus.

Mavra.

*2570. **GOLDOVSKY, Boris**
Mavra, a lyric masterpiece.
Chrysalis, 4, no. 11-12, 1951, p.3.

2571. **HEAD, Leslie**
Stravinsky and his opera buffa.
MMu, 13, Nov. 1964, p.21+.

The Nightingale.

2572. **CALVOCORESSI, M. D.**
M. Igor Stravinsky's opera: "The Nightingale".
MT, 55, June 1914, p.372-4.

2573. **MORRIS, R. O.**
Beecham Opera: The Nightingale.
Athenaeum, no. 4674, 28 Nov. 1919, p.1265.

2574. **HENRY, Leigh**
The search for The Nightingale: a parable.
MS, 16, 14 Aug. 1920, p.60-1.

2575. **PRUNIÈRES, Henry**
Igor Stravinsky's "Chant du Rossignol".
Ch, n.s., no.9, Sept. 1920, p.271-4.
This is the title given to the revised version of the opera in three acts which became a symphonic poem in three scenes.

2576. **DAVIDSON, Gladys**
Stravinsky. The Nightingale.
in DAVIDSON. Stories from the Russian operas, p.186-92.

Oedipus Rex.

2577. **SABANEEFF, Leonid**
Stravinsky's "Oedipus".
Ch, 8, July-Aug. 1927, p.258-61.

2578. **COPLAND, Aaron**
Stravinsky's "Oedipus Rex".
NR, 54, 29 Feb. 1928, p.68-9.

*2579. **SESSIONS, Roger**
On Oedipus Rex.
MM, 5, Mar. 1928, p.9-15.

*2580. **DONNER, Eugene**
Oedipus Rex of Stravinsky.
Outlook, 148, 28 Mar. 1928, p.504.

2581. **BURKE, Kenneth**
Musical chronicle.
Dial, 84, May 1928, p.445-7.

*2582. **GILBERT, Richard**
"Oedipus Rex" and "Pas d'Acier".
Arts, 17, June 1931, p.640-1.

*2583. **HENRY , Leigh**
Oedipus Rex and objective music drama.
MC, 103, 1 Aug. 1931, p.7+. illus.

2584. **BOYS, Henry**
Stravinsky's "Oedipus Rex".
L, 15, 5 Feb. 1936, p.277.

2585. **NOBLE, Jeremy**
Stravinsky's opera-oratorio.
LME, 14, Nov. 1959, p.22.

2586. **MELLERS, Wilfred**
Stravinsky's "Oedipus".
L, 16, 27 July 1961, p.149.

2587. **STRAVINSKY, Igor**
On "Oedipus Rex".
Encounter, 18, June 1962, p.29-35. illus.

2588. **MELLERS, Wilfred**
Stravinsky's Oedipus as twentieth-century hero.
MQ, 48, July 1962, p.300-12. mus.
Also *in* LANG, *ed.* Stravinsky, p.34.

2589. **GOODWIN, Noel**
Stravinsky at the cross-roads.
MMu, 14, July 1966, p.16.

*2590. **ZINAR, Ruth**
Greek tragedy in the theatre pieces of Stravinsky and Milhaud.
DA, 29, Sept. 1968, p.927A-8A.
PhD, Mus., thesis, New York University. 1968. 396p.

The Rake's Progress.

2591. **[GISHFORD, Anthony]**
Strawinsky's "The Rake's Progress".
T, no.20, Summer 1951, p.4-5. 4pl.

2592. **WHITE, Eric Walter**
"The Rake's Progress".
T, no.20, Summer 1951, p.10-18. mus.

2593. **CRAFT, Robert**
"The Rake's Progress".
SR, 34, 27 Oct. 1951, p.52-3. mus.

2594. **APRAHAMIAN, Felix**
Stravinsky's "The Rake's Progress".
World rev., n.s., 33, Nov. 1951, p.17-19.

2595. **CAPELL, Richard**
Stravinsky's opera.
MT, 92, Nov. 1951, p.498-9.

2596. **HAREWOOD, Earl of**
Strawinsky and "The Rake's Progress".
O, 2, Nov. 1951, p.610-16. illus.

2597. **RUTZ, Hans**
Stravinsky in Venice. Tr. by Hans Keller.
MR, 12, Nov. 1951, p.329-31.
On "The Rake's Progress".

2598. **MASON, Colin**
Stravinsky's opera.
ML, 33, Jan. 1952, p.1-9.

2599. **[CLEALL, Charles]**
"The Rake's Progress".
MO, 75, Feb. 1952, p.271.

2600. **REPASS, Richard**
Stravinsky and the music-drama.
MT, 93, Feb. 1952, p.66-9. mus.
Deals with "The Rake's Progress".

2601. **MURRILL, Herbert**
The Rake's Progress.
S, 6, May 1952, p.55-8. mus.

2602. **APRAHAMIAN, Felix**
Stravinsky and "The Rake's Progress".
L, 48, 25 Dec. 1952, p.1090.

2603. **WILLIAMSON, Audrey**
The Rake's Progress - a study.
MA, 73, 1 Jan. 1953, p.6-7+. illus.
Hogarth's paintings contrasted with Stravinsky's music.

*2604. **AUDEN, W. H.**
[The Rake's Progress].
Harper's bazaar, Feb. 1953, p.165.

2605. **NOTES on The Rake.**
ON, 17, 9 Feb. 1953, p.24.
Describes the lecture recital on the opera given by Auden and Kallman.

2606. **THE STORY of Igor Stravinsky's Rake's Progress.**
ON, 17, 9 Feb. 1953, p.18-21. illus., bib.

2607. **STRAVINSKY, Igor**
Reflections on The Rake: the origin of the music.
ON, 17, 9 Feb. 1953, p.8. illus.

2608. **KERMAN, Joseph**
Opera à la mode.
O, 5, July 1954, p.411-15.

2609. **CRAFT, Robert**
Reflections on "The Rake's Progress".
S, 9, Sept. 1954, p.24-30.

2610. **McFADDEN, George**
The Rake's Progress: a note on the libretto.
Hudson rev., 8, Spring 1955, p.105-12.
Ignores Chester Kallman's contribution to the text.

2611. **KLEIN, John W.**
"The Rake's Progress".
L, 60, 10 July 1958, p.69.

2612. **COOKE, Deryck**
"The Rake" and the 18th century.
MT, 103, Jan. 1962, p.20-3. mus.

2613. **KLEIN, John W.**
Stravinsky's "The Rake's Progress".
MO, 85, May 1962, p.465+.

2614. **DREW, David**
Licensed rake.
NS, 66, 9 Aug. 1963, p.179.
Discusses the act divisions in the Glyndebourne production.

2615. **STRAVINSKY, Igor**
Programme notes. The Rake's Progress.
London mag., 5, Feb. 1966, p.42-4.

2616. **ROSEBERRY, Eric**
Some thoughts on Stravinsky's "Rake's Progress".
L, 82, 20 Nov. 1969, p.710.

Le Rossignol, opera – *see The Nightingale.*

STREIKHER, Lyubov (1888-)

2617. **MOISENKO, Rena**
Lyubov Streikher.
in MOISENKO. Realist music, p.231-3.
One of the few Russian women composers.

SVIRIDOV, Georgy (1915-)

2618. **GROSHEVA, Yelena**
Austere yet straight from the heart.
in LIPOVSKY. Lenin Prize winners, p.135-41.

2619. **TAKTAKISHVILI, Otar**
Georgi Sviridov.
in LIPOVSKY. Lenin Prize winners, p.132-4. illus.

2620. **KREBS, Stanley D.**
Georgii Sviridov.
in KREBS. Soviet composers and the development of Soviet music, p.261-8. mus.

TAKTAKISHVILI, Otar (1924-)

2621. **TAKTAKISHVILI, O**
Young musicians.
SCR, 1, Jan. 1957, p.19-21.
Abridged from *Sovetskaya muzyka,* 4, Apr. 1956. Deals with Russian musicians.

2622. **KREBS, Stanley D.**
Otar Taktakishvili.
in KREBS. Soviet composers and the development of Soviet music, p.299-306. mus.

TANEYEV, Sergey (1856-1915)

2023. **PRING, S. W.**
Sergeyi Ivanovitch Taneyeff.
MSt, 12, Aug. 1915, p.277-8.

2624. **MONTAGU-NATHAN, M.**
Sergei Ivanovich Tanéyef.
MO, 38, Sept. 1915, p.799.

2625. **TIDEBÖHL, Ellen von**
Sergius Ivanowitsh Taneieff.
MMR, 45, Sept. 1915, p.277-8.

2626. **MONTAGU-NATHAN, M.**
Russian music. A Taneyef souvenir.
MMR, 46, Dec. 1916, p.313-14.

2627. **MONTAGU-NATHAN, M.**
Taneyef.
in MONTAGU-NATHAN. Contemporary Russian composers, p.201-30. illus.

2628. **MONTAGU-NATHAN, M.**
The story of Russian music. 12. Taneyef.
MSt, 10, Sept. 1917, p.28+.

2629. **KARATYGIN, V.**
To the memory of S. I. Taneev. Tr. by S. W. Pring.
MQ, 13, Oct. 1927, p.540-54. 1pl.
First appeared in the special Taneyev number of *Muzykalny sovremennik,* Apr. 1916. The author was a critic and composer (1875-1925).

2630. **SABANEYEFF, Leonid**
Sergey Taneyeff.
in SABANEYEFF. Modern Russian composers, p.19-39.

2631. **ABRAHAM, Gerald**
Sergei Taneief.
in CALVOCORESSI *and* ABRAHAM. Masters of Russian music, p.439-49. 1pl.

2632. **BOELZA, Igor**
A great teacher.
SL, 12, Sept. 1945, p.58-61. illus.

2633. **HARTMANN, Thomas de**
Sergeii Ivanovitch Taneieff.
T, 39, Spring, 1956, p.8-15. 1pl.

2634. **WEINBERG, Jacob**
Sergei Ivanovitch Taneiev.
MQ, 44, Jan. 1958, p.19-31. 1pl., mus.

2635. **TANEIEV, Serge**
Convertible counterpoint in the strict style. Tr. by G.G. Ackley Brower. With an introduction by Serge Koussevitzky.
Boston, Bruce Humphries. 1962. 7-355p. mus.
Taneiev's study of counterpoint on an algebraic basis, which took him twenty years, contains over 300 music examples. Still one of the most remarkable musical treatises ever written. Gerald Abraham calls it "a monument of misapplied ingenuity" *(Musical times,* 107, Jan. 1966, p.38).

2636. **GARDNER, John**
A Russian contrapuntist.
C, 17, Oct. 1965, p.6-7. mus.

TCHAIKOVSKY, Piotr (1840-93)

A. *General.*

2637. **SHEDLOCK, J. S.**
Obituary. Peter Iltitsch Tschaikowsky.
Academy, 44, 11 Nov. 1893, p.422.

2638. **STEVENSON, E. I.**
Peter Iltitsch Tschaikowsky.
Harper's weekly, 37, 18 Nov. 1893, p.1112. illus.

2639. **LEGGE, Robin**
Peter Tschaikowsky: a sketch.
MO, 17, Jan. 1894, p.234.

2640. **TSCHIKOWSKY'S early life.**
MS, i.s., 1, 6 Jan. 1894, p.10.
Said to be as related by the composer.

2641. **KASHKINE's recollections of Tschaikowsky.**
MT, 38, July 1897, p.449-52.

2642. **NEWMARCH, Rosa**
Tchaikovsky as a musical critic.
MS, i.s., 11, 14 Jan. 1899, p.22-3.
21 Jan. 1899, p.36-8.
28 Jan. 1899, p.50-1.
4 Feb. 1899, p.66-8.
The second article deals with Beethoven, the third with Schumann and Brahms and the fourth with Brahms and Wagner. There is one error which Newmarch does not correct (others she does): Bizet did not die at 30.

2643. **NEWMARCH, Rosa**
Tchaikovsky. His life and works, with extracts from his writings, and the diary of his tour abroad in 1888.
Grant Richards. 1900. viii-ix, 2-232p. illus., 1pl.
The original 1900 edition was supplemented in 1908 by Edwin Evans analyses of selected works, his essays *The relation of Tchaikovsky to art-questions of the day* and the addition of a classified list of compositions to the chronological list, but the

index was omitted. The diary extracts do not include Tchaikovsky's visit to England in 1888. Some of the material by both authors first appeared in periodicals. Still the definitive study of the composer.

*2644. **TCHAIKOVSKY, P. I.**
Guide to the practical study of harmony. Tr. from the German version of P. Juon by E. Krall and J. Liebling. Leipzig. 1900. Published in English in Leipzig, translated in turn from the German translation of the original text. It was written in 1871.

2645. **KEETON, A. E.**
Peter Ilyitch Tschaikovski.
Contemporary rev., 78, July 1900, p.74-82.

2646. **CARTER, Vivian**
The happier Tschaikovsky.
MS, i.s., 14, 20 Oct. 1900, p.242.

*2647. **SIMPSON, E. E.**
Tschaikowsky in Leipsic in 1888.
M. 19, Dec. 1900, p.100-9. illus.

*2648. **SIMPSON, E. E.**
Tschaikowsky as a musical critic.
M, 19, Mar, 1901, p.460-9.

2649. **NEWMAN, Ernest**
Essential Tschaikowsky.
Contemporary rev., 79, June 1901, p.887-98.
Also *in* LLA, 230, 3 Aug. 1901, p.288-98.

2650. **STUNT, Henry**
Tchaikovsky.
MS, i.s., 16, 20 July 1901, p.37.

2651. **TSCHAIKOWSKY.**
MMR, 31, Dec. 1901, p.269.
32, Jan. 1902, p.13-14.

*2652. **MASON, D. G.**
[Tchaikovsky and his music].
Outlook, 72, 1 Nov. 1902, p.548-54. illus.

2653. **NEWMARCH, Rosa**
Tchaikovsky and Tolstoi.
Contemporary rev., 83, Jan. 1903, p.112-18.
Also *in* LLA, 237, 4 Apr. 1903, p.58-63.

2654. **LEE, E. Markham**
Tchaikovsky.
Bodley Head. 1904. xi-xvi, 1-162p. 1pl., mus.
This useful early study of Tchaikovsky's music is one of the *Music of the masters* series. The list of works is based on the Jurgenson thematic catalogue and gives references to relevant page numbers in the text.

2655. **NEWMARCH, Rosa**
Tchaikovsky's last visit to England.
MT, 45, Feb. 1904, p.95-7.
This visit was in 1893.

2656. **KEETON, A. E.**
One of Tchaikovski's love episodes.
MMR, 34, Mar. 1904, p.43-5.
Says Désirée Artôt was two years older than the composer; in fact she was five years older.

2657. **LAW, Frederic S.**
Tchaikovsky (1840-1893).
MS, i.s., 21, 26 Mar. 1904, p.202-3.

2658. **TCHAIKOVSKY, Modeste**
The life and letters of Peter Ilyich Tchaikovsky. Ed. from the Russian and with an introduction by Rosa Newmarch.
John Lane, the Bodley Head. 1906. [1905]. viii-ix, 2-782p. illus., 22pl., mus.
Abridged and very inaccurate version of the German edition. The 3000 letters are arranged chronologically, and there is an annotated list of compositions. Still one of the most important books on the composer, but it should be read with great caution owing to the number of errors.

2659. **TIDEBOEHL, Ellen von**
P. I. Tschaikowsky and Mme. von Meck.
MMR, 35, Apr. 1905, p.65-7.
May 1905, p.87-8.

2660. **EVANS, Edwin**
Tchaikovsky.
Dent 1906. v-ix, 1-234p. [second ed.] 8pl. mus.
One of the *Master musicians* series and last revised in 1966, it contains a catalogue of works, and despite some minor inaccuracies of date in the personalia appendix, it remains one of the standard books on the composer.

2661. **LEE, E. Markham**
Tchaikovski.
George Bell. 1906. v-viii, 1-63p. 6pl., mus.
Not to be confused with Lee's earlier book on the composer, this is one of Bell's *Miniature series of musicians.* There is no index.

2662. **EVANS, Edwin**
On Tchaikovsky's musical opinions.
MS, i.s., 27, 30 Mar. 1907, p.198-9.
Actually on his instrumentation. Part one of the series *The relation of Tchaikovsky to art-questions of the day.*

2663. **EVANS, Edwin**
The relation of Tchaikovsky to art-questions of the day.
2. Tchaikovsky and form.
MS, i.s., 27, 18 May 1907, p.309-10.

2664. **EVANS, Edwin**
... 3. Tchaikovsky and idealism.
MS, i.s., 27, 1 June 1907, p.345-6.

2665. **EVANS, Edwin**
... 4. Tchaikovsky and nationalism.
MS, i.s., 27, 15 June 1907, p.374-5.

2666. **EVANS, Edwin**
... 5. Tchaikovsky and individuality.
MS, i.s., 27, 29 June 1907, p.410-12.

2667. **EVANS, Edwin**
... 6. Tchaikovsky and criticism.
MS, i.s., 28, 13 July 1907, p.25-6.

*2668. **TRACY, J. M.**
[Tchaikovsky - talented composer].
Mu, 14, Aug. 1909, p.351.

2669. **HADDEN, J. Cuthbert**
Tchaikowsky's peculiar marriage.
MO, 33, Feb. 1910, p.328-9. illus.

2670. **LAWRENCE, Frederic**
Peter Ilich Tchaikovsky.
London quarterly rev., 116, Oct. 1911, p.289-301.

2671. **BYRON, May C.**
A day with Peter Ilyich Tschaikovsky.

Hodder. [1912?] [Unpaged]. [36p.] 5pl.
Very chatty, supposedly authentic portrait. Of marginal interest.

2672. **RONALD, LANDON**
Tschaikovsky.
T. C. and E. C. Jack. [1912?] 8-63p. illus., mus.
Half biographical and half devoted to piano solos and songs, this was the first of Ronald's two books on the composer. It lacks an index.

*2673. **MASON, D. G.**
Yankee Doodle as it might have been treated by Tschaikowsky.
Outlook, 100, 27 Jan. 1912, p.219-24. illus.

*2674. **HADDEN, J. C.**
[His mysterious marriage].
NMR, 11, Nov. 1912, p.498-501.

See no. 395.

See no. 423.

*2675. **MASON, D. G.**
[Tchaikovsky's life and work].
NMR, 14, July 1915, p.260-4.

2676. **RUNCIMAN, John F.**
Tschaikowsky in 1916.
Saturday rev., 121, 15 Jan. 1916, p.58-9.

2677. **DUNCAN, Edmondstoune**
Tchaikovsky: a biographical sketch.
MS, n.i.s., 8, 16 Sept. 1916, p. 204-5.

2678. **MONTAGU-NATHAN, M.**
The story of Russian music. 11. Tchaikovsky.
MSt, 9, July 1917, p.clxix+. illus.

*2679. **STORER, H. J.**
Tchaikovsky, the student.
Mu, 22, Oct. 1917, p.737.

2680. **TSCHAIKOWSKY.**
Musical herald, no. 850, Jan. 1919, p.7-9.

2681. **BUCHANAN, Charles L.**
The unvanquishable Tchaikovsky.
MQ, 5, July 1919, p.364-89.

*2682. **FORSYTH, Cecil**
[A note on Tschaikowsky].
MMR, 20, Jan. 1921, p.57-8.
Mar. 1921, p.130.

2683. **RONALD, *Sir* Landon**
Tschaikovsky.
Murdoch. [1922]. 6-28p. illus., 1pl., mus.
One of the *Mayfair biographies,* it is unindexed. The second of Ronald's two books on the composer.

2684. **SCHOLES, Percy A.**
Tchaikovsky (1840-1893).
School music rev., 31, Dec. 1922, p.133-5.

2685. **FRAGMENTS of biography, no.7 - Tschaikovsky.**
Opera, 1, Oct. 1923, p.10.

*2686. **PAGES from a composer's diary.**
LLA, 324, 7 Mar. 1925, p.556-61.

2687. **FACSIMILE letters of musicians. 5.**
MMR, 55, May 1925, p.137. illus.
From Tchaikovsky to Francesco Berger, dated 1891.

*2688. **WALSALL, A.**
Tschaikowsky's adoration of Mozart.
E, 43, Sept. 1925, p.661.

2689. **TSCHAIKOVSKY.**
Paxton. [1927]. 3-17p. illus., 1pl.
Not always accurate, e.g. regarding the affair with Désirée Artôt. There is a brief list of works.

2690. **HOLT, Richard**
Tchaikovsky and the gramophone.
G, 6, Aug. 1928, p.94-6.

2691. **SABANEEV, L.**
Tchaikovsky. Tr. by S. W. Pring.
MT, 70, Jan. 1929, p.20-3.

2692. **LIMBERT, K. E.**
Tchaikovsky (1840-1893).
Parents' rev., 40, Apr. 1929, p.243-54.
The same article with two paragraphs added was published in the same periodical, vol. 55, Apr. 1944, p.92-100.

2693. **HEINTZ, John**
Tschaikovsky's black beast.
Open court, 44, Nov. 1930, p.641-6. illus.
"The bête noir of Tchaikovsky's existence was the dread of an endless death".

2694. **FELBEY, Rudolf**
Tchaikovsky and Tolstoy.
Ch, 12, Dec. 1930, p.65-9.

2695. **GREW, Eva Mary**
The childhood of great musicians. 12. Tchaikowsky.
British musician, 10, Sept. 1934, p.201-3.
Oct. 1934, p.228-30.

2696. **ABRAHAM, Gerald**
Tchaikovsky revalued.
in ABRAHAM. Studies in Russian music, p.334-50.

2697. **CALVOCORESSI, M. D.**
Tchaikovsky in the light of recent criticism.
L, 13, 22 May 1935, p.876.

*2698. **SLONIMSKY, Nicolas**
The most amazing romance in musical history.
E, 53, Oct. 1935, p.575-6+.
Nov. 1935, p.645-6. illus.

2699. **ABRAHAM, Gerald**
Peter Tchaikovsky.
in CALVOCORESSI *and* ABRAHAM. Masters of Russian music, p.249-334. 1pl.

2700. **LOCKSPEISER, Edward**
Debussy, Tchaikovsky and Madame von Meck.
MQ, 22, Jan. 1936, p.38-44.

2701. **BLOM, Eric**
Common prejudices about Tchaikovsky.
L, 16, 9 Sept. 1936, p.502.

2702. **BENNIGSEN, Olga**
A bizarre friendship: Tchaikovsky and Mme. von Meck.
MQ, 22, Oct. 1936, p.420-9. 1pl.

2703. **BOWEN, Catherine Drinker *and* MECK, Barbara von**
Beloved friend, the story of Tchaikovsky and Nadejda von Meck.
Hutchinson. [1937]. 5-528p. 8pl., mus.
Very informative skimmings from the first two volumes of the correspondence. Bowen's romanticised prose, the numerous inaccuracies and bad translation preclude any recommendation of this unsatisfactory work, which forms the basis of Ken Russell's film *The Music lovers.*

2704. **LOCKSPEISER, Edward**
Claude Debussy in the correspondence of Tchaikovsky and Madame von Meck.
MO, 60, May 1937, p.691-2.

2705. **ABRAHAM, G.**
The riddle of Tchaikovsky.
MMR, 67, July-Aug. 1937, p.129-31.

2706. **TOYE, Francis**
The greatest of Russian composers.
L, 18, 15 Sept. 1937, p.582+.

2707. **ABRAHAM, Gerald**
Tchaikovsky.
Novello [1938]. 2-14p.
One of the *Novello biographies of great musicians.* Contains a list of the principal compositions.

2708. **MANN, Klaus**
Pathetic symphony. A Tchaikovsky novel. English version by Hermon Ould.
Gollancz. 1938. 9-445p.
First published in German in 1935, it falls between the two stools of biography and fiction.

2709. **BENNIGSEN, Olga**
More Tchaikovsky - Von Meck correspondence.
MQ, 24, Apr. 1938, p.129-38. 2pl.

2710. **SLONIMSKY, Nicolas**
Further light on Tchaikovsky.
MQ, 24, Apr. 1938, p.139-46. 2pl.

2711. **MULLEN, James M.**
Tchaikowsky's visit to Baltimore.
Maryland historical mag., 34, Mar. 1939, p.41-5.
This visit was in May 1891.

*2712. **BARNETT, N.**
Neglect of Tschaikowsky's genius.
Mu, 44, Dec. 1939, p.210.

2713. **ABRAHAM, Gerald**
Tchaikovsky: some centennial reflections.
ML, 21, Apr. 1940, p.110-19. mus.
Also *in* ABRAHAM. Slavonic and Romantic music, p.107-15. mus.

2714. **TCHAIKOVSKY, Mme. Anatol**
Recollections of Tchaikovsky.
ML, 21, Apr. 1940, p.103-9.
By the wife of his brother Anatol.

2715. **BAYLISS, Stanley**
Tchaikovsky. 1840-1893.
Choir, 31, May 1940, p.73-5.

2716. **HOLT, Richard**
Peter Tchaikovsky, 1840-1893.
G, 17, May 1940, p.409-10. illus.

*2717. **ROSENFELD, Paul**
The minority and Tschaikowsky.
American music lover, 6, May 1940, p.2-5. illus.

2718. **SABANEEV, Leonid**
Tchaikovsky (Born May 7, 1840). Tr. by S. W. Pring.
MT, 81, May 1940, p.201-2.

2719. **SERGUÉFF, Nicolas**
Peter Tchaikovsky, 1840-1893.
DT, no. 356, May 1940, p.468.

2720. **LAMBERT, Constant**
Tchaikovsky today.
L, 23, 2 May 1940, p.905.

2721. **HUSSEY, Dyneley**
... Tchaikovsky's centenary.
Sp, 164, 17 May 1940, p.686.

*2722. **BEDENKOFF, Alexander**
The cheerful side of Tchaikovsky.
MA, 60, 25 May 1940, p.11. illus.

2723. **TURNER, W. J.**
Tchaikovsky.
NS, 19, 25 May 1940, p.668.

*2724. **BERTENSSON, S.**
[The truth about the mysterious death of Peter Ilyich Tschaikowsky].
E, 58, June 1940, p.389. illus.

2725. **LA MAIN GAUCHE,** *pseud.*
... Tchaikovsky in England.
MO, 63, June 1940, p.396.

*2726. **BEDENKOFF, Alexander**
Tchaikovsky in America: as told in his diary.
MA, 60, July 1940, p.5+. illus.

2727. **EVANS, Edwin**
Chaikovsky today.
ASJ, 1, July 1940, p.204-8.

2728. **FISHER, Margaret**
Peter Iljitch Tchaikowsky.
Nineteenth century, 128, Aug. 1940, p.180-95.

2729. **LLOYD, A. L.**
Chaikovsky in the Soviet Union.
ASJ, 1, Oct. 1940, p.321-6.

2730. **WESTBROOK, Francis**
Tschaikowsky reconsidered.
Choir, 32, Mar. 1941, p.34-5.

*2731. **HALLIDAY, John**
Tchaikovsky on records. With a foreword by Arthur [sic] Rodzinski.
New York, Four Corners. 1942. 89p.

*2732. **PURDY, Claire**
Stormy victory: the story of Tchaikovsky. With decorations by Vera Bock.
New York, Messner. 1942. xiv, 248p.
Like Gronowicz's biography, this is aimed at teenage readers. A catalogue of works is included.

2733. **PEYSER, Herbert F.**
Recalling a once-celebrated controversy.
MA, 63, 10 Jan. 1943, p.7+. illus.
How Seidl defended his idol, Wagner, after an article by Tchaikovsky in a New York newspaper.

2734. **ABRAHAM, Gerald**
Tchaikovsky. A short biography.
Duckworth. 1944. 6-144p. bib.
This revised version of the biography reprinted from *Masters of Russian music* (Calvocoressi and Abraham) contains a comprehensive list of Tchaikovsky's works but no index. One of the best short studies of the composer in English.

2735. **BERTENSSON, Serge**
The Tchaikovsky Museum at Klin.
MQ, 30, July 1944, p.329-35. 2pl.

2736. **ABRAHAM, Gerald,** *ed.*
Tchaikovsky. A symposium.
Lindsay Drummond. 1945. 5-252p. illus., mus., bib.
A valuable if rather uneven series of essays, it includes a list of compositions giving page references to the text. The American edition, called *The music of Tchaikovsky,* was published by Norton in 1946.
Contents: Tchaikovsky the man by Edward Lockspeiser. - The symphonies by Martin Cooper. - Works for solo instrument and orchestra by Eric Blom. - Miscellaneous orchestral works by Ralph Wood. - The chamber music by Colin Mason. - The piano music by A.E.F. Dickinson. - Operas and incidental music by Gerald Abraham. - The ballets by Edwin Evans. - The songs by A. Alshvang. - Religious and other choral music by Gerald Abraham.

2737. **LAKOND, Wladimir,** *tr.*
The diaries of Tchaikovsky. Tr. from the Russian, with notes, by Wladimir Lakond.
New York. Norton. 1945. 10-365p. illus., 9pl.
The eleven diaries (including number two which was lost) span 1873-91, and were made available by the composer's brother, Ippolit. Here they are arranged chronologically and are annotated. The lack of an index is to some extent offset by the detailed register of personalities.

2738. **LOCKSPEISER, Edward**
Tchaikovsky the man.
in ABRAHAM, *ed.* Tchaikovsky. A symposium, p.9-23.

*2739. **MAYO, Waldo**
Tchaikovsky; his life told in anecdotal form. Illustrated by Andre Dugo.
New York, Duell, Sloan and Pearce. 1945.
For younger readers.

*2740. **ZAVADSKY, V.**
Tschaikowsky the most personal of composers.
Mu, 50, Mar. 1945, p.54-5.

2741. **BROOK, Donald**
Tchaikovsky.
in BROOK. Six great Russian composers. p.73-135. illus.

*2742. **GRONOWICZ, Antoni**
Tchaikovsky. Tr. from the Polish by Joseph Vetter.
Drawings by George Avison.
New York, Nelson. 1946. 192p.
A biography for teenagers. There is a list of Tchaikovsky's compositions.

2743. **WEINSTOCK, Herbert**
Tchaikovsky.
Cassell. 1946. 8-388p. illus., 1pl. mus., bib.
Claims to be the first full-length biography written in English. A clear, very competent and straightforward, but slightly pedantic survey containing a very comprehensive list of works but a poor index.

*2744. **WILSON, E.**
Mice, headache, rehearsal: Tchaikovsky's diaries.
New Yorker, 21, 19 Jan. 1946, p.74-7.

2745. **ASSAFYEV, Boris**
The great Russian composer.
in SHOSTAKOVICH *and others.* Russian symphony, p.6-15.

2746. **DAVIDOVA, Ksenia**
The archives of the Tchaikovsky Museum.
in SHOSTAKOVICH and *others.* Russian symphony, p.198-211.

2747. **KELDYSH, Yuri**
Tchaikovsky: the man and his outlook.
in SHOSTAKOVICH *and others.* Russian symphony, p.16-39.

2748. **SHOSTAKOVICH, Dmitri**
Thoughts about Tchaikovsky.
in SHOSTAKOVICH *and others.* Russian symphony, p.1-5.

2749. **SHOSTAKOVICH, Dmitri,** *and others.*
Russian symphony. Thoughts about Tchaikovsky.
New York, Philosophical Library. 1947. 1-271p. 1pl.
Essays about Tchaikovsky and his work (that by Shostakovitch is only of four pages). Poorly translated and containing many errors, e.g., "Eugene Onegin" was first performed in 1879, not 1881; Petipa becomes "Petipas". There is a 54 page list of the composer's musical and literary works.
Contents: Thoughts about Tchaikovsky by Dmitri Shostakovich. - The great Russian composer by Boris Assafyev. - Tchaikovsky the man and his outlook by Yuri Keldysh. - Operas by B. Yarustovsky. - Symphonies by Daniel Zhitomirsky. - The ballets of Tchaikovsky by Vasil Yakovlev. - Chamber music by Arnold Alshvang. - The archives of the Tchaikovsky Museum by Ksenia Davidova.

2750. **GODDARD, Scott**
The enigma of Tchaikovsky.
Disc, no.1, Winter 1947, p.22-8.

2751. **SCHALLENBERG, E. W.**
Tchaikovsky. Tr. [from the Dutch] by M. M. Kessler-Button.
Sidgwick and Jackson. [1950]. 1-60p. illus., 1pl., mus., bib.
First published in Amsterdam and Stockholm. Chatty, badly balanced and poorly translated, with no index and, despite some perceptive remarks, many errors and misprints ("The Storm" is called "Thunder" and one key is given as H flat).

2752. **SHAWE-TAYLOR, Desmond**
The neglect of Tchaikovsky.
O, 1, Apr. 1950, p.15-21. illus.

*2753. **ROSENWALD, H.**
The unknown Tchaikovsky.
Music news, 42, May 1950, p.18-19.

*2754. **SLONIMSKY, Nicolas**
Musical miscellany: Tchaikovsky's method of work.
E, 68, Dec. 1950, p.7.

2755. **HOPE, Evelyn**
Tchaikovsky and the Von Meck letters.
FR, 170, Dec. 1951, p.842-7.

*2756. **FICKES, M. P.**
Master of melody.
E, 70, Mar. 1952, p.10-11. illus.

2757. **WELDON, George**
In defence of Tschaikowsky.
MMu, 1, Jan. 1953, p.11. illus.

2758. **WHEELER, Opal**
The story of Peter Tschaikovsky. Part 1. Illustrated by Christine Price.
Faber. 1954. 11-119p. illus.
Attractively illustrated and including some simple piano pieces, the book is largely devoted to the composer's childhood. Part 2 is *Peter Tschaikovsky and the Nutcracker ballet,* no. 2765.

2759. **SENIOR, Evan**
The man who knew Tchaikovsky.
MMu, 3, Jan. 1955, p.18-19. illus.
Vladimir Davidov, nephew of Tchaikovsky and keeper of the Klin Museum.

2760. **BERGER, Fred**
Music's great sensualist.
Coronet, 41, Apr. 1957, p.16+. illus., disc.

2761. **KOLODIN, Irving**
Tchaikovsky in America.
ON, 22, 2 Dec. 1957, p.12-13.

2762. **RABENECK, Nicolai**
To be or not to be: a portrait of Tchaikovsky in mid-career.
ON, 22, 2 Dec. 1957, p.10-12. illus.

2763. **BRIGGS, John**
The collector's Tchaikovsky and the Five.
New York, Lippincott. 1959. 11-256p. discs.
An interesting annotated discography (now very dated) with biographical sketches. Half the book is devoted to Tchaikovsky. It lacks an index.

2764. **GEE, John** *and* **SELBY, Elliott**
The triumph of Tchaikovsky.
Robert Hale. 1959. 11-206p. illus., 12pl., bib.
Bold, fresh, colourful treatment of the composer's personal life, but sketchy coverage of the music. The index is of limited use.

2765. **WHEELER, Opal**
Peter Tschaikowsky and the Nutcracker ballet. Illustrated by Christine Price.
Faber. 1960. 5-95p. illus.
A biography for young children, with only a small proportion on "The Nutcracker", and including some short piano pieces. The text includes too much fiction.

*2766. **SMITH, R.**
A fanfare for Piotr Ilyich.
HF, 10, Mar. 1960, p.48-9+. illus.

*2767. **SHAPORIN, Yury**
Master of melody.
MJ, 18, Sept. 1960, p.62.

See no. 423.

2768. **HOFMANN, Michel**
Tchaikovsky. Tr. by Angus Heriot.
Calder. 1962. 7-189p. illus., mus., bib.
Mainly for the younger reader, this hasty account is to be valued for its many illustrations. The catalogue of compositions is incomplete and the index scrappy.

2769. **PITFIELD, Thomas**
Letters from Tchaikovsky to Brodsky.
L, 67, 19 Apr. 1962, p.683-4. illus.

See no. 2407.

2770. **HANSON, Lawrence** *and* **HANSON, Elizabeth**
Tchaikovsky: a new study of the man and his music.
Cassell. 1965. ix-xii, 3-332p. 10pl., bib.
Companion volume to the same author's book on Prokofiev.
A distorted, hack biography containing many inaccuracies, e.g., the date of the "Character Dances" is spring, not autumn 1865; the authors confuse the two works called "The Voyevoda". There is a catalogue of Tchaikovsky's compositions.

2771. **HARLING-COMYNS, F.** *,tr.*
Tschaikowsky on the "Eroica" and "Fidelio".
MO, 90, Jan. 1967, p.201.
Taken from Tchaikovsky's critiques for the *Moscow news,* 1871-5.

2772. **YOUNG, Percy M.**
Tchaikovsky.
Ernest Benn. 1968. 5-76p. illus., mus.
A rather skimped, general life for use by children. The drawings are uncaptioned.

2773. **JACOBY, Susan**
Tchaikovsky's Russia: the lingering passion.
SR, 53, 14 Mar. 1970, p.75-6+. illus.

2773a. **GARDEN, Edward**
Tchaikovsky.
Dent. 1973. v-vii, 1-194p. 8pl., mus., bib.
Replaces Edwin Evans' study (no. 2660) in the *Master musicians* series. Thorough, serious and very informative, it treats the life and music in one sequence and contains a calendar of the composer's life, a personalia section and a detailed catalogue of works arranged by musical form; also a few minor errors carried over from Evans' book (Belaiev died in 1904, not 1907). Probably the best short biography of Tchaikovsky in English.

2773b. **WARRACK, John**
Tchaikovsky.
Hamish Hamilton. 1973. 9-287p. illus., bib.
An introduction to Tchaikovsky's life and work for the general reader. A handsomely produced volume with over 170 illustrations, many in colour, but the index would benefit from being in larger type, The list of works is very detailed, with dates of composition and first performance, and includes arrangements of works by other composers and also literary writings. The sources of the illustrations are given and there are two family trees.

B. *Works.*

Orchestral music.

2774. **BLOM, Eric**
Tchaikovsky orchestral works.
O.U.P. 1927. 5-51p. mus.
Covers "Romeo and Juliet", Concerto for piano no.1, Symphony no. 4 and "Casse-Noisette" suite. Brief, but of a high standard.

2775. **BIANCOLLI, Louis**
Tchaikovsky and his orchestral music.
New York, Grosset and Dunlap. 1944. 1-56p. illus., 4pl.
Very chatty coverage of the better-known works. Includes a short biography.

2776. **WOOD, Ralph W.**
Miscellaneous orchestral works.
in ABRAHAM, *ed.* Tchaikovsky. A symposium, p.74-103.

*2777. **BUDDEN, R.**
Tchaikovsky: orchestral works.
1952.
One of the *Decca music guides.*

Symphonies.

*2778. **MATHEWS, W. S.**
The symphonies of Tschaikowsky.
M, 17, Apr. 1900, p.612-14.

2779. **NEWMAN, Ernest**
Tschaikowsky and the symphony.
MMR, 32, July 1902, p.122-4.
Aug. 1902, p.145-7.
Sept. 1902, p.163-4.

2780. **WESTRUP, J. A.**
Tchaikovsky and the symphony.
MT, 81, June 1940, p.249-52. mus.

2781. **BLOM, Eric**
Tchaikovsky as symphonist.
L, 26, 25 Sept. 1941, p.449.

2782. **COOPER, Martin**
The symphonies.
in ABRAHAM, *ed.* Tchaikovsky. A symposium, p.24-46.

2783. **ZHITOMIRSKY, Daniel**
Symphonies.
in SHOSTAKOVICH *and others.* Russian symphony, p.86-131.
Includes sections on the Suites and "programme compositions".

2784. **WARRACK, John**
Tchaikovsky symphonies and concertos.
B.B.C. 1969. 5-55p. mus.
Includes the "Andante and Finale", "Sérénade Mélancolique", "Valse-scherzo" and other concertante works, but excludes the "Manfred Symphony". A useful, workmanlike guide.

Symphonies nos. 1-3.

2785. **ABRAHAM, Gerald**
The great unplayed. Tchaikovsky's earlier symphonies.
MS, 26, 11 July 1925, p.12.

Symphony no. 1.

2786. **CARSE, Adam**
First symphonies: studies in orchestration. 4. Brahms - Tchaikovsky.
MO, 44, Sept. 1920, p.957-8.

Symphony no.2.

*2787. **BARNETT, S.**
Tschaikowsky's Second Symphony, a neglected masterpiece.
Mu, 45, May 1940, p.94.

Symphony no.4.

2788. **BLOM, Eric**
Symphony no 4 in F minor (op. 36).
in BLOM. Tchaikovsky orchestral works, p.23-42. mus.

2789. **NEWMARCH, Rosa**
Tchaikovsky. Symphony no.4, in F minor (op. 36).
CL, 4, p.52-6.

Symphony no. 5.

2790. **EVANS, Edwin**
Tchaikovsky analyses. 4. Symphony no.5 in E minor, op.64.
MS, i.s., 28, 12 Oct. 1907, p.229-32. mus.
26 Oct. 1907, p.261-4. mus.

2791. **WHITE, R. T.**
... Tchaikovsky's Fifth Symphony.
MTe, 4, Oct. 1925, p.614+. mus.

2792. **NEWMARCH, Rosa**
Tchaikovsky. Symphony no.5, in E minor and major, op. 64.
CL, 1, p.48-52.

2792a. **TOVEY, *Sir* DONALD**
Tchaikovsky. Symphony in E minor, no.5, op.64.
in TOVEY. Essays in musical analysis, Vol. 6, p.58-65. mus.

Symphony no.6.

2793. **[EVANS, Edwin]**
The "Pathetic" Symphony. A new reading.
MS, i.s., 18, 1 Nov. 1902, p.271.

*2794. **CONCEPTION and working out of the Pathetic symphony.**
Current literature, 37, Oct. 1904, p.336-8.

2795. **EVANS, Edwin**
Tchaikovsky analyses. 3. Symphony no.6 in B minor, op.74 (The "Pathetic").
MS, i.s., 28, 17 Aug. 1907, p.105-7. mus.
31 Aug. 1907, p.137-40. mus.
14 Sept. 1907, p.165-7. mus.
28 Sept. 1907, p.197-200. mus.

2796. **GILMAN, L.**
... Tchaikovsky's Pathétique symphony.
North American rev., 213, Feb. 1921, p.266-71.

*2797. **BIART, Victor**
Great orchestral masterpieces: Pathetique symphony.
E, 43, Dec. 1925, p.851-2. illus.

*2798. **ANDERTON, M.**
Adagio from Tschaikowsky's Pathetic symphony as a piano study piece ...
Mu, 37, Mar. 1932, p.13-15. illus.

2798a. **TOVEY,** ***Sir*** **DONALD**
Tchaikovsky. Pathetic Symphony in B minor, no. 6, op. 74.
in TOVEY. Essays in musical analysis, Vol. 2, p.84-9. mus.

2799. **ABRAHAM, Gerald**
New light on old friends. B. The programme of the "Pathétique" symphony.
in ABRAHAM. On Russian music, p.143-6.

*2800. **GREW, Sidney**
Tschaikowsky's "Fate" symphony: the composer's exposition.
American music lover, 6, Aug. 1940, p.112-15.

2801. **SUCKLING, Norman**
The tragic symphony.
MMR, 81, July-Aug. 1951, p.143-9.

2802. **OTTAWAY, Hugh**
Some reflections on Tchaikovsky's Sixth Symphony.
MO, 80, Oct. 1956, p.15-17.

2803. **PIGGOTT, Joyce**
Tchaikovsky's last great symphony.
MMu, 7, Nov. 1958, p.15. illus.

Symphony no. 7.

2804. **SCOTT-MADDOCKS, Daniel**
Tchaikovsky's Seventh.
MMu, 11, Sept. 1962, p.30. illus.
The 1892 symphony reconstructed by Bogatyrev.

Francesca da Rimini.

2805. **NEWMARCH, Rosa**
Tchaikovsky. Symphonic fantasia, "Francesca da Rimini" (op. 32).
CL, 2, p.88-90.

Marche Slave.

2806. **NEWMARCH, Rosa**
Tchaikovsky. Marche Slave (op.31).
CL, 2, p.106.

Romeo and Juliet.

2807. **BLOM, Eric**
Romeo and Juliet, fantasy-overture.
in BLOM. Tchaikovsky orchestral works, p.5-12. mus.

2808. **NEWMARCH, Rosa**
Tchaikovsky. Overture-fantasia, "Romeo and Juliet".
CL, 1, p.79-80.

2809. **SUTTON, Wadham**
Tchaikovsky's Romeo and Juliet.
Music in education, 26, 15 Nov. 1962, p.171. mus.

The Snow Maiden.

2810. **GOODWIN, Noel**
The Snow Maiden. Music.
DD, 12, Sept. 1961, p.12-13.

The music for the ballet of this name is from Tchaikovsky's "The Snow Maiden" incidental music and Symphony no.1, and from the Piano Sonata, op. 37 and the last of the Pieces for piano solo, op.72, both orchestrated by Chagrin.

Suites.

2811. **NEWMARCH, Rosa**
Tchaikovsky. Suite no. 1, in D minor (op. 43), for orchestra.
CL, 3, p.57-61.

2812. **NEWMARCH, Rosa**
Tchaikovsky. Suite no.3, in G major (op. 55).
CL, 3, p.61-4.

2813. **NEWMARCH, Rosa**
Tchaikovsky. Suite no.4, "Mozartiana".
CL, 3, p.64-5.

The Tempest.

2814. **NEWMARCH, Rosa**
Tchaikovsky. Symphonic fantasia (op.18), "The Tempest".
CL, 2, p.87-8.

Ballets.

2815. **KEETON, A. E.**
Tshaikovski [sic] as a ballet composer.
Contemporary rev., 86, Oct. 1904, p.566-75.

2816. **EVANS, Edwin**
A great master of ballet music. The Tchaikovsky centenary.
DT, no.356, May 1940, p.468-9.

2817. **LAWSON, Joan**
Tchaikovsky and the ballet: some hitherto unknown facts.
DT, no. 375, Dec. 1941, p.124-7. illus.

2818. **EVANS, Edwin**
The ballets.
in ABRAHAM, *ed.* Tchaikovsky. A symposium, p.184-98.

2819. **YAKOVLEV, Vasili**
The ballets of Tchaikovsky.
in SHOSTAKOVICH *and others.* Russian symphony, p.132-59.

The Nutcracker.

2820. **BLOM, Eric**
Suite from the ballet "Casse-Noisette" (op. 71a).
in BLOM. Tchaikovsky orchestral works, p.42-51. mus.

2821. **NEWMARCH, Rosa**
Tchaikovsky. Suite from the ballet "Casse-Noisette" (op. 71a).
CL, 3, p.86-8.

*2822. **AUDEN, W. H.**
Ballet's present Eden; example of "The Nutcracker".
Center, 1, Feb. 1954, p.2-4.

*2823. **WEINSTOCK, H.**
Chronology of the Nutcracker.
Center, 1, Feb. 1954, p.5-6.

2824. **BARNES, Clive**
The Nutcracker. Music.
DD, 9, Feb. 1958, p.15.

*2825. **WALDEN, Daniel**
The Nutcracker. Pictures by Harold Berson.
Philadelphia, Lippincott. 1959. 45p.

See no. 2765.

2826. **GOODWIN, Noel**
The Nutcracker. What Tchaikovsky thought.
DD, 19, Apr. 1968, p.22+.

The Sleeping Beauty.

2827. **NEWMARCH, Rosa**
Tchaikovsky. Valse from "The Sleeping Beauty".
CL, 3, p.143-4.

*2828. **CARTER, Elliot**
The Sleeping Beauty.
MM, 14, 1937, p.175-6.

2829. **POSNER, Sandy**
The Sleeping Princess. The story of the ballet. With decorations by Joyce Millen.
Newman Wolsey. 1945. 9-96p. illus.

Mostly deals with how the ballet came to be written rather than with its plot.

2830. **HUSSEY, Dyneley**
The composer of "The Sleeping Beauty".
DT, no. 427, Apr. 1946, p.333-5. illus.

2831. **HASKELL, Arnold,** *ed.*
The Sleeping Beauty.
Bodley Head. 1949. 7-56p. 13pl., mus.
Dyneley Hussey writes on the composer and the music. The other contributors are Karasavina, Sacheverell Sitwell and Joy Newton.

2832. **CLOUGH, F. F.** , *comp.*
Tchaikovsky: the Sleeping Beauty ballet, op. 66.
G, 33, May 1956, p.486-7.
Lists which items are included in seven recordings.

2833. **CRISP, Clement**
Vsevolozhsky and the Sleeping Beauty.
About the house, 2, Nov. 1968, p.26-34. illus.
Vsevolozhsky was Director of the Imperial Theatres, 1881-99.

2834. **GOODWIN, Noel** *and* **PERCIVAL, John**
Tchaikovsky: the Sleeping Beauty, op. 66.
DD, 20, Mar. 1969, p.18-20.
A table of production sequences: the score compared with four productions.

Swan Lake.

2835. **CHURCHILL, Douglas W.**
"Le Lac des Cygnes": the ballet, the music and the records.
G, 20, June 1942, p.10-11. disc.

2836. **ROBERTSON, Marion**
The story of the ballet Swan Lake (Le Lac des Cygnes).
With decorations by Joyce Millen.
Newman Wolsey. 1947. 7-96p. [second ed.] illus.
Covers various productions of the ballet and includes a detailed synopsis of it.

2837. **SENIOR, Evan**
Tchaikovsky: music that dances.
DD, 1, Mar. 1950, p.10+. illus., mus.

2838. **BEAUMONT, Cyril W.**
The ballet called Swan Lake.
C. W. Beaumont. 1952, v-viii, 9-176p. illus., 1pl., bib.
Historical, critical and technical study, with some useful appendices, by a noted ballet historian.

2839. **CLOUGH, F. F.** , *comp.*
Tchaikovsky: Swan Lake ballet, op. 20. [A] concordance table.
G, 33, Aug. 1955, p.106.
Lists which items are included in eleven recordings.

2840. **LANCHBERY, John**
Tchaikovsky's "Swan Lake".
DT, 54, Dec. 1963, p.129. illus.

2841. **GOODWIN, Noel**
Back to the Lake. Music.
DD, 17, May 1966, p.33-5.
Compares the 55 numbers in the original score with various staged versions.

Concerti.

2842. **FISKE, Roger**
Tchaikovsky's later piano concertos.
MO, 62, Oct. 1938, p.17-18. mus.
Nov. 1938, p.114-15. mus.
Dec. 1938, p.209-10. mus.
Discusses concertos two and three, the Concert Fantasy and "Andante and Finale".

See no. 2859.

2843. **BLOM, Eric**
Works for solo instrument and orchestra.
in ABRAHAM, *ed.* Tchaikovsky. A symposium, p.43-73. illus.

See no. 2784.

Concerto for piano no.1.

2844. **EVANS, Edwin**
Tchaikovsky analyses. 2. Piano concerto in B flat minor, op. 23
MS, i.s., 28, 3 Aug. 1907, p.73-6. mus.

2845. **BLOM, Eric**
Piano concerto no.1, in a B flat minor (op. 23).
in BLOM. Tchaikovsky orchestral works, p.13-33. mus.

2846. **NEWMARCH, Rosa**
Tchaikovsky. Concerto no.1, in B flat minor, op. 23, for pianoforte and orchestra.
CL, 1, p.102-5.

2847. **BLOM, Eric**
A sin of omission.
MMR, 73, Mar.-Apr. 1943, p.60-2.

2848. **GRAVES, Norma R.**
Christmas concerto.
E, 72, Dec. 1954, p.11+. illus.

2849. **FRISKIN, James**
The text of Tchaikovsky's B flat minor concerto.
ML, 50, Apr. 1960, p.246-51. 4pl.
The article was left unfinished and completed by Mrs. Friskin and Malcolm Frager.

Concerto for violin.

2850. **NEWMARCH, Rosa**
Tchaikovsky. Concerto in D (op.35), for violin and orchestra.
CL, 4, p.121-3.

*2851. **RICH, T.**
[Master lesson upon Canzonetta from Concerto, op.35 in D major ...]
E, 58, June 1940, p.388+. mus.

Variations on a Rococo Theme.

2852. **MONTAGU-NATHAN, M.**
Displaced variations.
Strad, 57, Aug. 1946, p.108+.

2853. **FYODOROVA, Zoya**
They found what Tchaikovsky really wrote.
MMu, 5, July, 1957, p.11. illus.
Deals with Fitzhagen's alterations to the text of the Variations.

Chamber music.

2854. **ABRAHAM, Gerald**
The story of Russian chamber music.
Strad, 47, Feb. 1937, p.445-6.
Mostly devoted to Tchaikovsky.

2855. **MASON, Colin**
The chamber music.
in ABRAHAM, *ed.* Tchaikovsky. A symposium, p.104-13.

2856. **ALSHVANG, Arnold**
Chamber music.
in SHOSTAKOVICH *and others.* Russian symphony, p.160-92.
Includes sections on "romances and songs" and piano and violin solos.

Quartet for strings no. 2.

2857. **ABRAHAM, Gerald**
Tchaikovsky's Quartet in F, op. 22.
L, 16, 15 July 1936, p.141-2.

Trio for piano.

2858. **EVANS, Edwin**
Tchaikovsky analyses. 1. The Trio in A minor, op. 50 ...
MS, i.s., 28, 20 July 1907, p.41-4. mus.

Piano Works.

2859. **JOHNSON, Thomas Arnold**
The piano works of Tchaikovsky.
MO, 63, July 1940, p.438-9.
Includes the piano concertos.

2860. **DICKINSON, A. E. F.**
The piano music.
in ABRAHAM, *ed.* Tchaikovsky. A symposium, p.114-23.

Children's album for piano: No.21, Reverie.

2861. **LOVELOCK, William**
Master lessons in miniature: "Sweet dreams" by Tschaikowsky.
MTe, 16, Dec. 1937, p.677+. mus.

Dumka for piano.

2862. **LEE, E. Markham**
The amateur's repertoire.
MO, 53, Nov. 1929, p.136-7. mus.
The opus number is 59, not 56 as Lee states.

Mazurka for piano in D minor.

2863. **LOVELOCK, W.**
Some practical aids to the better playing of Mazurka in D minor by Tschaikowsky.
Piano student, n.s., 2, June 1936, p.198-9. mus.
The article does not say from which set of piano pieces this mazurka comes.

The Seasons.

*2864. **HAMBOURG, Mark**
A master lesson on Tchaikovsky's "April".
E, 68, Apr. 1950, p.26+. mus.

Songs.

2865. **NEWMAN, Ernest**
Tschaikowsky as a song-writer.
MMR, 31, Aug. 1901, p.173-5.

2566. **TCHAIKOVSKY as a song-writer.**
MS, i.s., 16, 10 Aug. 1901, p.87-8.

2867. **[ABRAHAM, Gerald]**
Tchaikovsky as a song-writer.
L, 16, 21 Oct. 1936, p.788.

2868. **EVANS, Edwin**
Tchaikovsky as a composer.
L, 23, 25 Apr. 1940, p.856.

2869. **ALSHVANG, A.**
The songs. Tr. by I. Freiman.
in ABRAHAM, *ed.* Tchaikovsky. A symposium, p.197-229.

Choral music.

2870. **ABRAHAM, Gerald**
Religious and other choral music.
in ABRAHAM, *ed.* Tchaikovsky. A symposium, p.230-5.

2871. **VANSON, Frederick**
Tchaikovsky - church composer.
Choir, 53, Oct. 1962, p.177.

Liturgy of St. John Chrysostom.

*2872. **STROM, Florence**
The Tchaikovsky choral settings of the Liturgy of St. John Chysostom.
Master of Music thesis, Eastman School of Music, University of Rochester, New York. 1948.

2873. **BECKWITH, R. Sterling**
How to write a Russian mass.
American choral rev., 10 Summer 1968, p.178-85.
Includes a table outlining the order of worship for the liturgy.

Operas.

2874. **NEWMARCH, Rosa**
National opera in Russia (Fourth paper). Tchaikovsky.
PMA, 30, 1903-4, p.57-73.

2875. **KEETON, A. E.**
Tchaikovski's operas.
Contemporary rev., 85, Apr. 1904, p.487-95.

2876. **NEWMARCH, Rosa**
Tchaikovsky's early lyrical operas.
MJIMS, 6, Oct. 1904, p.29-34.

2877. **GILMAN, Lawrence**
Music and the opera. Tschaikowsky as opera-maker.
Harper's weekly, 52, 15 Feb. 1908, p.28.

2878. **ABRAHAM, Gerald**
Operas and incidental music.
in ABRAHAM, *ed.* Tchaikovsky. A symposium, p.124-83.
Also in revised and enlarged form *in* ABRAHAM. Slavonic and Romantic music, p.116-77. mus. The title here is *Tchaikovsky's operas.*

2879. **YARUSTOVSKY, Boris**
Operas.
in SHOSTAKOVICH *and others.* Russian symphony, p.40-85.

2880. **SEAMAN, Gerald**
Tchaikovsky as opera composer.
L, 69, 4 Apr. 1963, p.613.

2881. **OSBORNE, Conrad**
The richness of Russian opera.
HF/MA, 16, Jan. 1966, p.74-5. illus., disc.

The Enchantress.

2882. **SEAMAN, Gerald**
Tchaikovsky in the theatre.
L, 60, 6 Nov. 1958, p.752.

Eugene Onegin.

2883. **TSCHAIKOWSY'S opera "Eugeny Onegin".**
MT, 33, Oct. 1892, p.585-6. mus.

2884. **DAVIDSON, Gladys**
Tchaikovsky. Eugéne Oniegin.
in DAVIDSON. Stories from the Russian opera, p.193-205.

2885. **NEWMARCH, Rosa**
Tchaikovsky. Valse from "Eugene Oniegin".
CL, 3, p.144.

2886. **ABRAHAM, Gerald**
"Eugene Onegin" and Tchaikovsky's marriage.
MMR, 64, Dec. 1934, p.222-3. mus.
Also *in* ABRAHAM. On Russian music, p.225-33. mus.

2887. **WESTRUP, J. A.**
Tchaikovsky's best opera.
L, 26, 16 Oct. 1941, p.545.

2888. **COOPER, Martin**
Tchaikovsky's "Eugene Onegin".
L, 39, 29 Apr. 1948, p.716.

2889. **BUSH, Alan**
Eugen Onegin.
O, 3, May 1952, p.269-72+. illus.

2890. **MONTAGU, George**
Tchaikowsky's "Eugen Onegin".
LME, 7, May 1952, p.24-5. illus.

2891. **SEMEONOFF, Boris**
Eugene Onegin - a synopsis and discography.
Record collector, 7, June-July 1952, p.141-9. disc.

2892. **GOLOVANOV, Nikolai**
The most popular opera in Soviet Russia.
MMu, 2, Nov. 1953, p.13. illus.

2893. **THE STORY of Tchaikovsky's Eugene Onegin.**
ON, 20, 5 Mar. 1956, p.22-4. illus., bib.

2894. **PELTZ, Mary Ellis**
Seen through a letter: notes on Eugene Onegin.
ON, 22, 2 Dec. 1957, p.4-7+. illus.

2895. **"EUGEN Onegin".**
ON, 28, 29 Feb. 1964, p.18-19. illus., bib.

2896. **STEDMAN, Jane W.**
A smiling sigh.
ON, 28, 29 Feb. 1964, p.24-5. mus.

2897. **PORTER, Andrew**
Tchaikovsky's finest opera.
About the house, 3, Christmas 1970, p.32-7. illus.

2898. **RUSSELL, John**
Onegin - an anti-opera?
About the house, 3, Christmas 1970, p.29-31. illus.

Iolanta.

2899. **DAVIDSON, Gladys**
Tchaikovsky. Iolanta.
in DAVIDSON. Stories from the Russian operas, p.206-24.

2900. **LLOYD-JONES, David**
A background to Iolanta.
MT, 109, Mar. 1968, p.225-6.

See no. 1407.

Mazeppa.

2901. **TIDEBÖHL, Ellen von**
Tchaikovsky's opera "Mazeppa".
MMR, 48, Aug. 1918, p.174-6.

2902. **NEWMARCH, Rosa**
Tchaikovsky. Danse Cosaque from "Mazeppa".
CL, 3, p.144.

2903. **PAULS, John P.**
Musical works based on the legend of Mazeppa.
Ukranian rev., 11, Winter 1964, p.61-4.

The Queen of Spades.

2904. **GILMAN, Lawrence**
... Tchaikovsky's opera "The Queen of Spades".
Harper's weekly, 54, 19 Mar. 1910, p.25.

2905. **NEWMAN, Ernest**
Tchaikovski's "Pique Dame".
Nation, 17, 5 June 1915, p.319-20.

*2906. **ARFWEDSON, C. A.**
Tchaikovsky and "Pikovaya Dama".
Twentieth century Russia, 1, Sept. 1915, p. 52-4.

2907. **DAVIDSON, Gladys**
Tchaikovsky. The Queen of Spades.
in DAVIDSON. Stories from the Russian operas, p.225-38.

2908. **COOPER, Martin**
Tchaikovsky's "Queen of Spades".
L, 43, 5 Jan. 1950, p.40.

2909. **MONTAGU, George**
Tchaikovsky's "The Queen of Spades".
LME, 5, Dec. 1950, p.26-8. illus.

2910. **MITCHELL, Donald**
A note on Tchaikovsky's "Queen of Spades".
Ch, 25, Apr. 1951, p.86-9.

2911. **SEAMAN, Gerald**
"The Queen of Spades".
L, 66, 7 Dec. 1961, p.1005.

2912. **GOLDOVSKY, Boris**
The third man.
ON, 30, 15 Jan. 1966, p.26-7. mus.
Refers to the third lover in the story.

2913. **ABRAHAM, Gerald**
"The Queen of Spades".
L, 76, 29 Sept. 1966, p.478. illus.

2914. **JEFFERSON, Alan**
Tchaikovsky's card-sharp countess.
MMu, 15, Oct. 1966, p.16-17. mus.

The Sorceress, opera – *see The Enchantress.*

TCHEREPNIN, Alexander (1899-)

A. *General.*

2915. **REICH, Willi**
Alexander Tcherepnin.
Ch, 13, Apr.- May 1932, p.161-4.

2916. **TCHEREPNINE, Alexander**
Music in modern China.
MQ, 21, Oct. 1935, p.391-400. 2pl., mus.

*2917. **TCHEREPNINE, A.**
Great Russian music of yesterday: how it has influenced the music of today. Ed. by G. Asklund.
E, 66, Dec. 1948, p.731+. illus.

*2918. **TCHEREPNIN, Alexander**
Let underprivileged instruments play!
MJ, 20, Jan. 1962, p.51+.

2919. **TCHEREPNIN, A.**
A letter from Alexander Tcherepnin.
T, 61-2, Spring-Summer 1962, p.17.

*2920. **TCHEREPNIN, A.**
The world of sound.
MJ, 22, Mar. 1964, p.33+. illus.
Includes a list of works.

*2921. **PETERSEN, J. E.**
Alexander Tcherepnin: molto spirito.
School musician, 37, Aug-Sept. 1965, p.68-9.

*2922. **TCHEREPNIN, Alexander**
Composers have a duty.
MJ, 25, 1966, p.71+.

2923. **TCHEREPNIN, Alexander**
A trip to the Soviet Union.
World of music, 9, no.4, 1967, p.17-22. illus.
His first visit for 49 years. English, French and German text.

2924. **KATIGBAK, A.**
A conversation with Alexander Tcherepnin.
Piano quarterly, 16, Winter 1967-8, p.24-5. illus.

2925. **CLARK, Frances**
A visit with Tcherepnin.
Clavier, 7, Mar. 1968, p.20-1. illus.

2926. **SLONIMSKY, Nicolas**
Alexander Tcherepnin, septuagenarian.
T, 87, Winter 1968-9, p.16-23, illus., mus.

2927. **ALEXANDER Tcherepnin.**
LME, 24, Feb. 1969, p.11. illus.

2928. **SMITH, Patrick J.**
Alexander Tcherepnin: "Today is the golden age..."
HF/MA, 19, June 1969, p.MA24+. illus.

B. *Works.*

Symphony no.4.

2929. **TRUSCOTT, Harold**
A note on Tcherepnin's Fourth Symphony.
T, 57, Spring 1961, p.28-30. mus.

Chamber Concert

2930. **SLONIMSKY, Nicolas**
Tcherepnin. Chamber Concerto for flute, violin and chamber orchestra.
in SLONIMSKY. Programme notes: 1947-1948, p.49-50. illus.

Bagatelles for piano.

*2931. **TCHEREPNIN, Alexander**
Master class.
Piano teacher, 5, 1963, p.2-4. illus., mus.
A lesson on two of his "Bagatelles" by the composer.

Song without words no. 4.

*2932. **DUMM, R.**
Piano footnotes: an analytical-interpretive lesson on Alexander Tcherepnin's Song without words no. 4.
Clavier, 3, no.2, 1964, p.27-30. mus.

Boris Godunov (Mussorgsky), *ed.*

See no. 1002.

TCHEREPNIN, Nicolas (1873-1945)

2933. **MONTAGU-NATHAN, M.**
Tcherepnin.
in MONTAGU-NATHAN. Contemporary Russian composers, p. 255-72. illus.

TRIODION, Sergei

B. *Works.*

Stenka Razin.

See no. 89.

TSCHAIKOWSKY - *see* **TCHAIKOVSKY**

USPENSKY, Victor (1879-1949)

2934. **BELAIEF, Victor**
Three Eastern pieces. Tr. by S. W. Pring.
MMR, 57, Sept. 1927, p.261-4. mus.
Three pieces from Uspensky's folk-song collection.

USSACHEVSKY, Vladimir (1911-)

A. *General.*

*2935. **USSACHEVSKY, Vladimir**
Music in the tape medium.
Juilliard rev., 6, Spring 1959, p.8-9+. illus.

B. *Works.*

2936. **WHITTENBERG, Charles**
Ussachevsky's film music.
A.C.A. bull., 11, June 1963, p.5.
On his music for the film *No Exit.*

*2937. **USSACHEVSKY, Vladimir**
The making of "Four Miniatures"; an analysis.
Music educator's j., 55, Nov. 1968, p.76-89.

VARTABED, Gomidas (1869-1935)

*2938. **BEGIAN, Harry**
Gomidas Vartabed: his life and importance to Armenian music.
DA, 26, Sept. 1965, p.1683-4.
Thesis, University of Michigan. 1964.

VASSILENKO, Sergey (1872-1956)

2939. **MOISENKO, Rena**
Sergei Vasilenko.
in MOISENKO. Realist music, p.234-42. mus.

2940. **KREBS, Stanley D.**
Sergei Vasilenko.
in KREBS. Soviet composers and the development of Soviet music, p.82-5.

VERSTOVSKY, Alexey (1799-1862)

B. *Works.*

2941. **SEAMAN, Gerald**
Verstovsky and "Askold's Tomb".
MMR, 90, Nov.-Dec. 1960, p.213-17. mus.
The title refers to one of his operas.

VOGEL, Wladimir (1896-)

A. *General.*

*2942. **VOGEL, Wladimir**
New drift in Germany's International Society for Contemporary Music.
MM, 8, May 1931, p.44-7.

See no. 769.

2943. **GATTI, Guido**
Current chronicle.
MQ, 35, Jan. 1949, p.140-1.

2944. **SKULSKY, Abraham**
Wladimir Vogel ... to create new forms for twelve-tone music.
MA, 79, 1 Dec. 1949, p.7+. illus.

2945. **CASTIGLIONI, Niccolò**
An "international" composer - Vladimir Vogel.
Ricordiana, 1, Oct. 1956, p.5-6. illus.

2946. **BONISCOTTI, Angiola**
Vladimir Vogel.
Ricordiana, 9, Apr. 1964, p.1-3. illus.

2947. **VOGEL, Vladimir**
Impressions of Feruccio Busoni.
PNM, 6, Spring-Summer 1968, p.167-73.

B. *Works.*

2948. **VOGEL, Vladimir**
My cantata on Modigliani. Tr. by Gwyn Morris.
Ricoriana, 8, July 1963, p.1-3.
The title of the cantata is "Meditazione sulla maschera di Modigliani".

2949. **APPIA, Edmond**
Vladimir Vogel's "Thyl Claes".
MQ, 36, Apr. 1950, p.300-2. illus.
The work is an "epic oratorio".

VYSHNEGRADSKY, Ivan (1893-   )

See no. 754.

2950. **SABANEEV, Leonid**
Vyshnegradsky's tonal system. Tr. by S. W. Pring.
MT, 74, Oct. 1933, p.886-8.

WEISSBERG, Yuli (1878-1942)

2951. **MOISENKO, Rena**
Julia Weissberg.
in MOISENKO, Realist music, p.243-8. mus.

YAVORSKI, Boleslav (1877-1942)

2952. **SABANEYEFF, Leonid**
Bolyeslav Yavorski and his pupils.
in SABANEYEFF, Modern Russian composers, p.208-13.

YURASOVSKY, ?

B. *Works.*

Trilby.

See no. 89.

ZHELOBINSKY, Valery (1913-46)

2953. **MOISENCO, Rena**
Valeri Zhelobinsky.
in MOISENCO. Twenty Soviet composers, p.63-4.

2954. **MOISENKO, Rena**
Valeri Zhelobinsky.
in MOISENKO. Realist music, p.249-52.

ZOLOTAREV, Vassily (1873-1964)

B. *Works.*

The Decembrists.

See no. 89.

Index of authors, editors and compilers

References are to entry numbers, not page numbers. Hyphenated surnames are filed under the first part.

Index of translators and illustrators

References are to entry numbers, not page numbers. Illustrators are asterisked.

Subject index

The following selective subject index excludes entries for Russian composers (these are listed in the contents list) and their works, except for the joint "Mlada"; musical forms such as opera; and most broad general terms like aesthetics and nationalism. References are to entry numbers, not page numbers.